THE
NOTRE DAME
STORY

BY FRANCIS WALLACE

THE
NOTRE DAME
STORY

BY

FRANCIS WALLACE

RINEHART & COMPANY, INC.
New York · Toronto

LD
4113
.W3

TO

MY OLD FRIEND AND CLASSMATE

Very Reverend John J. Cavanaugh, C.S.C.

PRESIDENT OF NOTRE DAME

FOREWORD

You may as well know, before we kick off, that while I try to be an accurate reporter, I have never exactly been accused of giving my alma mater the worst of it—except, occasionally, by somebody at my alma mater.

In 1928, five years after graduation, I was so well known in the sports writing profession as a neutral for Notre Dame that, when I met the late W. O. McGheehan on a train en route to South Bend, he smiled and said:

"Just before I left the office I wrote a column which said I was going out to Notre Dame to investigate the rumor there was a university located there. So tell me about it."

McGheehan was ranked by the craft on a par with Damon Runyan. So, as a loyal son of Notre Dame du Lac, I told him about it. When we reached the campus I gave him the fifty-cent grand tour. There were no hotel rooms so Rockne took us in his home—and took over McGheehan.

Just twenty-four hours after he had written the column which said he was going to investigate a rumor about a university, this starched cynic said, with complete sincerity: "Gee—I hope we win tomorrow."

We didn't win. We lost the first home game in twenty-two years; but as long as he lived Bill McGheehan was Notre Dame's attorney for the defense in New York City.

You see, there is a university located there.

It got McGheehan as it gets most people who go there expecting to see only a football factory—as it may get you, if you don't watch out.

But because of its football excellence Notre Dame has become identified in the public mind with football; so much so that, when motion picture companies have recently come with offers to exploit that success, the official answer has consistently been:

"Sorry. We've already had entirely too much football publicity. But if you are interested in the *real* Notre Dame story, with football reduced to its proper proportions—"

There is such a Notre Dame story, as there is of every college; a story of faith and good works by idealistic and practical men; of founders, builders, administrators, faculties, alumni and students; a story which could be told in terms of any of these backgrounds.

I have chosen to tell the highlights of the real Notre Dame story—as it impresses me and, of course, speaking only for myself—in the technicolor of football because I know it best from that angle and think you will find it more entertaining; because football, now an integral part of almost every university, has made a definite and unique contribution to the rapid growth of Notre Dame in this century; because I believe that the excellence of Notre Dame football is merely a reflection of the excellence of the University as a whole; that Notre Dame cannot help having good football teams *too*.

I have chosen to tell the story chiefly in terms of the man who has been the most spectacular figure, not only of Notre Dame, but of all American college history. The Rockne story is in the best American tradition. He came here as a boy of five; he was, you might be thinking, only a football coach; but the king of his native Norway was preparing to knight him when he tragically died; the American people did knight him with a mourning as sincere as any American of any station has ever received; and President Hoover called his death a national loss.

Through the years, as a writer, I've met many of the great

leaders—but none quite like Rockne. He operated from the football field but his activities flooded into many fields. He was teacher, fighter, psychologist, orator, scientist, strategist, actor, salesman, diplomat and business executive. A success at all these things, he could have been successful at almost anything. He had a flaming spirit and whirring brain. He knew the secret paths to the hearts and minds of men, instinctively followed that little light in the soul which can only be described as genius.

Extravagant claims? Hero worship? Go among the men who knew him best, whether friend or foe, and see how much of it you will still find.

When those of us who did know him best get together, we usually wind up talking about Rock—not of the celluloid saint nor of the sketchy figure outlined even in his own writing, but of a human being with very human faults, a saving sense of fairness and a rare charm.

In 1921, after an Army victory, he sat at dinner with the squad, in his best form. Roger Kiley, now a Chicago judge but a sophisticate even in college, said to me: "Look at that son-of-a-gun. He can make you so mad you want to kill him—then he smiles and you wonder what it was you were so mad about."

On March 31, 1931, I was in an express office in Miami when my wife called on the phone. She was crying. Rockne had been killed.

When we arrived at the Coral Gables house, a stack of telegrams was on the table. The one on top was from Rock:

LEAVING RIGHT NOW. LOVE AND KISSES.

Mrs. Rockne was unemotional, waiting, like the rest of us, for that second message, with the typical wisecrack. Little Jackie, playing around the house, said: "Did my daddy get killed in an airplane?" To him it was just another marvellous thing his wonderful father had done.

Finally the packing began. There was an old trunk which Rock must have had since student days, for there were initials painted on the inside with brusque strokes: K. K. R. A football that belonged to Jackie wouldn't fit in the trunk and I suggested that we deflate it.

"Don't—" Mrs. Rockne said. "Knute blew that up himself."

So the breath of Rockne is still probably somewhere in that old football.

Certainly it is still in his game, for it was he, more than any other person, who blew it up to its present proportions. His breath is in the radiant influence he had on the lives of his pupils and associates; in the progress of American sport and education; in the memory of a man who was, above all else, a hero to boys, symbol of success and of clean, inspiring sportsmanship.

In this story you will find much of Rockne, of Gipp and of all Our Lady's Tough Guys who have spread her gospel at other schools. There will be something of these other schools and of their men who have been influenced by Notre Dame men. And there will be enough about football itself to help you understand the manner in which this sport has so intricately twined itself throughout the entire college structure.

But there will be something more, ever present if not always expressed, of the things, so much more important than football, which have influenced Notre Dame men.

There is a belated but growing recognition of the fact, in the current state of the world, that the prime purposes of a college should not be merely research and professional education.

Winston Churchill recently put it this way: "There can be no hope for the world unless the people of Europe unite together to preserve their freedom . . . founded upon Christian ethics."

That *is* the Notre Dame story.

Before Rockne and before football, from the beginning, its primary goal has always been the production of moral leadership —sound, cultured *American* men in whom the spirit rules.

THE
NOTRE DAME
STORY

I

In every winning tradition, including the American, there is a confidence, based on historical fact, that the situation will always produce its man—that *somebody, somehow,* will do the right thing in time.

This feeling, which, as a nation, we all had after Pearl Harbor and have had throughout the "cold war" with Russia, helps mightily to produce the imperative result because it contributes to that poise under pressure which the champion must have to think and fight his way out of a storm.

It happens every year on the football fields. In my annual "Football Preview," now appearing in *Collier's* after nine years as "Pigskin Preview" in *The Saturday Evening Post,* I picture the season in advance from information furnished by the best qualified observers. Most of the predictions stand up well; and there are usually understandable reasons for teams which fall below or rise above pre-season anticipations. In almost all cases the results can be traced to performance of key players.

Almost any story can be clearly told by the football analogy because every football game, like war and all of life, is a battle which calls upon the full strength of every competitor—body, mind, emotion and spirit.

The champion wins the close ones because he *believes* that

3

he can; and he believes he can because he has done it before. That's what Bill Roper tried to instill in his Princeton squads with his famous aphorism: "The team that won't be beaten can't be beaten."

Conversely, the team which has been losing the close ones, in the crucial moments of a fight, begins to think of the games it has lost; and thinking of losing, it loses. There is no question of its physical courage; but it lacks that invincible confidence which is the basis of moral courage. Hard luck is the loser's alibi. The winner makes his luck.

That's what Rockne meant with his battle cry: "I don't want a man to go in there to die gamely—I want a man to go in there *fighting to live!*"

The Notre Dame tradition, from the date of its foundation in 1842, has been a constant fight for life. From the beginning it was a Spartan child, thrown on the hillside to live or die. Born under the most rugged conditions, it lived the hard way, came up from the other side of the collegiate tracks, after a long early struggle for survival that was one crucial scrimmage after another.

In each emergency, as in each winning football game, Notre Dame has found its man. It now has the confidence that it always will. It believes it has a special destiny for the very special reason that it is under very special protection.

In 1921 Notre Dame went to Iowa City for a game which has become a milestone of football history. Dr. Eddie Anderson, an Iowa boy and now coach of that same Iowa squad, was then the apple-cheeked Notre Dame captain. On the night before the battle he said to a pep meeting of Hawkeye students:

"I notice you have a sign on one of your buildings which says: 'Notre Dame—Notre Game.' I don't know what Notre Dame means to you—but to us it means Our Lady."

It did turn out to be Iowa's game; but the faith of Eddie Anderson was not shaken. Notre Dame does pray, before and during a game, as any religious person does in times of stress, as soldiers do in battle; but what it prays for is the strength, the courage, the intelligence and the will to do the things which will earn victory. It does not expect gridiron miracles and claims none in its football history.

It's *men of faith* who really move mountains, as Notre Dame proved in the famous Army game of 1928 when it called upon— and found—all of the elements which have made it great, in and out of football. The material was deficient and crippled, a justifiable 1-4 underdog against an undefeated Cadet squad.

Rockne, never more dangerous than when faced by such a challenge, called upon the spirit of George Gipp—sent the boys out to "win this one for the Gipper."

During the timeouts, the boys prayed; and after one of these prayers Tim Moynihan said: "Okay—now let's play a little football, too."

They did—but with two minutes to go the game was tied. The situation still needed its man. Rockne, fighting to live, found him on the bench—and sent Johnny "One-Play" O'Brien out to win his title and the game.

It was hailed as a master stroke by the master gridiron dramatist; but it was just alert thinking under pressure and sound football. O'Brien was a tall, obscure, pass-catching sophomore end. Army had a stumpy safety man; and when O'Brien came running in, Frank Carideo, the Irish quarterback, knew what play to call. Johnny Niemiec got the ball to the spot, O'Brien was there, caught it and was immediately taken out—not for dramatic effect but because he was, as yet, inexperienced on defense.

That's the Notre Dame educational and athletic tradition —work and pray, think and fight to live—but always work and think.

Its faith is the faith of Bernadette—and the physical testimony is on the campus.

Notre Dame is now one of the largest country clubs and most beautiful universities in America. At least half of it has been planned and built in the last twenty years but it all conforms to the Gothic of the early buildings which, with spires pointed to heaven like candles, is in itself the architectural expression of prayer. It is securely shut off from the encroaching town by a forest, two large lakes, its own eighteen-hole golf course and acres of parking space which surround the stadium. There's not much ivy but plenty of green grass and ancient trees.

It's a place its people like to show, particularly to those who may have come expecting to see nothing much more than a brick football factory. It has its church, of course; but there is also a replica of the Grotto of Lourdes hidden away among the trees where the lakes almost join. It's a spot you come on suddenly and usually there are boys there who have slipped off, alone, to light a candle, to kneel and pray for the strength and guidance to win their private battles.

The Grotto symbolizes the way of religion at Notre Dame. The school is frankly Catholic and this atmosphere umbrellas all of its training. But it is also assumed that the students are adults, beyond the stage of catechism and ready for the philosophical decisions of free will. The Grotto is like the church, and the chapel in every residence hall—there if you want it, quietly eloquent.

In 1947, during the week before the Army game, there were reporters from many metropolitan newspapers on the campus. One of these, a Georgia boy with, I suspect, little formal religion, said to me: "Let's go walk by that outdoor cathedral again."

The Notre Dame spirit, in its entirety, goes all the way back to The Founder—who was, by all accounts, quite a guy, himself. He came from France, as Rockne came from Norway, and as Father Nieuwland, whose experiments led to synthetic rubber, came from Belgium—as so many of the other pioneers who made Notre Dame, came from Ireland; but they were all spiritual brothers of the work-think-fight-pray tradition which also made America. Most of them arrived by roundabout routes and accidental detours. You may think what you wish about such things but at Notre Dame the word is *providential*.

II

Gridiron goobers of the future, poring into such ancient lore as this, will come upon the name of Jack F. Rissman and probably conclude that, though he cannot be found among the immortal lists, he surely must belong there because, in the great names on the trophies emblematic of the national championships, that of Jack F. Rissman leads all the rest. But to the best of my knowledge Mr. Rissman was just a Chicago sportsman fortunate enough to get in on the ground floor of a very good thing.

It was he who, in 1924, decided that the awarding of national championships should be taken out of the field of contentious post-season debate and be scientifically decided. He chose the Dickenson system of rating (now replaced by the Associated Press poll) and offered a trophy to be retired by the first school which won it three times; and since it was his money which bought it, the trophy modestly wound up with the name of the donor. It was presumably also his idea; but there is a version which states that the suggestion came from the great Rockne himself in one of his shrewder moments—for Rock won the first leg in 1924 and retired it in 1930, just before his death.

Notre Dame then provided the Knute K. Rockne Trophy, retired in 1940 by Minnesota which, in turn, put up the Dr. Henry L. Williams Trophy, in honor of its former great coach and exponent of the shift. This was retired by Notre Dame in 1947. Here are the official winners since 1924—before which the national champion was anybody's guess although the newspapers usually had arrived at accepted conclusions:

RISSMAN TROPHY

1924 Notre Dame
1925 Dartmouth
1926 Stanford
1927 Illinois
1928 Southern California
1929 Notre Dame
1930 Notre Dame

ROCKNE TROPHY

1931 Southern California
1932 Michigan
1933 Michigan
1934 Minnesota
1935 Southern Methodist
1936 Minnesota
1937 Pittsburgh
1938 Notre Dame
1939 Southern California
1940 Minnesota

WILLIAMS TROPHY

1941 Minnesota
1942 Ohio State
1943 Notre Dame
1944 Army
1945 Army
1946 Notre Dame
1947 Notre Dame

Notre Dame kept the award in competition by offering the Rev. J. Hugh O'Donnell Trophy (on which Michigan won the first leg in 1948) in honor of the man who, more than any other, had been the embodiment of everything the school typifies. A big, bluff and ruddy youngster, he had been regular center on the 1915 football team, and first president of the Monogram Club. The descriptive nickname of Pepper clung to him even after he joined the Order and finally became president of the school through the difficult wartime years from 1939 to 1946. He was preparing for a trip to South America in 1947 when he was sentenced to a quick death by unsuspected cancer. Pepper could take it—and the fortitude of his last days has become part of the Notre Dame tradition.

During his requiem Mass the sanctuary was crowded with the high rank of the hierarchy. As these men went through every meticulous detail of the ceremony, I felt I was watching a great and solemn play, which, as Clare Booth Luce recently observed, the Mass, superficially, is. The actors were all highly educated and masculine, like my classmate and friend, John J. Cavanaugh, who, as the current president of the school, was the chief celebrant. Many could have become brilliant in professional and business ranks.

Yet all, like Pepper O'Donnell, had taken the vows of celibacy, obedience and poverty, had given their lives to the Idea that the first duty of man is to love and serve his Creator. That calls for the highest type of guts—the moral courage of a great faith. The word the church uses is *vocation*.

There might never have been a Notre Dame if, back in 1836, Simon Bruté, the Bishop of Vincennes in the then Northwest Territory, had not visited the seminary in Le Mans, France, to plead for vocations to carry on the work of bringing the gospel to the Indians and whites of his diocese. One of those who listened was Edward Sorin, a young giant of comfortable background whose zeal and energy had brought him into the Congregation of the Holy Cross. Five years later, when the opportunity arrived, he sailed from France with six Brothers of the Order—a religious brother being a man who devotes his life to the more humble but very practical duties of service.

When Father Sorin, who was to wrestle with financial problems all his remaining life, found the passage money to be insufficient, he talked his band into the steerage, which they shared for thirty-nine days with, among others, "a company of French comedians and German Protestants."

Barney Ross, the ex-welterweight champion, when he first stepped on American soil after returning from the South Pacific as a Marine, kissed the ground. Father Sorin did the same thing when he stepped off his ship, as a sign of adoption. He was a good American from the beginning and always remained so—and that's Notre Dame, too.

None of the band could speak English; but they started for the wilds of Indiana, and wilds they were, for the trip from New York took twenty-four days by canal, by boat, by horse and cart. They survived storms and manfully fought off robbers; and the night when they knew they were approaching some sort of frontier protection, they stood "in the clear bright moonlight and sang all the hymns to the Blessed Virgin we knew."

They were assigned to a spot ten miles from Vincennes, in virtual wilderness—and the next day started to build a school! Sorin was a salesman and something of a promoter, as evidenced by the letter he sent to his superior in France: "We are not mentioning the fact that we shall have to use the attic for a dormitory; we are not mentioning the refectory; nothing has been said of the fact that the teachers will probably not understand their new pupils. Tell me, are we not men of faith?" He had also been very good at getting even the Protestants to come from miles around to help with the building program.

Faith—and work—made the school a success and Sorin wanted to enlarge it to a college. Vincennes already had a college; but the Bishop offered a tract of nine hundred acres near South Bend, warned of the hardships that would be met—and attached some stiff conditions. Sorin prayed—and then set out by ox cart in bitter cold and snow, for the north. Accompanied by seven Brothers—four of whom had come from Ireland—he made the 250 miles in ten days, arrived at South Bend November 26, 1842. They knelt in the snow, dedicated their efforts to Our Lady—and went to work. They made bricks from marl beds found near the lakes; and Sorin again talked the surrounding Catholics—and Protestants—into helping with the job. He started his school almost immediately, and on January 15, 1844, through the kind offices of a Methodist friend who was also a state senator, got a charter for The University of Notre Dame du Lac, with its meager endowment of flesh and blood.

At the beginning Notre Dame lived by barter. For one hundred dollars a year it guaranteed to feed a boy, wash and mend his clothes, give him medical attention and teach him the "complete English course—spelling, reading, grammar, history, surveying, astronomy." It would accept whatever dollars the parents could afford and take the rest in grain, produce, hogs, furniture or what-have-you? Certain electives were extra. Latin brought an added hog; and something very fancy, like the pianoforte, which the pioneers seemed to regard as the hallmark of culture—two big hogs.

The students, as might be imagined, were rough customers —the sons of plainsmen, trappers, farmers and storekeepers, the advance guard of civilization. Sorin's method was the French device of keeping them so busy they had no time to get into jams. Some did, of course, but Sorin did everything possible to retain the hard-to-get students—and positively never expelled one until his father had fulfilled all financial obligations.

The early days were a series of goal-line stands which required all the faith and work and thought of the valiant little squad. But the Coach always found a way.

Fire was a constant hazard and finally destroyed the first ambitious college building which housed two hundred students. Once, the working capital was reduced to fifty cents and Sorin sold a valuable team of horses. When cholera became a serious menace during a national epidemic, he correctly diagnosed its local cause as a dam on a nearby property which caused swampland near the lakes. But the owner would not raze the dam, and held out for an exorbitant price.

"There are moments when vigorous action upsets the enemy," the man-of-prayer-through-action decided. He sent his men, equipped with crowbars, to destroy the dam—and got away with it because public opinion supported him.

During the gold rush of '49 he financed a company which did manage to reach California—but alas, found no gold. That brought censure from his superiors in France; and there were other difficulties from that quarter, caused by the slowness of communication and the usual lack of understanding by the home office of the problems of the man in the field.

But the thing that brought him there, he never forgot. He is quoted: "If all men fail me, there is one treasury that is always full, the treasury of Our Most Holy Lady. In the darkest hours of our need, in the moments of deepest discouragement, never once has she failed me. So great has been our protection, I am compelled to go right ahead with this work, knowing that her power and kindness will not fail us in the days that lie ahead. And when this school has grown a bit more I will raise her aloft, so that men will know, without asking, why we have succeeded here. To that Lovely Lady, raised high on a dome, a golden dome, men may look and find the answer."

Like all other small businessmen, Sorin was affected by fluctuating currencies during the frequent financial panics. But he worked and prayed and was not above begging; and in critical moments donations dropped in from sources even he had not thought of tapping. He took students of every age, from first grade on through high school and college; added professors and new courses as conditions warranted. He founded the school for girls, which is now the proud St. Mary's, just across the Niles Road from Notre Dame—but still much too remote for the students of, let us assume, both institutions?

Oddly enough, registration increased rapidly during the Civil War. At its end there were nearly five hundred students; all were housed and taught in a "huge" new five-story building—the physical proof that Coach Sorin had finally got his school across the fifty-yard line.

The Congregation thought so too, made him Superior-General, the head of its activities throughout the world. He appointed a new president at Notre Dame and began the series of ocean crossings which were to total fifty before his death in 1893.

He was in Montreal, April 23, 1879, preparing to sail for Europe, when the word came that every college building except the church had been destroyed by fire; and that only $40,000 of the $200,000 loss was covered by insurance.

He returned at once, found the religious community assembled at the church by Father William Corby, president of the school, who, as an army chaplain, had himself contributed to the Notre Dame tradition by giving mass absolution to The Irish Brigade at the Battle of Gettysburg.

There was a reasonable fear that the shock of seeing his life's work in ashes might break the 65-year-old Sorin. But he met them at the altar, prayed with them, and gave them a fight talk Rockne would have envied, for it ended: "If all were gone I would not give up." After which he picked up the first wheelbarrow.

That was in April. By September the nucleus of the present University was ready to receive students—a better Main Building, with a bigger statue of Our Lady looming higher in the sky from a wider golden dome, so that all men might see and know the answer.

13

It was this disastrous fire of '79 which first brought Notre Dame and its fighting spirit to national attention. Help came from many outside sources, including, as always, Sorin's beloved Protestants—the original synthetic alumni.

On his way to becoming a patriarch, Sorin exercised a firm but constantly decreasing supervision over the University which was now only a part of his international sphere. And that may have been providential, too; for Sorin's idea had been restricted by hard necessity to a "tight little boarding school" which could not hope to compete with the heavily endowed schools.

Notre Dame had a brighter destiny. The new men were on their way.

Among the things they brought was the new sport of football—which was one headache, at least, that Sorin never had.

Football *is* a headache to college presidents. They are uncomfortable about the money they make from this amateur sport, and disturbed about its exaggerated importance in the collegiate structure—the fact, for instance, that not just Notre Dame but the average educational institution is much more apt to be identified, in the mind of the general public, by its football coach and stars than its prestige professors and mental athletes. Try that out on yourself with the first twenty schools that come to mind.

Let's go into this tail-wags-dog phenomenon quite thoroughly because of its importance to the Notre Dame, and the entire college, story.

III

One of Rockne's best stories told of the Irishman just over from the County Galway, to whom football was explained as a game "where the ball is kicked off and the fight begins." He was enthusiastic, wanted to begin at once but was told there was no ball available.

"To hell with the ball," he said, "let's start the game."

Rock's stories usually had a point and this one just about explains the appeal of the sport to the young men on the field. They are vital. They like contact. The ball is the excuse. This is the frame of mind in which every coach tries to send his team on the field—the reason for his fight talk. It is the message the cheerleaders drum: "Fight! Team! Fight!"

But football is more than that; like all sporting spectacles it is *outdoor theater*, with mental, emotional, even spiritual aspects, as well as physical. It is intensely human and sometimes quite dramatic because those are young boys down there and kids make mistakes. The crowd grows frenzied because the crowd becomes part of the game, part of the spectacle, part of the show. Emotionally and mentally attuned, they become highly vocal, transmit their feelings to the players.

It's a grand afternoon, when you can be part of the Big Game; like golf, it will make you forget your other troubles; it

15

is well worth the icy roads, the rain and cold, the joust with pneumonia germs. That is, if you win; but somebody almost always wins.

There are other things about football too—financial backdrops, muted music, all sorts of things which may surprise you.

The legend, take it or leave it, is that the game originated late in the Eleventh Century when English workmen, excavating on an old battlefield, unearthed the skull of a Danish invader and gave it a good kicking around—a feature which has not disappeared entirely from the modern game. (At least Chic Harley, the Ohio State immortal, seemed to think so when, after a boot glanced off his headguard during a high school contest, he winked at the booter and said, "Nice going, Red.")

The legend continues that English kids enthusiastically continued the sport of "kicking the Dane's head"—until they ran out of skulls, after which they substituted an inflated cow's bladder which was also much kinder to bare feet. The earliest form had other reminiscent characteristics—was accompanied by "lusty yelling, fierce argument and brutish behavior." It finally came under the disapproving eye of the authorities who banned "futeballe" because it was keeping too many young men from the practice of archery, proficiency in which was then vital for national defense. But after firearms had made archery archaic, James I gave it his blessing as a manly pastime that would "develop character" —which also has a familiar ring.

In 1823 William Webb Ellis, a student at Rugby College, chagrined at his failure to kick the cussed ball skillfully, picked it up and ran across the goal. This was considered very unsporting at the time and Master Ellis was in disgrace; but like so many other revolutionaries, a monument was later erected to this daring young man who thus became the father of rugby and the grandfather, so to speak, of American Football.

There may have been informal contests between other neighboring schools; but our first college football contest of rec-

16

ord, a form of soccer, was between Princeton and Rutgers at New Brunswick, November 6, 1869. Rutgers won, 6 goals to 4. They played again at Princeton the next week and the Tigers won this one, 6 goals to 0. A man still lives who saw it—Henry Green Duffield, Treasurer-Emeritus of Princeton, who was then a boy of ten.

The early facts are in dispute but the following version will be close enough for us. The first intersectional game, between Cornell and Michigan, was played at, of all places, Cleveland, presumably a halfway spot, in 1873. The nucleus of the present Ivy League was formed this same year among Princeton, Rutgers, Yale and Columbia. They arranged games for the following spring, which was thought to be the best season for football at that time.

Proud Harvard seems to have been the first victim of schedule trouble, for when it wanted to get in on the fun, it was told that the spring cards had been completed. The Cantabs then did what Rockne was forced to do later, and what Leahy is being forced to do now—ranged far afield, to Montreal, and brought in McGill University. But when the Canadians arrived it was found that they were playing the Rugby version introduced by Master Ellis, whereas the Americans were still playing soccer.

Harvard, as the host, deferred to the guests and played rugby. The score, perhaps traceable to McGill manners, was 0-0. The next year, 1875, Harvard challenged Yale, but insisted on the new rugby style. There was an argument, of course; but since no international amenities were now involved, Harvard was not so polite. Neither was Yale. They finally agreed on a compromise form in which they *kicked* and *ran*. This game, which Harvard won 4-0, seems to have been the first played under the basic rules which have since been developed into our great Autumnal Madness.

The Yales liked it, joined with Harvard in an attempt to force the other schools to adopt the new version. Princeton, Rutgers and

Columbia finally admitted the running, twisting and dodging features but insisted the kicking departments, in which they excelled, should count for more points in the scoring.

There was angling, you see, from the beginning. In fact, football might be defined as a smooth-surfaced ellipse full of submerged angles—like those which sunk the Army-Notre Dame game. There have been, through the years, other and less courteous interruptions of famous series—Army-Navy, Harvard-Princeton, Yale-Army, Penn-Yale—and on down the line to intense neighborhood rivalries between smaller colleges and high school squads.

Each season produces its squabbles which are hung out in the sectional and national press, ponderously discussed at regional meetings and the semi-annual sessions of the National Collegiate Athletic Association, which is the U. N. of college football. The acrid accusations and debate follow the same pattern as those of the political U. N., accomplish about as much and for the same basic reason—because each is more an advisory than a regulatory body, with bitter tongues but baby teeth.

As an average football fan, with only a seasonal interest, you have probably often puzzled about all this excitement over a simple game which an irritated Cornell president once described as "the agitation of a bag of wind." In a general way you have probably decided that it all seems to boil down to arguments over the eligibility and financial payments to college players.

And you have probably come to this general conclusion: So what and who cares? Since you have to crack down at the box office for college and professional football alike, you are not likely to be too much concerned about the hair-splitting distinction between amateur and professional.

From your observation it seems to be a fact that all the college heroes are paid, in one form or another. You may know players in your town who couldn't possibly go to college if they didn't get financial help. The boys and their families make no

18

secret of that and the local press sometimes proudly refers to numerous "offers" from even the most piously proclaiming colleges.

You probably wish they'd stop boring you with their silly arguments and get on with the games—particularly the ones you'd most like to see.

Well, it all seemed that way to me as far back as twenty years ago when I wrote "The Hypocrisy of College Football Reform" for *Scribner's Magazine*—an article which, incidentally, I had previously shown to Rockne, who not only okayed it but gave me some added material and said: "Any time they all want to come out in the open I'll take my chances."

Since that time I've written consistently about the same subject for *The Saturday Evening Post, Collier's* and other magazines; and the title for each article could have been the same as the *Scribner's* original. Each year, in covering the highlights in the "Football Preview," I get a lot of confidential information which confirms my belief that the great majority of coaches, including practically all of the better ones, agree with Rockne's sentiments of twenty years ago.

There *is* a lot of hypocrisy in college football, of politics, finagling and some downright crookedness. Nobody knows that better than the harried college presidents, who are even more anxious to get rid of it all than you or I or the coaches. That's why they work so hard at it. You may wonder why, as highly educated men, they cannot solve what seems to be a simple and minor problem in their own field. So let's go into that.

IV

The college presidents, like Frankensteins fleeing their football monsters, are caught in the switches of paradox, hung on the horns of dilemma.

As educators they are intellectually concerned with ideas and ideals; but making money out of an amateur sport is contrary to both because, by very definition, an amateur cannot profit financially from the sport in which he engages. However, as practical executives and administrators, they need football money, know there is nothing really wrong with taking it and making good use of it.

The Southern colleges made an effort to square this circle a few years ago with various forms of legal athletic scholarships which, in effect, admitted the principle that an athlete whose labor they sold for gain was entitled to some financial return, at least to the extent of a free education. But they weakened their own position in too many cases by using the legal scholarship as basic pay and going on from there to compound the problem. Threatened with schedule sanctions they were whipped back into line in 1948.

So temporarily, at least, the colleges have again "solved" their dilemma by insisting upon the Job Plan (now called the Sanity Program), but, for the most part, taking care not to scrutinize practical operations too closely or to find out whether the hot stove is being handled with asbestos gloves. Many college presidents do make honest efforts; but since most of them make much the same noises at the annual N.C.A.A. prayer meetings, it is difficult to distinguish the pharisees.

That's the way it is and has been; and that's the way it will continue to be as long as they try to make the square practice fit into the round theory or vice versa. Unfortunately there is still more vice than versa and that's what all the shooting is about.

Still, the faculty men would be very happy if you or I would help them get off the horns of their dilemma. So let's give it another and perhaps presumptuous whirl. And let's try the method Rockne used whenever things began to get out of line on the field—by going back to fundamentals.

Leaving the Yale bowl after an Eli victory over Cornell two years ago, I paused briefly to watch the young men playing soccer in an open field.

They were as seriously energetic as the lads had been in the Bowl, though less destructive. At least none seemed in danger of brain concussion, which was what had happened to Levi Jackson earlier that afternoon.

This may also have been a soccer team match between Yale and Cornell. Nobody seemed to care and few of the streaming crowd even gave the game a mildly curious glance.

Yet, it struck me that this was a duplication of the scene in the earliest days of football. These were students, too; but there would be no arguments over this game. These were all pure amateurs who would give the faculties no headaches.

The pointed difference was: The game of football had been played inside the concrete Bowl and for gate receipts.

I shall now give you a primer, of a sort, which will trace the significant steps, each innocent enough at the time it was taken, which brought the college boys from the open field, landed them inside the closed Bowl—and ultimately led to the situation which causes so many college prexies to hate themselves in the morning.

As we go, please give close attention to the italicized words; for in them you will find most of the virtues and vices of football, the sources of its appeal, the keys to most of its "problems."

Early class football was encouraged by the faculties because it provided a healthy outlet for student energies and fitted snugly into the Grecian ideal of *the sound mind in the sound body.*

The first intercollegiate games developed *school spirit* and fostered the *alumni loyalty* which all colleges seek, with at least one eye slanted toward future *endowment.*

The *public* began to attend the games; and then the *newspapers,* which first follow public interest and then stimulate it in a mushrooming growth.

As rivalries and enthusiasms mounted there came the first *emphasis on winning teams.*

Zealous alumni who wanted to gloat over and perhaps win *bets* from pals from other schools, began to "go out after them," to get superior athletes who normally would have gone to other colleges. Thus began *proselyting.*

Professional *coaches* were brought in and these began to *take the game away from the boys.*

The first wooden stands and fences went up. *Gate receipts* were charged. This opened the Pandora Box, was the beginning of the *end of the amateur system;* but nobody realized this at the time because the motive was not to profit but to make up a deficit.

Alumni finally began to influence boys *who would not have gone to college at all* if they had not been superior athletes. Naturally these needed financial help which was cheerfully provided. And so proselyting developed into *subsidization.* The venial sin against the holy ideal of amateurism had become mortal;

but as usual in such cases, nobody seemed to realize it, so gradual had been the transition.

The sport spread to all sections, became a definite part of the college scene and of American life. This was a *uniquely American game which grew out of the American character* with its stimulating qualities of *incentive, competition,* and *dramatic conflict.* And it took its definite place in our *outdoor theater.*

The bigger colleges made the astonishing and pleasant discovery that the roistering alumni had prospected a *bonanza* and laid it on their doorsteps for *exploitation.* It was realized that football could not only *finance the entire athletic program* but also stimulate the highly desirable factors of *undergraduate spirit, alumni morale, public support* and *institutional publicity.* Since colleges are chronically hard up, this new and easy source of revenue was regarded as a windfall.

So the *colleges took over the football business.* Stands were enlarged, prices went up, following the law of supply and demand. The *first stadium* was built at Harvard, the citadel of amateurism. Others followed and those which could not afford their own fields rented baseball parks. The *gold rush* was on.

When the ghost of old Simon Pure, the Spirit of Amateurism, began to groan and grunt in the new sepulchers of stone and steel, he was quieted by the first of the *rules* which have since become as numerous as the seats in the stadia.

Eligibility requirements aimed at the *tramp athlete* only emphasized his skidding, caused bitter disagreements and broken relationships when he turned up in the uniform of opponents. Insistence on higher grades put severe strains on the consciences of friendly instructors who were sometimes *pressured* to *give a break* to star players. So *the athletic tail began to wag the academic dog.*

The problem of financing the better type of proselyted athlete was settled by the *Job Plan* which brought on *conspir-*

acies by athletic departments and alumni to fool front office men who were not always too hard to fool.

Administrators who might have faced the problem squarely were *shackled by heavy indebtedness on the stadia* and the necessity to meet payments—which led to further involvements in all directions, since it was now more necessary than ever before to *attract and retain superior material* for winning teams to attract big gates.

The harried faculty men banded together in *conferences* which are nothing more than police bodies, with the commissioner as chief, designed to keep athletic crime within reasonable limits —and sometimes, or so it seems, to see that the right people do not get caught.

Bowl games, with pots of gold on the rainbow of season's end, added the final pressure.

You should now have a clearer idea of the complexities which have transformed the simple agitation of the bag of wind into *Dementia Pigskin.* Granting that the simplification may be a bit rough in spots, it all seems to boil down to two major conclusions:

(*a*) College football *is an amateur sport operated as a business for profit.* This poses the question: How can the colleges logically deny a financial return to players whose *labor they exploit* for handsome profits? The colleges have answered by insisting that the definition of an amateur applies to the player but not to themselves—an uneasy solution that begs the further question: How can the college insist that a player remain an amateur when the colleges themselves were the first to scrap the amateur idea?

(*b*) The cause of the immediate arguments is the manner in which help is given to players—which leads to constant charges of hypocrisy, bad faith and outright chiseling.

It's not a happy situation in which the Keepers of the Ideals have found themselves through the years. To my mind, and, I be-

24

lieve, the minds of most of the working people in football, the *practical* solution is obvious.

The colleges could abandon the classic *English* definition of an amateur, create and substitute a new definition of an *American amateur*—one who, because of his unique contributions to the general good of the school, is entitled to some financial return. This would legalize the things they actually do in football and intend to go on doing.

There is ample precedent for such action because the colleges openly give financial help to students whose mental and musical talents contribute to the well-being of the colleges.

Here's the rub: The colleges don't make money out of such amateur activities as the band, glee club and publications. They do make money out of the amateur sport of football. They cannot deny that fact, but they will not follow through to the logical conclusion—player subsidization—because that would mean they would have to admit that they themselves have scrapped the amateur system.

The modern philosophers, you see, can also do quite a bit of dancing on the point of a needle.

V

The football team you see on the field on any given day is no more a product of that day—or year—than is the man who happens to be president of the United States. Both are products of the years.

The football team is the sum of: (*a*) Material. (*b*) Coaching. (*c*) School policies. (*d*) Tradition. These are so interrelated that the team in the championship flight must almost of necessity have a high mark in all four factors.

No coach can win consistently without superior material. Superior material finds it hard to win with inferior coaching. Neither material nor coaching is apt to be high-grade if school policies are unfriendly to football; or if academic requirements are too difficult for the average athlete to get by. Winning spirit comes out of a tradition of victory which presupposes a favorable background in material, coaching and policy.

An easy proof of this contention is found in the football fortunes of Army and Navy. Their material and traditions are equal as could be; but Army has had much better recent success because it has had a definite advantage in *coaching policy*.

No civilian college ever willingly dissolves that pigskin pearl of great price—an efficient coaching staff. Nor, in recent years, has Army. But Navy did. Every three years it sent to sea the head

26

man who was just getting acquainted with his squad—and brought in another who had been out of contact with the game. The results were obvious in performance: Navy played with gallant spirit which was occasionally enough to produce a flaming victory; but over the long run it lacked the mechanical polish which only a continuous staff can apply.

In 1948 Navy recognized that its coaching policy was injurious to morale. So it installed a civilian coach who will stay on the job. As a result, Navy should pull up to parity with Army again; it might eventually be even better because life at Annapolis is a shade less grim than at West Point and an equal shade more attractive to superior athletes.

As long as we remain within the orbit of Mars, there should be no dearth of athletic talent at either service academy; nor, for that matter, is there apt to be in peacetime, if they continue the aggressive and realistic recruiting policies which have been in effect since World War II began. Army and Navy value superior athletes, not only for the usual reasons of prestige and morale but because the competitive athlete is considered superior officer material.

General Maxwell D. Taylor, Superintendent of the Military Academy, while discussing this general question with me at West Point, referred to a great Army tackle who had just flunked out. "He might not excel at mathematical calculations; but if I wanted somebody to take that hill over there—"

In normal times of peace, however, the service schools are definitely handicapped in their search for athletic talent, for three reasons: (a) Their stringent academic requirements, emphasizing higher mathematics, automatically shut out the physical type of athlete who is inclined to ride through high school as easily as possible. (b) Many of those who could get by academically, back away from military discipline and the obligation of at least four years of service after graduation. (c) Others are di-

27

verted by financial offers, open or covert, from civilian institutions, which also provide a more attractive social existence.

The most vital ingredient of the football mix is superior material. That's why all big-time colleges go to such lengths to attract it, some to the extremes of illegality and immorality. The minority of flagrant violators are in the position of the elderly seducer who has nothing much more than money to offer. The majority are more venial than venal because they have normal attractions which keep a constant flow of material coming their way. And, as a general rule, those schools which insist on rigid amateur virtue also happen to be in the best position to afford it. That's a cynical statement; but you will find, when you start exploring, just about as much realism in football as in other human relations.

The major conferences, for instance, are composed of big state-supported institutions with obvious advantages in competing for player talent. They are closer to the student's home, have bigger and more influential alumni groups, are less expensive, and their academic requirements are less stringent because they must be geared to the standards of the high schools they serve. They are usually coeducational, which means a more pleasant social life.

The more affluent private institutions, typified by those in the Ivy League, are penalized by higher costs and stiffer requirements, but compensate somewhat by social prestige and more prominent—and promising—alumni influence, both of which operate in subtle, but effective ways.

All of these selling points, concrete and intangible, are aggressively used by smart recruiters in the football business which —and you may as well keep this firmly in mind—is a *sport operated for profit* by the colleges in competition with each other. Athletic talent is the raw material of this business.

Now let's see where Notre Dame fits into this picture.

It is a private school; but its alumni are predominantly middle class and its permanent endowment is comparatively meager. In competition with the average state schools its expenses are higher and its academic requirements a firm shade tougher. (Specifically it demands two years of foreign language and two years of mathematics for entrance; and to remain eligible for athletics a student must maintain a general average of 77 percent —seven points higher than enough to keep him in school.)

But, in the application of our yardstick for football excellence, Notre Dame has certain definite and powerful advantages which clearly explain its consistent superiority:

1. Material. Notre Dame has always had, and will continue to attract, high-grade athletic material for these reasons:
   a. It is a leading Catholic school which has also long ranked among the top ten colleges in the country in geographical representation.
   b. Seventy-five percent of its widespread alumni have been graduated since 1930 and are youthful, enthusiastic and energetic.
   c. It has the largest unofficial alumni group—the celebrated and sometimes maligned (though not by Notre Dame) "synthetics."
   d. It is the second largest male boarding school in the world —with a democratic masculine atmosphere that forbids fraternities, hazing and other freshman regulations; with the aid of religious discipline, it provides an ideal athletic climate.
   e. Its highly publicized and spectacular victories have a strong appeal for young athletes, most of whom come from families with no previous college background.

2. Coaching. In nineteen of the last thirty-one years Notre Dame has been guided by the two most successful coaches of the era—Rockne and Frank Leahy. All of its leaders since 1918 have been former players.

3. Policies. These have always been favorable to a sane athletic program. While conforming fully to the regulations of the Western Conference and N.C.A.A., Notre Dame has been realistic in its approach, has recognized that football is a profitable business, has never apologized for football money, has, as a low-endowment school, made valuable use of it.

4. Tradition. A successful football team is like a successful man. It has body, mind and heart, and makes the best use of all of these. The body and the mind are scientifically trained, and the emotions are stimulated by evangelistic pep meetings and coaching psychology.

College spirit is just that—a calling back of the ghosts of tradition. How they respond depends upon various factors—the age and quality of the tradition, the intensity of the situation, the receptivity of the players. Where teams are otherwise near equal the stronger spirit usually wins.

Occasionally, when the situation is right, usually against an old rival or in a game where school prestige is threatened, the spirits soar; and when they do, the team rises far above its normal ability, performs with a valorous efficiency against which no rival can stand that day.

Over the years Notre Dame teams have had this high spiritual quality to a more marked degree than their opponents. The Irish frequently upset but seldom are upset. The explanation is simple enough. The goal of Notre Dame education is to produce a cultured man in whom the spirit rules. And that training reflects, logically, in all its activities—including football.

Rockne was once asked who his first assistant coach was. Though he was not a Catholic at the time, he pointed to the priest who was then Prefect of Religion, now Bishop John O'Hara.

This frankly religious character of Notre Dame education has been the x-quantity in its greatest gridiron triumphs—and some of its gridiron troubles.

VI

The keystone on which Rockne built was the Army series, the most famous and unique in gridiron history. For twenty-four years it was New York City's own game, the one annual event guaranteed to stir the metropolis. Always a spectacle, it usually found some way to be dramatic, was frequently the competitive gem of the season.

The initial contest, back in 1913, became a football landmark posted by two tablets—the first outstanding use of the forward pass and the national introduction of Notre Dame which was to become the leading gridiron power of the next four decades.

It is possible that the historians of the future may see the final game in 1947 as another landmark—the beginning of the decline of Notre Dame as the football leader. For the real meaning of the cancellation of the Army series was that it dramatized and brought into the open what had been no secret to even the casually informed—a quiet but persistent flight of major Big Nine schools from the Notre Dame schedule.

When a national landmark is demolished and a fine tradition broken there must be reasons. Army gave these: The game had got too big for its own good; the ticket situation and public participation had got out of hand; the Notre Dame game had become more important to the Cadet Corps than the one with the more traditional rival, Navy; and while Army had always made a good showing against the Irish, it had to put out so much effort that it sometimes couldn't get its emotional batteries recharged in time for Navy.

Notre Dame accepted these explanations from an old friend and honored foe, went along in a joint statement that made it look like a joint decision. It was an Army decision entirely but Army was nice about it, observed all diplomatic amenities. General Taylor made a special trip to the Notre Dame campus to soften the blow; and though Army had intended to break off abruptly after the 1946 0–0 tie, the '47 game was added as a concession to Irish sensibilities.

That was how the famous series finally came to Notre Dame after thirty-four years—for sentimental burial. Everybody on both sides leaned over backwards to wind it up pleasantly. The game itself was typical—a dramatic runback of the opening kick-off for 97 yards and a score by Terry Brennan; a gallant Army; a respectable 27–7 Notre Dame victory. The Irish students put on a nostalgic show between halves, and gave up their best girls to Army first-classmen at a campus dance that night.

It was such a splendid wake that people went home predicting this lively corpse must rise again and before too many years. As Arthur Daley wrote in the New York *Times:* "They were like people who, after the divorce had been granted, smiled and asked just what they had been mad about, anyhow?"

Army and Notre Dame will do all right in their separate ways. New York will get along without its game; as will the millions of people throughout the country to whom it had become the national game. But it will be missed and people who miss it will continue to ask: "Why?"

As a Notre Dame insider who has also been friendly to Army ever since 1921 when I first made the trip to West Point with the Irish squad, I will give you a strictly personal opinion which may also be fairly classified as special pleading.

We had grown to like Army through the years. We freely admitted and appreciated that Army had been our sponsor in national gridiron society, had been a friend when we had, as you will later see, sorely needed a friend. We knew that there had always been a minority among the athletic-minded at West Point who wanted to cancel the Notre Dame game on the understandable theory that the benefits derived were not worth the consistent damage to Army prestige.

We admired the way Army always came to the Yankee Stadium, usually as an underdog, fought its heart out, and left without a squawk, whether it won or lost. We were somewhat embarrassed by the fact that we won so consistently; we frequently said, among ourselves: "If we've got to lose one, why can't it be to Army, our good friend?" But we also knew that the games were usually close, that the underdog was always dangerous, that several of the Irish victories developed from games we were supposed to have lost. It was that kind of a series, which was why it became what it was. We loved it, thought the Army football squad, Cadet Corps and Alumni Association also loved it too much to allow anything to happen to it.

Much was made in the press and other discussions about how the "subway alumni," most of whom had never seen Notre Dame, had taken over the game with somewhat riotous behavior. There might have been something to that in the early days; but in the later years it was more of a blue-chip audience. Notre Dame distributed less than half of the seats and these, quite frankly, were spread by alumni among close friends and business contacts. You almost had to "be somebody" to get a ticket to the game and "somebodies" do not scalp tickets. Each year Notre Dame bounced New York scalpers from its campus and finally went so far as to allot student tickets only to those who actually boarded the student train.

The crowd was well-behaved and I don't recall any of those mass riots over goalposts which sometimes follow games in

33

strictly collegiate atmosphere. The disciplined Cadet Corps always marched off and Notre Dame students were usually too happy about the finish to provoke "incidents." The games on the field were rough but that was part of the tradition and the players enjoyed it. Army officials were irritated by some scurrilous mail from the more untutored synthetics; and there was an organized postcard campaign by a section of the Irish student body which, for many months before the '46 game, daily notified Cadet authorities that the Army dominance was about to end. This was good-natured in motive but may have been annoying to the recipients and a contributing item.

If Army wants to play again, Notre Dame will go along; and there are indications that the game may be resumed on a home-and-home occasional basis, rather than a permanent status, before too long. The Irish will never feel quite the same again about their good friends from West Point; but they have recognized Army's right to its own decisions and have never considered that Army had been influenced by any cabal out to "get" Notre Dame by schedule intrigue.

Is there such a combine? If so, why? And how important is the movement and its possible results?

There is no plain evidence of concert but everybody seems to agree by now that it does exist. The only Big Ten schools that now play Notre Dame are Iowa, Indiana, Purdue—all of which, because of small stadia, have trouble getting games in their own league—and Michigan State, which has recently joined the Conference. Other doors in other sections have also remained significantly closed when the Irish have tried the bells.

Why is something else. There have been neither charges of unethical conduct nor criticisms of academic standards—the usual reasons for schedule sanctions. Now and then something does come from behind this gridiron curtain but from "anonymous" sources. Some of these we will discuss later on in connection with other subjects; for the moment let's deal with the two factors which seem to be concrete and probably contain the real substance.

1. Notre Dame is just too tough. This is the verdict the press and public seem to have arrived at—and with which Notre Dame has no quarrel. Football, after all, is a business.

2. Frank Leahy. The one plain fact in the situation is that the flight from the schedule definitely accelerated, if it did not actually begin, when Leahy returned from the Navy in 1946, spurned professional offers and signed a ten-year contract at Notre Dame. It is also a fact that Leahy is hard to beat. In his eight years as a head coach—the first two at Boston College—he has won 71 games, lost 5 and tied 5. In his last four seasons at Notre Dame he has won three national championships and run second (to Michigan in '48) with another undefeated squad.

There have been innuendos about his "salesmanship" and aggressive recruiting—but again no charges. There are criticisms about his personal mannerisms and affectations. It all seems to boil down to a vague accusation that no man can actually be as good, either on or off the field, as Leahy seems to be. Notre Dame would like all these things brought into the open and weighed on the scales—in fairness to the man and his school.

Leahy's troubles, and Notre Dame's at the moment, are rooted in his elusive personality, his coaching efficiency and the obvious fact that, as an athletic director, he has not been able to match Rockne. The Master could beat them and make them like it. The Pupil beats them and they seem to wind up hating his guts (in a professional way, because, personally, he is one of the nicest men in football).

Nobody else has approached Rockne as an athletic director at any school. He was a genius in personal relations and Notre Dame has come to a belated recognition of the fact that no one man should be expected to try to match him. It has moved Moose Krause, with Leahy's approval, into the schedule picture, as Director of Athletics. And that brings us to the question: How serious is the schedule situation and what might come out of it?

To Notre Dame the situation is irritating but not serious. It did not make the situation but, now that it has been made, will see it through. The only fixtures it has lost are Army, Illinois and Northwestern; these have been readily replaced by Southern Methodist, Washington, Michigan State, North Carolina and Tulane. It isn't flattered when old friends don't answer the doorbell; but it has shown that this is still a big country where new friends can be made—friends with fine teams and also big stadia. It isn't mad at anybody; if any of the old friends should want to come back in the future, it will look over its schedule situation at the time and see if it can conveniently fit them in.

The significant development is that there has been, for some time now, a sharp division on policy matters between the Northern and Southern Conference groups; and that Notre Dame, the powerful lone wolf and acknowledged box-office champion, has been forced to veer from its natural orbit and normal alignment with the Big Ten, toward the South. It is a rather amazing fact that some stadiums are actually being enlarged to meet the Notre Dame crowd-power and that others might be so enlarged.

Out of all this could come a new alignment of championship games among schools which want to play the best and are willing to lay their prestige on the line in sporting competition. You can guess where the public interest will go, on the days when Notre Dame meets SMU and Doak Walker, North Carolina and Charlie Justice.

Actually, as we shall see a few pages along, Notre Dame is following a path blazed by Jess Harper and Rockne forty years ago when the Irish, rank outsiders in their own section, were forced to go out of their section for games.

The football followed Notre Dame then, when the odds were terrific against them.

The football might just follow Notre Dame again, when it starts with a powerful hand and plenty of blue chips.

That's why Notre Dame isn't mad at anybody, why it will go on trying to hold its unique position as par for the course. If all they can say about you is that you are the best—that's pretty good. And that is all they've really said about Notre Dame.

Michigan?

Okay—and now we're getting into something entertaining as well as illuminating.

VII

Notre Dame and Michigan have been fighting it out for years—in the weekly Associated Press poll, a guessing game based on the fallacy of comparative scores, but nevertheless the most satisfactory method yet devised for deciding the mythical national championship between teams which do not get together on the field.

The Irish won in '47, though the AP did confuse itself and all concerned by holding a "second poll which, however, was not to supersede the first." Minnesota settled that by delivering the national championship trophy to Notre Dame. And after the '48 season Notre Dame dutifully brought the trophy to the Wolverines. So, with honors even, they go on battling fiercely every week—in the polls.

Notre Dame has said, with what must be embarrassing frequency to Ann Arbor, that it would much prefer to settle these things on the field. It is sincere enough; but it has also obviously enjoyed sticking the needle into the Wolverine hide because these two, in a quiet way, happen to be the Hatfields and McCoys of the Midwestern gridiron. This is one of those situations submerged in the smooth ellipse, a dormant feud resulting from an ancient quarrel and enmeshed in the bigger and frequently asked question: "Why doesn't Notre Dame belong to the Western Conference?"

They did get together in 1942-43 with honors even between Crisler and Leahy; but that was after a lapse of thirty-three years—and from all appearances it may be that long before they get together again, though they are natural rivals and there's even tradition of a sort involved. Some of the early coaches at Notre Dame were Michigan men; the first three games Notre Dame played were against Michigan; it was the Wolverines who first taught the Irish how to play the game in 1887, just eight years after Princeton and Rutgers formally began to agitate the bag of wind.

Notre Dame had survived its early fight for life, was an established college, with a student body drawn from every state in the union, and was growing in all directions like the vital youngster it was. Football was only one of many informal campus sports, a form of soccer that class teams, with as many as forty on a side, played for a barrel of apples or a keg of cider. So when Michigan, the "Champion of the West," suggested that it drop in at Notre Dame for a game of the rugby style, the Irish eagerly accepted but said the visitors would first have to show them how the new game was played.

Michigan arrived on the morning of *Wednesday*, November 23, was met by a committee of students, shown around—and then two teams were formed, each composed of Michigan and Notre Dame players. After "some minutes" of this demonstration, the real game began, with eleven men on a side; but there was just time to play "one inning" which Michigan won 8-0. After a hearty dinner, President Walsh thanked the visitors who departed by carriage for Niles, en route to Chicago where the next day they defeated an eleven picked from alumni of Yale and Harvard, 26-0.

The following year the Wolverines came back, this time in April, and gave the Irish two more lessons. The first was played at the Green Stocking Ball Park in South Bend before four hundred spectators, with Michigan winning 26-6. The next day the visitors came out to the campus, for noon dinner, and after a "short ride on the lake" took the field again, but with a change in the lineup. R. S. Babcock, a Wolverine who had been injured the preceding day and was too lame to play, exchanged jobs with E. M. Sprague, who had refereed the previous day's game.

Then, the first rhubarb developed, described in the *Notre Dame Scholastic:* "Ann Arbor could do nothing until the last two minutes of the first inning. Then, while the players were settling some dispute, Sprague took the ball and made a touchdown for Michigan. Notre Dame claimed the touchdown was illegal, asserting that Sprague neglected to put the ball in play and furthermore went out of bounds near the goal. The referee Babcock, however, could not see it in that light." It ended Michigan 10, Notre Dame 4.

In the spring of '89, Notre Dame, resplendent in new uniforms "which had the great advantage of being padded" challenged Michigan, no doubt hoping to call themselves Champions of the West. But, according to the aggressive *Scholastic* editor, "Michigan backed squarely out, alleging various excuses. The secret of the matter probably is that their best men have left the team and it is in a weak state." At any rate, the fine camaraderie seemed to have been definitely dissipated because the teams did not meet again for nine years.

The first great contest of Notre Dame tradition was against Northwestern, which was to become a consistent rival through the years; and, of course, it was won or it would not be so well remembered. It was played away from home and old Brother Hugh used to tell about it at later football banquets, just before he fell asleep. According to his version, which amplified through the years, with his waistline, the Notre Dame players were still being brought back to the campus—in ambulances—a week later. The inference was that any man able to return under his own power was not considered to have done his full duty to the University.

That was the only game played in '89 and perhaps the *Scho-*

lastic editor referred proudly to an undefeated season. In his most ambitious dreams he would not have predicted that Notre Dame would not have a losing season in the next forty-three years. Actually, excepting those first three "practice" games with Michigan, Notre Dame has had only one losing season, in 1933, when Hunk Anderson's last squad lost five and tied one of nine games; but even this goat team found enough strength in tradition to upset Army 13-12 in the finale.

Not even a bumptious college sports editor could have seen a mighty football tradition in the making, nor much future in the sport itself, from the evidence of the first seven years at Notre Dame. Only twenty-one games were played, against whatever outfits were available, including folks like Illinois Cycling Club and Indianapolis Artillery.

In 1894 the need for "a coacher" was realized and James L. T. Morrison, who had played with Michigan the preceding year, was brought in. His regime got off to an auspicious start with a 14-0 victory over Hillsdale; but this seemed to cause Hillsdale also to realize the necessity for a coacher; when they went home, they took the Notre Dame mentor with them, which seems to have been par for the course in those days. Morrison was followed by H. G. Hadden, who seems to have come from parts unknown and disappeared into same after one season. But the fickleness of these gentlemen may also have been providential; for Hadden was succeeded by a man who, typifying the brighter side of the free and easy era, became one of Notre Dame's illustrious sons.

Frank E. Hering had played quarterback at Chicago but came to Notre Dame to coach, play on the team and study law. He was an outstanding student and natural orator, and after graduation became associated with the Order of Eagles as editor of their magazine. In 1930, after the entire nation had adopted the custom of Mother's Day, the War Mothers traced its source and credited the original impetus to Frank Hering, one of Our Lady's tough guys, who had advocated the idea at a speech given February 7, 1904 to an Eagles' convention at the English Opera House in Indianapolis, where a tablet now marks the spot.

Hering, who served for four years and was the first authentic coach in the Irish tradition, was succeeded in the next decade by a transitory group, most of whom seem to have been players brought in from other schools, who coached the team, played on it and sometimes continued their studies. It was a fitful procedure, typical of the state of football at a time when an eleven usually meant just that; when the men who started invariably finished, often from necessity, because those who could not make the first team showed little inclination to serve as scrimmage fodder. This was fertile territory for the tramp; and when one of these sturdy characters dropped in he was eagerly welcomed by the coach and players who, no doubt, also had ingenious methods for "taking care" of him academically.

Notre Dame undoubtedly had its share of these colorful birds of flight and one of them remained, as a vestigial remnant. James Francis Farragher, recently dead, was a native of Youngstown and a pipe-fitter by trade, who liked football better and followed the glory road. When I met him he had one eye and a distinctive terminology which referred to *New*braska, and to Duquesne by its earlier name of Holy Ghost College, and to West Virginny where he served under Fielding Yost, who also played on the team, in the fashion of those days.

Jim finally settled down at Notre Dame, where he played under the famous Pat O'Dea for two seasons and then coached the team himself in 1902. He never impressed me as a man who had spent much time in class but he did have the student's viewpoint —at least, in his years as a campus cop, whenever an emergency arose we always felt that Jim would be more loyal to us than to the University. He had a keen scent for lager at reunion parties, and I remember one of these where he sat recounting his experiences while a distinguished alumnus and former gridiron great po-

42

liced the ceremonies, wearing Jim's cap, badge and gun. The gun
went off, incidentally, but fortunately without incident.

The romancers of life always receive more than their share of
publicity; but the great majority of the grid heroes at all schools
around the turn of the century were of the solid class, and some of
our best citizens of later years came out of this rugged era. One of
these at Notre Dame was Louis "Red" Salmon, who played four
years and coached in 1904. He is the first great legendary hero of
Notre Dame football, a fullback of the Nagurski type whom old-
timers well remember and who is often listed among the all-time
players. Another was Angus McDonald, who played both baseball and football, later became Chairman of the Board of the
Southern Pacific Railroad and was a familiar figure at alumni gatherings and in the upper councils of the school until his death just a
few years ago.

Thomas A. Barry, who died in 1947, was an excellent example.
He graduated from Brown, where he was captain of the 1902
football squad, and later finished law at Harvard. But football men
frequently are unwilling to leave the sport and Barry coached two
years at Notre Dame, and later at Tulane, Wisconsin and Bowdoin
before he finally settled down to a successful business career. He
was secretary of the Rhode Island branch of the National Metal
Trades Association for thirty years and advised member companies on labor relations.

There was another group of vagabonds around Notre Dame
who provided background atmosphere. These were knights of the
road, mostly of Irish extraction, who dropped off freight cars for
temporary hospice, liked the place, and remained to exchange
light labor, light as possible no doubt, for food and living quarters
in a row of outlying shacks attached to the fence around the baseball field which waggish students christened Rockefeller Hall.
They finally faded as quietly as they had come, victims of progress.

VIII

There comes a time when every healthy teen-ager begins to get too big for his pants. If neglected, he is on his way to juvenile delinquency. If curbed too tightly he loses vitality or develops inhibitions. The average parents strive for—and are usually happy to settle for—a middle course where Junior has his fun, kicks over the traces now and then, but in the main stays fairly well on the beam.

That's just about the way the colleges have handled football. Where there are abuses, the faculties are mainly responsible. The tightly restricted Simon Pures either don't amount to anything much in a football way or get secret aid from conniving alumni. The great majority seem to admit that boys will be boys and settle for a reasonable compromise.

In the beginning it had to be worked out from scratch. The East handled it on an individual basis and still does. The Ivy League is a loose-knit informal grouping where each president is responsible for his own school. Tight organization has always been difficult along the Seaboard because of the variety of classifications, with private schools in the position of major importance.

In the Midwest, however, the big state institutions have dominated from the beginning; and these made their first move to bring the vibrant student activity of football back in line when the Western Conference was formed in 1896 by Wisconsin, Michigan, Minnesota, Chicago, Purdue, Northwestern and Illinois. Later Indiana and Iowa were added to make it the Big Nine. Michigan withdrew in 1905 but Ohio State came in; and when the Wolverines returned in 1917 the group operated as the Big Ten until Chicago retired in 1939 with a pessimistic valedictory by Dr. Robert Hutchins, who left a bucket of dead fish on the doorstep—his opinion of the football business. Michigan State has now been added to make it the Big Ten again.

The Western Conference has had its troubles and is still having them; but through the years it has done a fairly efficient police job and has served as the model for other sectional groups. Like most of them, it gives full lip service to the rigid amateur idea but operates on the elastic Job Plan, which has proved to be the most realistic solution of the subsidization problem for practical men of reasonable good will and intentions.

Shortly after the Conference was organized Notre Dame applied for admission but was told it was not big enough, which, at the time, it probably was not. The ambitious Irish, then coached by solid Tom Barry, didn't seem to be particularly offended, and made moves to qualify for future membership. They put their house in the then-accepted order by limiting athletic eligibility to six years by bona fide students; banning those who had ever been paid for athletic services; and requiring a general average of 75 percent for athletic participation. Such virtue was apparently rewarded by an increasing number of victories over major Conference opponents.

When Michigan withdrew in 1905 Notre Dame again applied, presenting its new eligibility and playing standards as proper credentials. They were put off diplomatically, much as Pitt has been in the last few years; but when Ohio State was taken in almost immediately, the Irish began to get the idea. Their pride was hurt, they made no secret of it, and the first lines were drawn for the showdown that was soon to come.

They had not played Michigan since 1902, which was just as well for them, as Yost was then in his heyday, with a four-year victory record that still stands. But when the Irish again appeared on the Wolverine schedule in 1908, they held the mighty Champions of the West to a 12-6 score, the only Notre Dame loss of that season and the second in three years.

A new power was rising, everybody knew it and looked forward to the 1909 meeting between the perennial champion and the husky young challenger. Notre Dame, still changing coaches almost every year—a definite handicap to an ambitious school trying to upset the master of the period and one of the great gridiron teachers of all time—came up with another new one but seemed to have used good judgment in his selection because he was Frank C. "Shorty" Longman, who had been an end on Yost's "point-a-minute" teams.

The dressing room speeches that day at Ann Arbor must have been interesting. Yost, a vigorous orator, no doubt called upon his champions to go out and put the bumptious upstarts from South Bend in their places. Shorty Longman, a thunderer whose idea of showing who was boss was to lick personally every man on the squad, or try to, was undoubtedly fired by the terrific yen every pupil has to upset the Master. And the situation was psychologically perfect for him.

Notre Dame had a lot of fish to fry that day—the chance to beat Michigan after eight previous defeats; the prestige of usurping that proud title, Champions of the West, which Michigan held so long that it is in the school song which Governor Dewey, a Wolverine, once quoted on the radio. Michigan was not then a member of the Western Conference but only because it didn't want to be. Notre Dame wanted to be but had been high-hatted. Then, to add spice, there had been some rumblings from Ann Arbor about the eligibility of two Notre Dame linemen, Ralph Dimmick of Hubbard, Ore., and George Philbrook of Olympia, Wash.

It must have been quite a ball game. For many years thereafter, and perhaps still if his health permits, Father Matt Walsh, one of Notre Dame's presidents, indoctrinated incoming freshmen with an engaging and expanding tale of how Pete Vaughan had hit the line so low for the winning touchdown of the 12-3 victory that the mark of the goalpost, then on the line, showed on his *back*. The *Scholastic* sports editor of that year, Leo J. Cleary, had this modest say:

"In the banner game of the season at Ann Arbor, Notre Dame clearly demonstrated her superiority in the West. For years the Yost machine had held sway. Michigan had given Syracuse a drubbing one week before which showed her wonderful strength; and competent critics, allowing Notre Dame due credit for her victories, prophesied a close score in Michigan's favor. Michigan men were in the best of condition, their linemen were heavy and their repertory of plays well rehearsed. Every artifice was employed by Yost's pupils; but the plays were smothered as fast as they were started. Michigan was out-generaled, out-fought and out-played at every stage of the game, and their show of gameness dwindled when they faced a bitter line-up. The victory over Michigan places Notre Dame far in the lead for Western honors and with a claim to Eastern superiority as well."

One of the by-products of Notre Dame athletics, which I will go into later on, has been a quite remarkable group of influential sports writers, none of whom has ever been exactly accused of giving his alma mater the worst of it. All, in their student days have probably served on the *Scholastic* where Notre Dame has never come close to being wrong in any argument or ever lost a game without explainable circumstances. But this may be a defensive mechanism, as the following clip from the South Bend *News* of November 23, 1909, will explain:

"At the close of what is pronounced the best football season since the rules were changed in the winter of 1905-06 Notre Dame is recognized by the authorities as the champion of the west. Eckersall, the Chicago football expert and critic, while admitting that Notre Dame must be considered the logical champion because of the defeat of Michigan, qualifies the statement by saying that 'Coach Yost's players were not at their best when they met Notre Dame and if the two teams were to meet next Saturday Michigan would in all probability be the winner.'"

Even the great Eckersall took another poll!

The day after the 1909 game Harry "Red" Miller, the first of the famous Miller clan of football players with all-Americans in two generations, went to Yost's office to pay his respects. He told me recently that he had been shocked and hurt by the Master's rudeness. He also said that "Notre Dame was much better than the score indicated."

The next year brought the payoff.

IX

Notre Dame, again en route to Ann Arbor, got only as far as Niles, six miles from home, when they were called back. Michigan had cancelled the game. This clipping of November 12, 1910, again from the *Scholastic*, gives the Notre Dame version of what it was all about:

THE CASE WITH MICHIGAN.

Michigan's cancellation of the Michigan-Notre Dame football game, which was to have been played at Ann Arbor last Saturday, has been the cause of much discussion here the past week. The trouble centered on our intention to play Dimmick and Philbrook, Michigan claiming that both these men were ineligible because of the fact that they had played out their time as collegiate football players. A review of the athletic careers of both of these men shows that in 1904-05 they were preparatory students at Tullatin Academy and competed on teams there. The following year both men were students at Peason's Academy, an institution apart from Whitman College. In September, 1907, they registered at Whitman College, taking two freshman studies and three or four preparatory studies. Dimmick remained at Whitman until February, 1908, and Philbrook until June of the same year. Whitman College is not named in the list of conference colleges issued in September, 1907. Because of that it is only reasonable to presume these men as participating in preparatory athletics prior to their coming to Notre Dame. On these grounds we maintain that Philbrook and Dimmick are eligible and will continue to hold these grounds.

Last January when this game was arranged, Manager Curtis inquired as to whether we would be allowed to play these men in the game this fall, and Director of Athletics Bartelme gave his assurance that there would be no trouble on that score. Mr. Bartelme also assured Coach Longman to the same effect. The reason for Notre Dame's desire that this matter be settled was brought about by various reports which originated from the Michigan camp last fall, after the Notre Dame game concerning the eligibility of these men.

The fact that Michigan sent down the names of Cole and Clarke as being eligible for this game leads to the one conclusion that they should consider Dimmick and Philbrook eligible, for Clarke and Cole, according to conference rules are ineligible, as Cole played the seasons of '05, '07, and '08 at Oberlin, and Clarke too has played his allotted time according to conference rule.

The *Scholastic* editors generously recognized that there might be another side to the case by reprinting this quotation from the Washington *Post:* "There is no reason why the word of a man like the vice-president of Notre Dame should be doubted, yet Mr. Bartelme, Director of Athletics at Michigan, flatly denies ever having agreed to the use of these men, and asserts that the three years' clause in the contract was especially designed to govern such disputes as have arisen."

I recently came upon a story from a Notre Dame source which would support the Michigan position. According to this admittedly hazy recollection, Notre Dame had issued orders not to take the two disputed men to Ann Arbor, but these instructions were "forgotten." There was no mention of this, however, in the printed accounts at the time.

The controversy was thoroughly aired in the newspapers, where the Irish cause was vigorously defended by Father Tom Crumley, a brilliant and tenacious philosopher who was then vice-president of the school and chairman of the Athletic Board. In recent years Notre Dame has enjoyed a friendly press, another Rockne accomplishment; but in 1910 they were still outsiders. They lost the publicity battle and were, formally or otherwise, banished from Conference football schedules for almost a decade.

These ancient events had a decisive effect on Midwestern and national football history; have had a scarred influence on Notre Dame's relations with Michigan and the Western Conference ever since; are reminiscent in the current Irish schedule troubles. They should also clarify two of the muddled points in the Irish gridiron legend: Notre Dame had definitely established itself as a major power before the arrival of Rockne; and it could hardly have been "obscure" when Army scheduled it in 1913.

What were the facts in the controversy? I don't know and I doubt if, at this late date, anybody knows—or cares much. The dispute obviously revolved about eligibility of players at a time when the three-year rule was just coming in; and the Notre Dame statement seemed to infer that it was, at worst, another case of the pot-and-the-kettle variety which is still familiar in such situations. Rockne, who was a freshman in 1910, dismissed the incident humorously in his autobiography:

"On the Notre Dame squad in my first year of football were two stars charged with being ringers, Philbrook and Dimmick. As a matter of fact they weren't, for Notre Dame never knowingly enrolled a ringer; but when Notre Dame went to play Michigan, controversy raged and for awhile it looked as if Dimmick would be barred. He saved the day himself when, recognizing a Michigan player who had seen college football experience elsewhere, Dimmick walked up and loudly commiserated with him. 'You've heard the bad news? It's terrible. Your youngest son has been dropped from the eighth reader.' "

The only trouble with that is that the Master seemed to be slightly misquoting himself. This may have happened in 1909 and Rockne would have been in position to have heard it repeated by Dimmick; but the 1910 game, when Rock was a freshman, was cancelled. The difficulty with trying to get the facts in such cases is that people are usually neutral for their own side, and arguments over eligibility always narrow down to precise interpretation. As late as 1948 Michigan protested the ruling of Big Nine officials who finally decided, after long deliberation, that Bump Elliott was ineligible.

Michigan no doubt has its version of the 1910 rhubarb. I can only give you the frankly Notre Dame case. The records show that all of the important Notre Dame players in the 1909 game had appeared in the losing 12-6 battle of the preceding year; that Dimmick played for three seasons and Philbrook four; that all of the members of the Irish cast proved their solidity in later life, including Philbrook who was killed in World War I. They definitely were not tramps. They may have been recruited and they may have received financial help. That was and is still being done in the best circles. The question then, as now, is whether it was done within the terms of existing rules and, perhaps more accurately, tacit practices.

Other factors were pertinent. Notre Dame was then still a small school, and a poor school by comparison with the state institutions: it is easy enough to understand why the Conference members may have suspected its rapid rise to football parity. After the controversy had ended Father Crumley made the stinging observation that "the dispute seemed to have been settled

more on theological than on athletic standards." People sometimes take sides about the Irish, too—even at Notre Dame, where
Sorin himself never liked them too much because they were not
"obedient by nature," which nobody with the Gaelic strain
would ever trouble to deny.

Notre Dame's remarkable national following has been due
primarily to the fact that it has been a spectacular, and at times
almost a magical, winner. Sportsmen follow it as they do a Jack
Dempsey or a Joe Louis because of its color, punch and sweep.
The school is never quite divorced, however, from its religious
and racial tradition. Millions of people undoubtedly wish it well
because it carries the Catholic banner and the Irish tag; so it is to
be reasonably expected that others may find themselves disposed
against it for the same reasons. There's no point in kidding ourselves about such things—religion and race are strong potions and
bigotry does rear up in the pinches now and then; but the record
certainly proves that Notre Dame progress has never been seriously hampered by it.

There's another and much more important angle of the football business which is all bound up with the preceding factors. You
have probably never given much thought to the *social* side of
schedule-making; but it's there, operating intangibly but effec-
tively, and along the same pattern as outside the game.

People naturally associate with those of the same general
background. There's nothing wrong with that, particularly since
most American ranks are open for the up-and-coming individual
who has the stuff to make the transitions—though these do have
uncomfortable moments now and then, when new-found friends
look backward.

The colleges also have social positions, defined by their alumni
and students, with the usual qualifications of old family, long and
honorable tradition, wealth, culture and manners. In an institutional sense colleges also fraternize with those of like academic and
athletic standards, and along private and state lines.

The swineskin elite are found, logically enough, in the Ivy League, a tight old gridiron-family group, with circles within the circle, through the Big Three, beyond Princeton to Yale and the Ultimate—Harvard. Army and Navy can mingle with these, as could certain older New England colleges if they should decide to go for football in the grand manner. When Harvard went to Virginia two years ago it was a significant gesture toward another "gentleman's school" because Harvard seldom goes anywhere and is discriminating about who comes to Harvard, as are all of the Ivy Leaguers.

(Nothing written here is to be construed as a slap at Harvard. I like the place and the people who conduct its athletics; as I do all of the Ivy Leaguers, always excepting those minority members who, after three drinks, start burping sneers about all colleges south or west of the Connecticut line, which, of course, includes other Ivy Leaguers. Such characters are known far and wide as Ivy Jerks.)

The state schools have their Conference Crowds with the Big Ten as the most pretentious. Michigan is also the social leader here, and, with Ohio State, Illinois and Minnesota, completes the Big Four. In the Pacific Coast group Stanford and California form the exclusive social twosome. The Southern conferences don't amount to much in gridiron social circles these days because of their attitude on amateurism, the holy religion among the elite.

As a general rule private schools rank the state institutions, socially. And a big stadium is a definite, though not always a conclusive asset. If you want a further check on all this, the complete volume of Football's Blue Book, take a close look at all the schedules and watch how the old friends gather in intimate groups, particularly toward the season's end, when the traditional games are played.

In this field, Notre Dame, operating as a lone wolf, without benefit of any Conference support, has also been sensationally successful. The Army sponsorship provided the wedge and Notre

Dame's ability to fill stadiums didn't hurt any; but here again the most vital factor was the Rockne charm and personality; and Notre Dame not only followed where he led but was able to march on after his death—until Leahy came back from the wars.

At the moment it is in the relative social position of the Boston Irish Catholic who, through exceptional vitality, ability and personality, made his mark, then his money, and, while doing these things, also gradually filled in the cultural, educational and social gaps in his "minority chart." Notre Dame has made the grade in record time and despite unusual handicaps; it knows it, is proud of the accomplishment, feels that it is definitely on its way to truly wonderful heights as an American institution of learning, prefers to regard its football eminence as a reflection of the true excellence of the University.

But it also has a little of that old inferiority complex lingering on, may be a little too sensitive, even today, when snobs, whom it feels it has outstripped in everything but antiquity, make those cracks about shirtsleeves, racial and religious origins—and football factories with Polish names.

Back in 1910 Notre Dame may have been unduly sensitive about such things, may have placed entirely too much stress upon them. But whatever the reason, it was on a spot, caged up within its own territory by the ruling powers, sentenced to obscurity.

It could accept the edict and give up the effort to be a major gridiron power—and there were some who counseled just that, particularly since football had been a losing venture, and never did pay its way until 1913.

But its Irish pride had been wounded; its fighting spirit had been aroused.

For Notre Dame there has always been, as now, only one decision—*fight to live*.

It faced to the East—and a new and glorious chapter in football history.

Up to now its men had been chiefly of Irish stock, supported by the Germans and sons of other pioneers.

Now, though Notre Dame did not know it, the new men were coming, the second wave—Italian, Slav, Pole, Syrian—but all Americans and including, as always, the Jews and the Protestants.

In various parts of the country boys were being born—Carideo, Savoldi, Schwartz, Brill, Metzger.

Living through the Montana winter in a tent was a hardy blond infant christened by his homesteading parents William Francis Leahy.

Starting to school were Layden, Stuhldreher, Miller, Crowley—the Four Horsemen.

In the grades were Hunk and Eddie Anderson, Mohardt, Shaw, Kiley, Wynne, Madigan—and the son of a Congregationalist minister, George Gipp.

A Chicago quarterback was thinking of a coaching career—and at West Point somebody had the glimmer of an idea about bringing in a small Western school.

Already on the campus as a freshman was the balding young genius from Norway whom nobody, including himself, thought big enough for a football player. He was a student of chemistry and a track athlete who had quit his job in the Chicago post office with every intention of entering Illinois University. But he had been detoured by one of those accidents which Notre Dame, with its strong sense of destiny and of ordained vocation, dares to believe *providential*.

X

MGM once made a picture during which Spencer Tracy muddled around for nearly two hours trying to decide whether he should remain a sports writer or become an *important* writer as Katherine Hepburn was nagging at him to do.

The flesh-and-blood characters of the sports-writing craft sometimes debate the same general subject during informal seminars which form such a pleasing sedative to, perchance, being considered unimportant; but their problem is mainly concerned with whether they should exchange a job at which they are perfectly happy for the privilege of developing artistic ulcers in lonely cubicles.

Sports writing is not only just about the most pleasant way of making a living you can imagine; it is also the field in which a writer can most completely develop because he is encouraged to shoot the works and suffers little of the editorial supervision which restricts "important" writers. His brain-children are Spartan babes, left on the daily hill of print exactly as born, to live or die; but they are usually lusty infants, of all shapes and colors, because that's the kind of people he writes about. He is not only a critic but a dramatist of the outdoor stage. Because he is not expected to create literature, he sometimes does; and when he moves on to another field he usually goes on writing in much the same manner.

All of which explains why sports have contributed men of the wide variety of style and subject as Damon Runyan, Ring Lardner, Westbrook Pegler, Heywood Broun, Quentin Reynolds, John Kieran and Paul Gallico, to name a recent few. And there are and have been many others who could "graduate" but whose preference is expressed in the press box phrase: "All I want is my job and a million bucks—and I'm not too particular about the million."

Punts, pitches, putts and punches *are* unimportant; but after all, and this is what the literary pontiffs seem to overlook, *athletes are people, too,* each with a story just as much affected by his sport as the sailor by the sea or any other fictional character by his environment. And each story is usually all the more dramatic because, like the movie star, the athlete is apt to be mentally and emotionally unprepared for the publicity and other pressures under which he lives.

The sports story can become as important as the writing makes it. Ring Lardner proved that. Runyan did it with fighters long before he celebrated his *Guys And Dolls.* Bill McGheehan's columns were acid portraits and Grant Rice finds poetry in all sports. Others do it right along in hurried marriages of sweat and inspiration whose quality escapes the attention of critics who do not look for gems on sports pages.

All sport has the flame of youth and the power to influence impressionable youth. Its people are vital and exciting. College football has the added background advantage of education. Its players and coaches, with higher mentality and culture, sometimes expand into other fields, become authentic heroes to youth and beloved national personalities. Stagg, Camp, Yost, Sutherland —and the greatest of all these, Rockne.

His story begins, like that of so many of our outstanding Americans, overseas, in the village of Voss, Norway, March 4, 1888. He was baptized in the Lutheran faith in a church which had begun as Catholic seven hundred years before, an interesting item since he was to die a Catholic. He came from a progressive and inventive-minded family, a pertinent observation because throughout his career he was usually a step ahead of his field, as was his carriage-building father whose "kariols" became so famous that he numbered Emperor Wilhelm of Germany among his customers.

His daring nature as a four-year-old once got him marooned on an ice floe, an adventure which brought the entire village to his rescue. He won a bad-acting horse, appropriately named Satan, by the simple method of accepting a challenge to ride the animal. When the family took him to the seaport town of Bergen, he fell off a gangplank and a sailor had to fish him out of the deep water with a grappling hook.

His father came to America to exhibit one of his carriages at the World's Fair, won a prize, decided to remain and sent for his family. When the ship docked in New York young Knute was missing—and they finally located the inquisitive five-year-old in the crow's nest. His first day at the Fair he was gone again—this time visiting Indians.

As a boy in Chicago grade school he was an exceptional student, an omnivorous reader and, as might be expected, a persistent pest to his four sisters, one older and three younger. He worked at odd jobs, faithfully attended church services and found outlets for his energies in all sorts of athletics. He was always small for his age but never let that bother him. His broken nose, at which Pegler later took a characteristic jab in print, thereby causing Rock to take considerable umbrage at Pegler, was a souvenir of a gang fight that followed a neighborhood baseball game.

Somebody swung a bat and mistook Rock's nose for a baseball —a blow which pained him all the more because his father had refused to allow him to play football because it was too rough! With the shrewdness he was later to use so well, he convinced his father that it was baseball which was really rough and thereby got permission to play football.

The Rocknes lived in the Logan Square neighborhood chiefly

inhabited by Irish and Swedes, with all the Nordics lumped as Swedes. You can imagine the carryings-on; but Rock himself wrote: "It was not unpleasant going, with its endless corner lots and tolerant police—a great place for a kid to grow up, with excitement for everybody." His early passion was for baseball and his heroes were Rube Waddell and Three-Fingered Brown; but the diamond interest waned after he first saw Walter Eckersall perform in a high school game.

As a freshman, 110 pounds, he went out for his Northwest Division High (now Tuley High) football squad but never got by the scrubs; never made the first team, in fact, until he was a senior. But his size was no handicap in track and he developed into a superior pole vaulter and half-miler, with a mark of 12 feet 4 inches in the former which probably brought the name of Knute Kenneth Rockne to the sports pages for the first time.

As happens so frequently, however, in high school as well as college, the young man's passion for athletics seems to have reduced his devotion to academic matters, which produced the usual complications. Finally came a day when the entire track squad absconded from school to practice. They were broken up as a unit and spread among the other high schools in the city; and, as also frequently happens, Rock's father suggested that, since his son obviously was not taking advantage of scholastic opportunities, it might be well if he went to work. So the future coach never finished high school, went to work instead, in the Chicago post office.

This is the official record of his service:

KNUTE ROCKNE: Appointed substitute clerk March 21, 1907. Promoted to regular clerk same date—salary $600 per annum. Assignment, Stamper Mailing Division, Main Post-Office. Transferred to Dispatcher Mailing Division, July 1, 1907. Salary advanced to $800 April 1, 1908; to $900 April 1, 1909; to $1,000 April 1, 1910. Resigned Nov. 28, 1910.

He worked from midnight till eight in the morning, every day in the week. The work was muscular—lifting fifty-pound sacks—and mental, for he had, seeking to avoid boredom, deliberately chosen the dispatcher's job which required him to memorize routes and timetables.

This was the crucial period in Rockne's life, during which he did the things which were to shape his later career. He continued his track activities, became a member of the Illinois A. C. He resumed his reading. And having decided there was no future in the civil service with its "political unfairness," he set himself a goal—he would save $1,000 and go to the University of Illinois.

Then came the accident which was definitely to affect the future of football and whatever else Rockne influenced.

He had saved his $1,000 but seemed slow about making the decisive break, which can become a difficult decision for a young man.

Rock's track activities had brought him into contact with other big-time amateurs. At the moment of his indecision, two of these, Johnny Devine and Johnny Plant, had decided to go to Notre Dame. When Rock told them he was thinking of going to Illinois, they suggested he go along with them.

"What swung me," he wrote, "was the argument that I could probably get a job, and certainly get by cheaper than at Champaign."

As a student editor I was characterized in our yearbook, *The Dome*, as "Hamlet at a sporting desk." The capsule was concocted, I believe, by the then head of our English department and now head of Hunter College, Dr. George Shuster. The phrase might well describe all sports writers who see something more on the field than punts and passes. I lived with the athletes I wrote about; and perhaps because I majored in philosophy, was always mooning in print about the nontechnical aspects of the game.

I have always been fascinated by the opportunity which the physical accident of athletic ability, in most cases football, gives a

61

young man to skip an economic generation. I have always been incensed at the injustice visited upon the players by the hypocritical aspects of such subsidization. Out of these convictions I later wrote several novels which became magazine serials and motion pictures, and finally realized that I had a social formula, was working, in fact, the vein of Alger and Cinderella—the American story of the boy who lifts himself from down here to up there.

One of the reasons, no doubt, that Rockne got to college and was able to stretch his thousand-dollar nest egg over four years, was because it is always easier for a good athlete to get college jobs—the very matter about which the colleges become so concerned and which they legislate against.

Where the system is flagrantly abused the college is responsible. But the system also produces the Rocknes, Sutherlands and all like them, successful men of today and the future, who would never otherwise have had their opportunities.

Then there is the matter of juvenile delinquency and the service of sport in salvaging boys who might have been taken over by vicious influences. Rockne lived in a rough neighborhood. He happened to be the type nothing could have spoiled; but there have been thousands of others whom sport has saved. I am thinking of one boy to whom his high school coach said: "In grade school you were the orneriest kid I ever saw and I was afraid for you. But once you got interested in football—" That boy became a college star and a business executive.

The harried, worried gentlemen of the N.C.A.A. might give a little thought to such things while tightening the hair shirts; might be less concerned about classic amateurism for the boys, particularly, to repeat, and this I cannot do too often, as long as they themselves conduct this *amateur sport for profit*.

IX

The feeling of a man toward his college usually describes an emotional circle.

The reverent freshman proceeds through sophomoric doubt and junior sophistication to such a senior cynicism that his alma mater is usually happy to be rid of him through graduation.

This path is reversed during the returning years. The wayward son at first comes back for football games, complaining about his seats and other things. The spacing organized class reunions bring on a romantic rheumatism which gradually develops into a magnificent magnification of his original devotion, and the arc is closed as the old grad pathetically gropes for his lost youth.

I saw a graphic demonstration of this when our twenty-five-year group convened at commencement time. We were quartered in Lyons Hall where there were also some graduating and hospitable seniors. The bridge of years was quickly gapped by a few remaining cans of student beer judiciously mixed with a bottle of fifteen-year-old alumni scotch and all was nicely sentimental until the inevitable sad senior began to sound off pessimistic opinions about the world in general and Notre Dame in particular.

We took turns with him in a corner, patiently trying to straighten him out. He had all the familiar words and arguments, we had the faith and wisdom of maturity. We got exactly nowhere but left him with the optimistic prediction that he would also be back for his twenty-fifth reunion and probably trying to convince some other rebellious senior that it wasn't going to be such a hopeless world and that he had been extremely privileged to have spent four golden years under the Golden Dome.

Still, the young man's attitude had been rather shocking and we were inclined to worry about both him and Notre Dame until the other seniors informed us that we had come upon an aggravated case which had baffled even their efforts. This was a consoling disclosure which confirmed our belief that neuroticism does not ordinarily flourish in a healthy masculine environment with spiritual overtones; and that Notre Dame probably has fewer sad young men in its student body than the average college.

I prefer to think that the more normal Notre Dame reaction was that of a football player on Rock's last team whom I met on the train as we travelled to Los Angeles. It was the final game of his career and he was going into it, he said, with a letdown feeling that was a complete contrast to the idealism of his freshman year. He was disillusioned about everything, particularly football. I gave him no pep talk, perhaps because I was still young enough to be of his generation and to have some doubts of my own.

The weather was too warm for my heavy overcoat so I borrowed his topcoat to wear in the press box. After the game—a glorious 27-0 victory in a contest we had entered as an underdog —I went to his room to return the coat.

I learned that he was in the hospital, which was surprising news since I hadn't remembered him being injured.

He hadn't been injured.

This disillusioned young man had played himself into exhaustion. And he's been doing much the same thing for Notre Dame ever since. I met him at the last Northwestern game. He had brought his family all the way from Wyoming where he is state governor of the Notre Dame Foundation. His name is Tom Kassis.

College boys have been doing things like that for their schools ever since that anonymous young immortal cried out: "I'd die for dear old Rutgers." Modern sophisticates choose to consider such expressions on the corny side now, just as they laugh at Brooklyn and Texas and as some even ridicule national pride and patriotism. But it will be a sad day for America when American boys can no longer feel such loyalty; as it is a sad day for any college campus when its athletes don't care enough to go all out in a game and its students don't care enough to be depressed by defeat.

The great day on any college campus is still the day when the football team wins a spiritual victory, does something it was not expected to do. That's easily proved. There were many great days and great victories during the '48 season; but quickly now, what games do you remember most vividly? Probably the Navy tie with Army; the Southern Cal tie with Notre Dame; the game that Ohio State *almost* won from Michigan; and for Notre Dame people, not the many victories but that last touchdown against the Trojans when the squad knew it had only two minutes to come all the way for the score that would preserve the first undefeated three-year stretch in Notre Dame history.

The spirit is still the important thing and college leaders are increasingly aware of the dangers of moral sterility which lie in too much emphasis on merely mental training. General Dwight Eisenhower expressed it this way in his installation speech as President of Columbia: "At all levels of education we must be constantly watchful that our schools do not become so engrossed in techniques, great varieties of fractionalized courses, highly specialized knowledge and the size of their physical plant, as to forget the principal purpose of education itself—to prepare the student for effective personal and social life in a free society."

There is not the slightest chance of a denominational school forgetting this principle because it is the essential reason for its existence. How strongly Notre Dame believes in education of the complete man was demonstrated after the Supreme Court had decided against released time for religious education in the public schools. Catholics were not directly affected by the ruling because the expansive parochial school system is maintained so that religious training may be fully and freely emphasized; but, nevertheless, almost the entire broadcast on Universal Notre Dame Night was devoted to a justification of released time by President John Cavanaugh and criticism of the Court decision by Dr. Clarence Manion, Dean of the Law School.

Cynicism is a thing of the mind; and Notre Dame, in its purely mental training, not only permits but encourages the mind to doubt—to the extent that its own philosophical courses sometimes turn Catholic students into atheists, as happened to one of my own classmates who had been preparing for the priesthood.

But loyalty is a thing of the heart, spirit a thing of the soul, and Notre Dame emphasizes such things more than even most religious schools. It doesn't stop at giving its boy things to learn —it gives him things in which he can *believe*.

It teaches him to believe in God and an immortal soul; in the right of each individual to earn temporal and eternal happiness by the decisions of his own free will. Its doctrine of social justice insists that the state is the creature, not the master, of the individual. Thus its firm support of our American form of government as opposed to totalitarianism, is a logical development of its theology.

The only political advice I ever had from a Notre Dame professor was from Father Bolger, head of the department of economics, who said to our group of freshmen as he probably said to all of his yearlings: "My advice to you young men who are about to have the right to vote, is to look around carefully and select the party least liable to loot the treasury." Notre Dame can produce any shade of political opinion among its students as long as that opinion includes a belief in God and the immortal soul. That is why I have never heard of a Notre Dame man becoming a Communist; and why nobody has ever heard of the existence of a Communist cell upon the campus. It would have to exist in an intellectual vacuum because the true Communist cannot believe in either God or an immortal soul.

There are Catholics, including some members of the clergy, who embrace economic doctrines also advocated by socialists and Communists; and who justify these by passages in the Papal Encyclicals. It is true that, up to a point, these do travel on the same track; it is equally true that the Church immediately parts company with any political doctrine which switches to a line that threatens the rights of the individual.

Theoretically, as a Catholic I could go along with the present English experiment in social democracy as long as it conforms to its announced purpose of protecting individual rights while enlarging government controls; but I must be prepared to veer away from the experiment as soon as it begins to threaten essential individual rights and thus point toward totalitarianism.

Actually, I would not go along with such an experiment in our country because I think it would inevitably develop into totalitarianism. I want no more government than is necessary to protect the common welfare; I want as much freedom for the individual as is possible. And that is a realistic political opinion based upon my own instincts and experience with other people. So I find it very easy to be a Catholic because I find myself in *intellectual* agreement with the Church teachings that affect that "personal and social life in a free society" that Eisenhower spoke of; and in *instinctive* agreement with the only basic spiritual things it tells me I *must* believe—that there is a God, that I have an immortal soul, that I should love my neighbor as myself and treat him accordingly—which means that I must recognize and respect his rights as firmly as I insist upon my own.

I believed these things before I went to Notre Dame; but Notre Dame education, in addition to training me for my profession, gave me facts and philosophy which strengthened my instinctive beliefs. I pity the person who cannot believe in things and people; and most of all the young who cannot bring themselves to believe in anything, who therefore are deprived of that most comfortable and heart-warming feeling of loyalty. I think that a university which turns out brilliant cynics has failed in its duty to youth, is itself guilty of delinquency just as much as parents who have not taken the trouble to comfort and strengthen the hearts and spirits of their children as well as their minds.

I have inserted this personal political credo because this is a Notre Dame story and I believe it is also the credo of the average Notre Dame student and graduate.

Jack Chevigny was a Notre Dame man, handsome, spirited, smart in the ways of the world, sophisticated in the superficial sense; but in the Army game of '28, after Rockne had given the squad George Gipp's deathbed request to "some day go out and beat the Army for me," it was Jack Chevigny who scored the first touchdown and cried exultantly: "There's one for the Gipper."

Sixteen years later, as an overage Marine lieutenant, he clenched his fist and with all his youthful faith and fire, said to me:

"Marines are expendable."

Three months later he hit the beach at Iwo Jima with a suicide squad. You can imagine how he died.

American boys and men have always done things like that for America because they have been taught to believe in America and a man fights and works hardest for the things in which he most truly believes.

My *team;* my *school;* my *town;* my *family;* my *friends;* my *faith;* my *country.*

That is the American credo—and Notre Dame's.

That is why Notre Dame, with its French name, Irish nickname and other foreign names, has always been a truly American university; and why, as it reaches toward physical and financial facilities comparable to the older universities, its people choose to believe that it is destined to become one of the great universities of the country, perhaps *the* university; because more than any of the others it will continue to avoid the dangers of barren mental training and insist upon the training of the full man, the cultured man in whom the spirit rules.

In its second century Notre Dame is not forgetting the lessons of the first; it will continue to build upon its two great sources of strength—God and the Melting Pot—upon which our country was also built.

XII

The old grads who have come back to the campus in recent postwar years have been shocked and appalled by bulging dormitories and classroom microphones, have moaned about educational factories, and mourned the lost charm and intimacy of their own student days. The Grand Central atmosphere is less apparent now, as the GI overflow has come back within the dam; but the social thought of the immediate future still moves in the direction of more higher education for more young people.

The postwar assault was heaviest on the big state schools. Notre Dame, apart from the inevitable Vetville (also known as Fertile Valley and Catholic Action), did a sensible job of containing its entrants within its facilities. It held its enrollment at about 5,000 and most of its projected $20,000,000 building program will go toward facilities other than dormitories. The long-term idea, already in operation, is to *pick the best and give them the best;* but administration officials, somewhat influenced by the alumni voice, are aware of a subtle danger.

A recent American Alumni Council report, reflecting the record of alumni financial support in 1947, listed 165 colleges. Notre Dame was a national champion in this field also—first in percentage of giving, first in per capita giving and second in total amount, following only Yale in this department, with $376,013

70

from 7,887 alumni against $420,034 from 15,846 sons of Eli. Here are the figures for the leaders:

SCHOOL	NUMBER	%	AMOUNT	PER CAPITA
Yale 15,846		40%	$430,034	$25.35
Harvard 15,242		36	366,836	24.58
Dartmouth 13,539		63	372,103	27.48
Cornell 12,965		25	353,822	27.29
Princeton 8,445		43	230,740	27.30
NOTRE DAME 7,887		72	376,013 [1]	47.68
Chicago 6,230		13	292,352 [2]	46.90
Columbia 4,931		9	104,254	21.19
Northwestern 4,860		9	183,030	10.76
Georgetown 3,105		18	60,575	19.50
Holy Cross 1,711		19	24,693	14.43

[1] Including capital gift of $101,000
[2] Including capital gifts of $202,000

Interesting conclusions can be drawn from this table. The eleven leaders are all *private* schools—which reveals their dependence upon private giving and their stake in private enterprise. Dr. Harold W. Dodds, President of Princeton University, emphasized this last February: "It is clear that if private enterprise fades out of our national pattern of education, private enterprise in other areas will fade out with it. . . . It is essential that the positions of the private college and university to track and investigate the social sciences and humanities must be kept free and unhampered by political control."

Statistics from the same source for 1948 are even more impressive from the Notre Dame viewpoint. The number of donors dropped to 6,973; but Notre Dame led the country in total amount ($614,939) and with a capital gift of $112,000 excluded, was second only to Harvard; and one of the two alumni groups which gave more than a half-million. Its 50% followed only Vassar (64%)

and Dartmouth (63%) in percentage of giving; its $75 per capita led the field by a wide margin. These reports are quoted to support the Notre Dame thesis that its men "put out" on all fields; that its football excellence reflects its general excellence; that its men believe in its product.

But in picking the best qualified freshmen, some sons of alumni began to be shut out—not in large numbers but sufficient to create an embarrassing problem, and one which promised to become more difficult because the large classes which followed World War I are now furnishing a crop of high school graduates who have been "brought up" on Notre Dame and have never considered entering any other college. In a closely-knit and fiercely devoted family such as this, it is hard, as has been done, to tell a loyal son that his son is just not good enough to get into the family school. As a father of a boy who will soon be knocking at the gates, and as an official of the Alumni Association who has had to face other fathers, I have personal knowledge of this situation.

The present thought is to meet it in two ways: By impressing on such fathers that their sons must come out of high school prepared to meet the academic competition; and by making concessions, when at all possible, for alumni freshmen, by giving them a year of grace during which they must prove themselves and catch up with the parade.

Out of this situation comes a much more fundamental thought: Notre Dame old-timers look with some misgivings toward a Brain Trust student body which might also lack the aspects of physical virility and mental hunger which have been the hallmark of the Notre Dame student. In plain words, they want to be careful not to sacrifice too much of the guts and rugged ability of the melting pot for the more cultivated brains of second and third generation kids who have been brought up the easy way and might lack some of the drive necessary to real accomplishment and leadership.

At one meeting of the Alumni Board the members frankly went over their own entrance qualifications and agreed that most of us could not have got into Notre Dame under existing requirements; and we proceeded to other men, great men of Notre Dame, including some of the most important academic leaders, who also could not have got in today.

I believe that the thing Notre Dame men like most about their school is the fact that, in their own experience, they found it to be a place where a boy was never asked *who he was* but was judged and rated entirely upon *what he did;* where the valedictorian got there for exactly the same reason as the football star—because he could hit harder and think faster.

That's why Melinkovich and Sheeketski have always had an equal chance with Hogan and O'Brien; why Czarobski played the opposite tackle from Connor; why the two greatest men of Notre Dame football—Rockne and Gipp—were neither Irish nor Catholic students.

Sure, Notre Dame is a football factory, a religious factory, an educational factory; but it is also something more, that stems from all of these—a factory of American democracy, operating in the best traditions of incentive, opportunity, initiative, competition and sportsmanship to produce the best in leadership and citizenship. That's what boys like, and why the Notre Dame boys who have gone through it swear by it, love it and support it any time its representatives step on any field.

That may also help to explain why the American public, and not just the Irish and Catholics, like it and root for it. The real things on the stage the public never sees may shine through the football curtain—just as the real qualities of an actor shine through the character he portrays on the screen.

There was no more zealous guardian of the rugged masculine atmosphere of Notre Dame life than Rockne—perhaps because he had found, in its practical democracy, the most fruitful climate for the development of his own brilliant, and I'm certain, mostly unsuspected talents.

And Notre Dame loves Rockne, not for himself alone, but because in his life he demonstrated just what Notre Dame can do with the right kind of human material, on and off the football field.

For "the lone Norse Protestant," invading the Irish stronghold, became part of it and it of him. He became, as he often jokingly said in explaining the foreign names in the football lineup, "Irish by environment"; and he finally became a Catholic, died with his rosaries in his hand.

Notre Dame isn't just a place where a boy goes to buy four years of formal education. It's a place that gets a piece of his heart, and his soul, because it reaches out for these things, as well as his mind. It gets even casual visitors like Bill McGheehan and the Georgia boy who felt the pull of that outdoor cathedral.

Are you still, perhaps, wondering about the spirit of its football teams?

XIII

Every basic situation is an effective reagent which brings out the latent potentialities of the personalities involved. An accident of background might produce either a cop or a crook; a lucky break might be the difference between a movie star or a tramp; a peacetime failure might become a wartime hero.

The human tragedy is that most people are miscast, and that is also true in America; but our way of life has also been the most successful experiment in human happiness because it gives the individual more of an opportunity to break the bonds in which he was born and to fight or stumble toward a new field more suitable to the development of his own talents.

That is also the American strength, the thing Americans fight to preserve—the priceless *opportunity* of the *individual* to his own destiny as against the herding of humans by a master state.

Our educational system is designed to help the individual decide upon and battle his way to his most productive role. A man doesn't have to go to college to be successful; but it helps; and the ambitious young man usually wants to go to college for that very reason. He may not know exactly what he is best suited for but he believes college will help him find it. His hungry mind wants

75

something and he goes, if only by instinct, to the place that feeds his mind.

Rockne had no family urging other than that of his sister. It is probable that each of them was motivated by nothing more than an instinctive belief that it would be a step in the right direction, that he had the type of mind which belonged in college and which college would so something with. They probably agreed aggressively on only one point—that he definitely would never get very far in the rigidly confined government postal service. (Socialists might give a thought to that item.)

That probably explains, by-passing the providential theory, why one college seemed about as good as another to him. Illinois, the big state school, had probably been a symbol and convenient objective; but Rock's immediate problem was financial; he had $1,000 to see him through four years; and when somebody told him he could stretch it farther at Notre Dame, that decided him; and Notre Dame's reputation as a poor boy's school was to pay off in a bonanza.

If he seemed to have made a quick decision, that was characteristic and explains much of his personality and career. You could never be sure what Rockne would do or say next; but you could be pretty sure he would be right.

The philosophers call that quality "intellectual perception" —the ability to make a decision before the mind has had time to think it out. Athletes call it "coming up with the right answer in the pinch." Regardless of what you call it, it adds up to the mighty powers of the real leader in action—the confidence he inspires in his followers, the doubt he puts in the minds of opponents.

There is a reasonable explanation for it in Rockne's case. Even when he seemed to act in emotional heat, which was almost always, he had probably done a lot of quiet thinking beforehand; so that when the moment came for electric action, he knew what to do—he had the courage, born of confidence in past success, to do

76

it, and the personal drive to follow it through and give it the greatest chance of success. He was the Patton of football.

Rockne was successful in so many fields because his hungry mind and aggressive spirit looked upon the unknown as something to explore and conquer, rather than to fear. He was the rare combination of the artist in inspiration and the mechanical perfectionist in execution. Add humor and vibrant charm, and to these a genuine interest in and feeling for human beings, and you have the sum of an always interesting man.

One of the fascinations of any job that deals with youth is spotting star material among the raw material, watching it develop and helping it find its proper niche. This is a hobby with such people as sports writers and drama critics; a duty with business executives; and a combination of the two with teachers, particularly so to the priests of Notre Dame who devote their entire lives to the task of bending and nurturing the masculine twigs which come to them.

It is hardly likely that any of the contemplatives on the campus saw a future spectacular in Rockne. He was undersized, overaged, with a face Pegler was later to compare to a battered oil can; and his blond hair had already begun to vacate toward early baldness. "So I went down to South Bend," he wrote in his autobiography, "with a suitcase and a thousand dollars, felt the strangeness of being a lone Norse Protestant—if the word must be used—invader of a Catholic stronghold."

Certainly nobody, including Rock himself, saw in him the great man of football. He was a track man; and regardless of what favors might have been given to football prospects at that time, track men were not especially preferred people. "The university gave me a chance to work off my board and room," he wrote, "as janitor of the chemical laboratory, cleaning out the slop buckets and doing minor chores," and he was assigned to live in Brownson Hall—an experience old students usually brag about in their later sentimental years but about which they were not exactly enthusiastic at the time.

In 1910, when Rock entered, the campus was still much as Sorin had left it, a "tight little boarding school" with about seven hundred students of all classifications from first grade to college seniors. The colorful "minims" were off by themselves in St. Edward's Hall, though they added color to the campus and were a noisy unit at the athletic contests. The prep school kids were quartered in Carroll Hall, a dormitory which occupied one side of the main building. Brownson was the companion dormitory on the other side and here were quartered the college students, mostly freshmen, who had to get by as cheaply as possible.

Brownson and Carroll had housed all the students after the rebuilding following the fire of '79. In Rockne's time, the majority of undergraduates lived, usually grouped by classes, in Sorin, Corby, Badin and Walsh Halls. Walsh, the most recently built, was then known as the Gold Coast; and while a boy didn't exactly have to apologize for living there, he usually felt he had to explain it away and hope it would sort of be forgotten.

The residence halls have private rooms with wash basins. There are showers and other facilities on each floor, something like the arrangements at most country clubs. There is also a "rec" room in the basement, and one telephone in the rector's office. Most rooms have double-decker beds, two desks, two clothes lockers and two chairs. After that there isn't much room for much else, including trunks, which are usually stored in the basement.

Sorin is the traditional senior hall and still the preferred place. In his senior year Johnny Lujack lived in a tower room which, because it was a little bigger, housed three students with the usual furniture; and when they were all present, you had to thread your way through the traffic. The newer halls have more modern touches here and there but conditions are essentially the same. Life is still rugged for the Notre Dame student of today.

78

Brownson and Carroll have, to practically nobody's regret, now been turned into offices; but this is the way they were: You slept on the top floor, with a hundred or more roommates; had the exquisite privacy of a boudoir, walled off by sheets and big enough for one single bed and a chair. Lights were out at ten and the bells began ringing at six in the morning.

You then went all the way to the first floor where you had a locker, washstand and mirror, also with a hundred others. Here you washed and shaved. You also ate on the first floor. You had a desk in the study hall on the second floor, with the same roommates and without sheets; and here you kept your books. You wore what you had on; and if you wanted to change clothes you went to another building, back of the tiny swimming pool, where the hundred trunks were. The showers were also here and toilets were on every floor. The recreation room was on the first floor of Washington Hall, which also contained the theater and Music Hall—and for a while, a ghost.

I did a stretch in Carroll Hall where, as a sophomore, I lived among the prep scholars—a tough lot. I always figured they were there because their parents couldn't handle them at home. It all sounds rugged now but nobody seemed particularly discommoded at the time, and there were things you could do in the dorms that you couldn't do in private rooms—like rolling a bowling ball down the long corridors, holding hurdle races and such—and getting back under the covers before the prefects arrived.

Two of my most embarrassing moments came in Carroll. I worked on the downtown newspaper, was a sort of campus Walter Winchell, complete with column, and since I was always careful never to slight Carroll's athletic activities, had a general "per" (permission) which included getting in late and sleeping late. I had an alarm clock which I was careful to hide under my cap under the bed; but one morning the alarm went off at two o'clock, the beds began to go over and—I couldn't find the clock. I always thought Father Gassensmith was very considerate about that.

79

Another time, in the refectory, the monkeys at my table decided to sing the then-popular "Avalon." I thought, "Surely they won't hit the high note"; but they did; and out we went, me too. I had to see the prefect of discipline to get back into school. It seems they thought, as a dignified soph, I should have had a better influence on the preps.

This is the essence of Notre Dame life the old-timers don't want the new-timers to miss.

XIV

The status of Knute Kenneth Rockne as a common man freshman was made clear when they assigned him to Brownson; but he found it right down the alley of Logan Square; as he found Notre Dame to be exactly the place for a fiery young individualist who wanted room to expand with no more cramping of his native style than is ever necessary for human beings to live in reasonably ordered peace with each other.

And he survived the entrance examinations without benefit of high school diploma—another thing that could not happen to-day when a boy has to rank high in his class to get in college at all—which must shut out a lot of high-grade material, and I don't just mean athletic material. But he had done a lot of reading during his postal years, had always been seriously concerned about serious things, as was proved when he first entered that service. With his application he had to present an essay. He wrote about how "the result of the Russo-Japanese War demonstrated the advisability of our having a large navy."

I have never heard nor seen in print why he chose to major in chemistry, unless he intended to become a doctor, because he did make an effort to get into medical school immediately after graduation. He revealed little of his private self in his autobiography; and though he talked a great deal, it was seldom about

81

Rockne. He had a very definite sense of personal dignity, once responded with swinging fists as students, welcoming him home after a *losing* game, carried him to a baggage truck for a speech.

I wrote about that in *The Scholastic* but felt he resented it —just as he let me know he was not too keen about my first book, *Huddle,* a fictionalized story of Notre Dame football in which he was the thinly-disguised coach. My publisher couldn't understand that because, he said, I had practically "apotheosized" the man. But Rock just didn't like being apotheosized or having people probe into his personal life—even though it was exemplary. I doubt if he ever had a "steady" girl other than his wife. He met her, courted her, married her and that part of his life was forever set. I've never known a more faithful and devoted family man, a cleaner living man nor a cleaner spoken man.

Regardless of why he took up chemistry, he was good at it, as he always was at everything he did. Father Nieuwland called him "a most remarkable student who often audited foreign courses to get a slant on other subjects than those he was carrying." He was later an excellent chemistry instructor until his athletic duties made him close that book, and probably regretfully.

One of his closest friends wrote that Rock occasionally yielded to depression. I saw him only three times in such moods— after he had lost his first game in three years; on the sands of Miami Beach after he had received a report from his doctor that his phlebitis was not yielding to treatment; and during the ruckus when the chairman of the Columbia Athletic Board was trying to force him to honor a penciled memorandum he had signed to coach at that school—one of several such jams he was to get into.

Normally he was a dynamo whirring over his scene, leaping at life with invincible confidence, full of fight and fun and an insatiable hunger for knowledge and excitement. And he got plenty of all these things as a student.

He was interested in music, played a flute in the college orchestra and took it on all his football trips, according to report, though I never saw it. He was an active figure in student smokers and entertainments, where the boys made their own fun, and was something of a star in dramatics, specializing, believe it or not, in a succession of shopworn female roles—squaws, Negresses and society ladies. He reveled in argument on any subject although he was never a formal debater; he took part in campus politics, at which the Chicago boys at Notre Dame have always been quite adept; and, like most men who become firm disciplinarians when they succeed to positions of authority, he was not exactly drawing his own model.

The halls at Notre Dame are so built that the basement rooms have windows on the ground level. Stern discipline requires the young men to be in at respectable hours, after which the doors are locked and late-comers are required to "sign in" with consequent explanations required. Since there are always occasions when even the most exemplary young men have reasons for being out late which, unfortunately, are not always acceptable to the judge, ground-level windows prove very convenient—providing they have also been conveniently left unlocked.

The "subway" rooms have all the facilities of the others but are a little cheaper and so, in the old days at least, were occupied almost entirely by athletes receiving financial help. Rockne and Dorais had a room particularly well situated for a "working-window"; but they improved on the custom by exacting a small fee upon the passers-through. Like most levies, it was unpopular; so the night-crawlers once made a collection of lanterns, ladders and other such bric-a-brac from a building project on the way home and left them in the Rockne-Dorais room where they were found in an early morning inspection before the occupants had awakened. For that they were sentenced to live in Brownson, or Siberia, as it was sometimes called, for two weeks; and the taxpayers had their revenge.

I assume this time-honored window custom still exists. I remember, one night after a dance downtown, when the student body would have been sans most of its prominent leaders and athletes had the prefects been on the welcoming committee. Or perhaps they were careful on this occasion to be more indulgent than diligent.

We had an eight o'clock class in Spanish one year, a very large class presided over by a very pleasant Mexican, at which everybody always answered "present." But one morning, after roll call, the "Prof" called six names, no doubt carefully selected, to go to the blackboard. None responded, and our José proved himself not nearly so naive as we had imagined when he said: "You see, I was once a student myself and I know all your tricks."

The students do have tricks and get away with their share; but discipline is quite firm at Notre Dame. For such things as drinking and gambling, expulsion is automatic, regardless of personalities. In my time cigarets were also forbidden; and since this was after World War I, it seemed very contradictory to think that the ex-captain whose picture was in *The Dome* (yearbook) with General Pershing, would be on his way home if he were caught smoking a "coffin nail." That remnant of Sorin's continental ideas has now gone the way of progress; but enough others remain to assure parents who send their boys to Notre Dame to be "looked after" that they will definitely be looked after.

George Gipp was "kicked out" when he was football captain, finally managed to get back but lost his captaincy. Not too long ago the team lost a quarterback who had been out after hours—and who became an overnight star in pro football. Another very famous player was caught in a crap game and given the gate in the spring; but he went to Indianapolis, worked as a soda jerk, sent letters home via his roommate, returned to summer school to make up his work, became an all-American the next fall—and his family never knew he had been expelled, perhaps doesn't know yet.

Such discipline doesn't hurt the football situation either, particularly when many are waiting to get in. (The very reason why there has never been such a well-behaved college generation as that which came out of World War II. The boys were just too scared to fool around.) The athletic climate at Notre Dame is also favored by the absence of coeds, fraternities, freshman caps and sophomore tyranny. Nobody bothers a first-year man as long as he acts like a man.

There's plenty of fun, the wholesome type of fun which healthy boys, gathered from all sections of the country and from much the same cultural and social levels, make for themselves. As long as you behave yourself, you're okay; and most boys are glad to react to that formula; but if you step out of line, you are brought back in by a subtle and marvellously effective student custom known as "goofing."

The Notre Dame student is a remarkably modest and non-bragging individual because he doesn't dare to be otherwise. If you are an impossible sort, they just throw you in the lake; but if you merely have an idea you're good at anything, and are indiscreet enough to admit it—brother!

Everybody agrees with you. Strangers come up and slap you on the back, compliment you, encourage you to demonstrate your particular excellence. Crowds gather to watch you; they will match you up with the local champion of your specialty and you'll find yourself the people's choice. And if you are "robbed" by palpably unfair judges, you'll find influential leaders to support you and demand another contest; and this will go on until you finally awake to the fact that you have been *goofed*.

Thereafter, unless you are a particularly dense or egotistical fellow, you will never again admit you're good at anything.

And nobody else will, either. As the local columnist I was usually in, very early, on a goofing party, and helped it along; but once in my senior year when a suspicious number of people, including some close friends, began suddenly to imply that I was a combination Shakespeare and Damon Runyan, I took a quick refresher course in modesty, just in case.

We had a chap who thought he had a body beautiful—and that went on for months. We had a barber, not even a student, who thought he could run—so he was matched up with Frank Thomas, later Alabama coach but then varsity quarterback—and shamefully "robbed" of first place by a committee of athletes who, it was loudly proclaimed, "were partial to Thomas because he was a monogram man." Though there are no real fraternities, a "secret one" was invented to goof a freshman football player, with Frank Thomas, Harry Stuhldreher and "Judge" Carberry as the presiding officers.

In his student days Rock was usually the campus champion at checkers, marbles, cards, oratory or whatever else the goof thought he was good at. Rock was chosen, not only because of his athletic eminence, but because he was a natural actor whose quick mind and humorous flair helped with the ad libbing such a role always requires.

The goof usually has it coming and the goofing is supposed to have a beneficial effect on his future life, as well as act as a deterrent on the entire student body. The goofers, of course, are looking for entertainment; and when this threatens to go overboard, the authorities usually step in. I doubt if Rock was ever cruel about it; once, when a softheaded fellow appeared who thought he was quite an athlete, Rock, as head coach, called a halt when the humor was about to cross the line.

There was another student activity which might have got him into serious trouble had the authorities been more diligent or perhaps less indulgent. He had a flat nose that could have been a souvenir of football; but it has also been ascribed, and sometimes in print, to surreptitious journeys on Saturday nights when he appeared in boxing bouts in neighboring towns under the name of Kid Somebody-or-Other. I never heard Rock mention it but it popped up so often that I began running the rumor down.

86

Joe Gargan, brother-in-law of Joseph Kennedy, former Ambassador to Great Britain, was a classmate and pal of Rockne's and a campus character in his own right—the only man who ever dared, during World War I, to appear at Notre Dame in a Marine uniform, carrying a swagger stick and leading a bulldog. A short while before his recent death, Joe told me Rock had been a fighter, all right; that Joe had been his manager and second; that Rock had, perhaps, violated his amateur standing by accepting a few needed bucks for such jobs; that he had been good at it, too, but had never got beyond the six-round semi-final class—perhaps because it would not have been discreet for a star Notre Dame athlete to become too prominent in the fight game.

Rock's student activities reflected the future man. He was fighter, thinker, worker, actor and humorist—and all these things are qualities of a great football coach.

His versatility and wide interests also help to explain why he did not become a scientist, even though he was under the influence of one of the great ones in this field, studied under him and taught under him for several years after graduation. Conceivably Rockne might have gone on with Father Nieuwland in the experiments which eventually led to the basic formulae for synthetic rubber—and on which, incidentally, the University still draws royalties.

Father Nieuwland slept in his laboratory, lived with his test tubes, went about in a very smelly raincoat which may have been the first ever produced by chemistry.

But Rock liked to be out where people were, where the excitement and the drama were. Everything else being equal, people usually become what they *are*; as puppies grow into different dogs; and similar-appearing seeds produce astonishingly varied products. And if you like the *providential* idea, or its more mundane expression, that each situation in a winning tradition produces its man, you might look at it this way:

Notre Dame already had its synthetic rubber man in the Belgian Nieuwland.

The football job was to be taken care of by the Norseman Rockne.

There was also another job—the major job of coordinating all the academic, scientific, athletic and spiritual activities, fitting each into its proper place in the transitional period; and Notre Dame already had its man for that too, the Irishman, Cavanaugh.

XV

The "Fighting Irish" nickname of Notre Dame teams is supposed to have come, though for this I cannot vouch, out of the 1909 Michigan game when Pete Vaughan, at a time when the boys were trailing, shouted: "What's the matter with you guys— you're all Irish and you're not fighting." After which they fought.

Actually it had probably been used before that because it comes, as they say in Hollywood, "out of characterization."

The student body has always been predominantly Irish and the priests even more so. Of the fifteen presidents, all but Sorin and his nephew, Auguste Lemmonier, who died in office, have been of Irish extraction.

There were seven presidents during Sorin's time but they always knew who was the real boss; and since the Irish are not "too obedient," there were differences of opinion and, for the most part, short terms of office. When Sorin died in 1893, Andrew Morrisey, a native of Ireland, as had been many of his predecessors, had just begun his term; but Sorin's idea was so strongly impressed that under Father Morrisey, Notre Dame became more of a prep school than ever. "We can never compete with those colleges that have such tremendous endowments," he said. "Our

89

very existence depends on giving Catholic boys a good preparatory foundation."

When John W. Cavanaugh took over in 1905, the time was ripe for a change and he was the man for the time—a native-born American who had not come up under the personal dominance of the old French taskmaster. Brilliant and forceful, he became the architect of the modern University. His term, from 1905 to 1919, was, except for Sorin's, the longest and most influential of any Notre Dame president and probably will remain so, since regulations now retire the academic leader after a maximum of six years.

Thereafter he served, as I think all ex-presidents of the country should also serve, as an ambassador-at-large and counsellor to his successors. Like Rockne he was never old in his head, was interested in all things and particularly in the boys who came to Notre Dame. I first met him in a revolving door at the library and before we got away from there he had my complete history up to that point, seemed especially friendly because I came from his native state of Ohio. He taught a few selected literary classes and I had him in The Novel, The Essay, and Shakespeare, Dante and the Bible. He would start dutifully from text and then delightfully ramble all over the face of the earth, up and down the highways and byways of history, literature and people. He made you want to come to class; and was also popular because he never called the roll until the class was over.

"Cavvy," as we privately called him, which he probably knew and liked, was the sort of faculty man you took walks with and talked things over with—any old thing—the old professor you kept in touch with and always visited when you returned, and who would have been hurt if you hadn't. His room in the Community House was a shrine in later days for such old grads as Frank Walker, Roosevelt's friend and Postmaster General.

It was my good fortune to know him well; and when my son was born, I asked him to come to New York as the godfather. Illness prevented that but he asked me to "pick out some hand-

90

some young man" to represent him. He is the godfather on record; so when, as and if the Wallace lad turns up as a freshman, he will have excellent sponsorship because the handsome young man I picked out to represent Father Cavanaugh was Jimmy Crowley, one of the Four Horsemen gridiron immortals.

I went into newspaper work in New York shortly after graduation and there became enamored of the style of Heywood Broun; but one day my new idol shocked me by giving Shakespeare a kicking around. I sent the column to Father Cavanaugh who replied: "This reminds me of a criticism I once read of a book: 'In this volume are many good things and new; but the new things are not good and the good things are not new.'" That took care of Broun—and a great lot of other people and things I've read, particularly in the economic field, in recent years.

Such student-teacher relationships, one of the nicer things about all college life, are strong at Notre Dame where the priests have no boys of their own. It was par for the course with Rockne and all of his football boys; and like the rest I seldom made an important move as long as he lived without making an effort to talk it over with him. He was always a great man to have in your corner; he fought for his kids, his game and his school; and it would be very interesting if he were around during the present sniping at his monument of schedule-building. But then, if he were still around, there might be no sniping—which is a tribute to Rock rather than a criticism of Leahy.

Few boys really know what they're best fitted for when they enter college; many never find out even there, and plenty don't follow the course they graduated from. I was one who went looking for a vague *something*, as Rockne himself probably did, who entered with ideas about law but switched to writing. You might be interested, through my case, to observe how the college and the boy work out such a problem, how one little thing leads to another and finally to the answer.

In freshman English Father Charles Miltner, a great teacher

91

and philosopher who later became president of Portland University, first said I had "some power over words." Dr. John Cooney, the homey old dean of journalism, encouraged my first efforts in that field and supplied the background romance of the craft. My first sonnet was printed in *The Scholastic* where it came to the attention of Father Charles O'Donnell, the poet who was later to become the twelfth president. I had just been struggling to fill out the fourteen lines but he said in his class that it was "a daring subject" for a sonnet, which I suppose it was, since I had chosen a steel-mill background.

In my sophomore year I had a financial problem which I brashly presented to the president, Father James Burns, who practically created a job for me—covering campus doings for the South Bend *News-Times*—and that started me as a professional journalist (twenty bucks a month) on the same paper where Ring Lardner, J. P. McEvoy, Frank Ward O'Malley and others got their start. This led into interhall sports and finally to the attention of the great Rockne himself who offered me the job of official athletic correspondent when Arch Ward left that spot to go to the Chicago *Tribune* to become the most influential sports editor in the country.

Rock gave me the same sound training in sports writing—another of his intensities—as he gave his players in football; and I was in the extremely fortunate position of learning the game from the growing master of the craft. My financial problem was now settled but, as a senior, I was flirting with the law again when George Shuster, during the course of a routine lecture in literature, hit me on the button at the right time with a pep talk that made me gamble on writing as a career. My knowledge of Notre Dame football was the crutch which later helped me break into New York and eventually into magazines and pictures.

I hope I won't give ideas to any Hunter students by confessing that I still owe Dr. Shuster my graduating thesis, a grandiose concept about Love and Courage. I finally conned him into com-

promising on a review of the football season for *The Scholastic*, of which he was faculty supervisor, in a blank verse parody of Dante's *Inferno*. That was another daring idea, like the sonnet; but when I got as far as the Army game, about the Fifth Circle, I was up against the deadline and finished the thing in slangy American sporting prose.

But I did follow the Professor to New York, got a room around the corner from his Flatbush honeymoon cottage and finally turned out to be a handy guy in an emergency. Doris needed rum for a fruitcake and this was prohibition; and since I was in the newspaper business, I was supposed to know about such things. I didn't but I found out. And if that didn't quite square the thesis rap, maybe George will consider this grandiose effort.

I hope I haven't bored you; but all this may help to give you a further idea why Notre Dame guys like the place and each other. It does have a lot of heart.

My mother came to Notre Dame for the first time for my graduation and met Father Cavanaugh. I had been looking forward to the meeting of these two great people who could give the most ordinary idea the imaginative lilt of blarney. They bounced it back and forth for a few sentences and then:

"Well, Mother, and what do you think of Notre Dame?"

"Father, it's heaven number two."

His biographer writes that Father Cavanaugh was never at a loss for words among the great. But that got him—as I think it will get all Notre Dame people, as it still gets me. For in thóse few words my mother said what I'm trying to say in this entire book.

Father Cavanaugh was never a football enthusiast in the sense that most Notre Dame priests are, including the current president, John J. Cavanaugh, his protégé but no relative. The younger Cavanaugh was brought up on it, and it was he to whom I always went as a New York reporter when I wanted to find out things even Rockne wouldn't, or perhaps couldn't, tell me. As

prefect of religion, Young Father John was closer to the boys than the Coach himself.

As a young president at the time of the Michigan-Western Conference rhubarb in 1910, the elder Cavanaugh was inclined to consider the matter not worth the fuss it had kicked up. His feeling was that each school should adopt athletic rules to fit its own situation—which is still the ideal position and the one all college presidents would undoubtedly adopt, if football had not become such a profitable business. But like all hard-pressed college administrators, Father Cavanaugh had a friendly eye toward any-thing that would bring in an honest buck. So, like the rest, he went along with the football business when it gradually became profitable; and he had the sound judgment and shrewd appraisal of men to appoint Rockne as the first homegrown coach at a time when that was considered so much of a radical move that those close to the situation thought it necessary to put on a letter-telegram campaign to bring it about.

XVI

Men like Tex Rickard and Flo Ziegfeld, with a magnificent disregard for decimals, confounded bankers with munificent money returns. Henry Ford set a price for his new models without benefit of cost sheets. Roosevelt did much the same with votes and Dreiser with words. The dreamers are men of instinct rather than of calculation. Often poor businessmen with personal affairs, their grand designs pay off because they know what people will buy.

Their business *is not business but people;* they have a medico's thumb on the public pulse because they like to be around people and to have people around them. The great showmen are easiest for reporters to see and their offices become loafing shanties for the press. This was so true of Rickard's quarters at Madison Square Garden that when old Tex wanted to talk a little private business he had to take his man out on the fire escape.

Rockne was definitely like that except that he had no private business. When a person he trusted walked into his office, he seemed to be actually relieved because that gave him a chance to talk, to get opinions on whatever it was he was working on. So it was one day when he told me he was dictating material for a transcription of a pep talk to his team. I liked it, as you may also have liked it when it later appeared in one of the two motion pictures about him; but I was surprised that he had bothered to

dictate it because he was strictly a rapid-fire ad lib speaker who never bothered with script or notes.

"Imagine my embarrassment," he quipped, "if I found myself misquoting myself." Then he laughed, for nobody appreciated his humor more than Rock himself.

Well, in his autobiography, I found the master frequently misquoting himself. He was a good reporter—every football scout has to be—but never allowed a minor fact to mar a major point and, in the motion picture manner, took plenty of license in rearranging historical sequence for dramatic emphasis. He was probably relying more on memory than research; and his material was put into final shape by a staff writer. And now let's pause to set the record straight on the disputed point of his writing ability; and if you don't think that important, I assure you Rockne did.

He was very proud of his authorship and would, I believe, in his later days, rather have been considered a writer than a football coach. His feud with Westbrook Pegler was based upon his artistic indignation when Peg callously lumped him among the ghost-written athletic morons. For the record, Rock not only could have written anything that appeared under his name but would, like all writers, have preferred it that way.

His newspaper stuff for Christy Walsh, to the best of my knowledge, was emphatically his own; but, understandably, his news sense was not always keen. He dictated his syndicate articles to Ruth Faulkner, his secretary, and in his typical manner, sometimes asked me to read and criticize them. So one day, buried down near the end, I found the startling threat that the coaches might break away from the national rules committee and make their own rules. I told him this was a magazine article, suggested that he kill it in the newspaper story and allow me to sound out editors; that it would not only receive more attention that way, which he wanted, but would also bring him in a nice check, which he always wanted—as who does not?

I arranged for the piece to appear in *Liberty Magazine*. Rock wrote the article himself, about 5,000 words, and capably enough; but magazines have their own problems and Denny Morrison, the editor, asked that I recast it. Rock made no objection; all I did was rearrange his paragraphs, put the salient points up front and add a few ideas I had heard him express. It was titled "The Coaches' Rebellion"; when he saw what he had written Rock got a bit afraid of the hot potato, stalled around for awhile; but then, courageously and characteristically, gave it the green light.

This was probably just about what John Kennedy later did on the *Collier's* articles; and he certainly did a faithful job of transmitting Rock's staccato style—for Rock wrote as he talked, like a quarterback barking signals and hoping somebody would want to argue about it. Few ever did argue or take him on in repartee and Bob Zuppke, of Illinois, was the only one who ever came out with anything like a draw.

Wally Steffen had him on the hip after the 1926 season when Carnegie Tech upset Notre Dame while the chagrined Rock was watching the Army-Navy game at Chicago. They frequently appeared on the same speaking program that winter and Wally delighted in referring to the game as a "setup" instead of an upset. But Rock took care of that two years later—though he actually had to risk his life to do it.

He was a good writer and speaker because he was witty, hardhitting and clear; but he also loved to play around with a fancy new word and could wrap up a situation in such a phrase as his description of football as "a pleasantly rough recreation." He knew how to illustrate with an effective anecdote and his wit was true because it came out of characterization and sharpened his point—which is why so many of his stories are still used by other coaches and sports writers to illumine similar situations. Typical of these was his remark to a boy who enjoyed dancing more than training but who was pleading to get into a game

Notre Dame was losing: "It's all right, Max, I'm saving you for the junior prom."

I have heard from people who should know, though from neither of the men involved, that John W. Cavanaugh and Rockne used to walk out in the forest environs where the President, a gifted speaker, would put the fledgling coach through elocutionary routines. Certainly Rockne, once he realized that a coach should be able to speak, would have gone about learning and from the best man available; he had that humble and valuable knack of going to headquarters for information. I once heard him ask George "Chunky" Murrin, now a Houston attorney, just which of two varsity guard candidates hit the hardest. Chunky was then a lowly freshman center but he had the answer because he was the guy who was being hit; and his vote for Noble Kizer did the later Purdue coach and athletic director no harm at the time.

As an orator, Rock was close to the top. His dressing room efforts were dramatic gems, his after-dinner speeches forceful and humorous; and he received $10,000 from Studebaker Corporation for a series of six inspirational pep talks to salesmen—a field in which he was successfully pioneering at the time of his death. But his writing never had the fluid drive of his speech; he was still sort of muscle-bound, had too much of the awe of the faithful servitor to let himself go in this medium. I believe, had he lived, he would have done a lot of useful writing of constantly improving quality. He did do two books early in his career—a technical volume on coaching and a boy's book called *The Four Winners* of which he was very proud. There may still be a few copies of these around but I loaned mine out!

The job of a football coach requires many talents, more so at Notre Dame than at any other school; so the personality of the coach becomes an important part of the system. Rockne worked on himself as much as he ever did on a tackle or a quarterback; and the secret of the remarkable success of Rockne-trained coaches was the fact that they copied their mentor's personality, psychology and versatility as well as his technical methods.

Frank Leahy, faithfully emulating the master in all things, had no flair for writing and found public speaking painful; but he applied himself to this problem with the same deadly thoroughness with which he attacks all other problems—and which seems to frighten some of his opponents—with the same excellent results. His efforts come out smoothly and capably but with that florid grace and mathematical precision which mark the synthetic.

Rock loved to be with people. Leahy would like nothing better than to coach his team and then go home to "Floss" and their five kids, occasionally play poker with his close friends or delve into gridiron calculus with other masters of the science. He does what he has to do on the public platform and does it very well; but he doesn't enjoy it. People have sharp eyes for such things in public figures and that explains a lot about the personal popularity of celebrities.

Gene Tunney once frankly analyzed for me his own early lack of facility with crowds: "I never should have been heavyweight champion. When strangers approach me and, either figuratively or actually want to feel my muscles, I cringe inside. But Dempsey and Babe Ruth love all that." I once repeated that to Leahy, told him I thought he and Tunney were essentially alike; and he agreed. Gene is now a smoothie; and one day Leahy will be.

Truman had the common touch—Dewey didn't—and that, as much as any one thing, may have explained their astonishing election "upset"; just as the political history of our country is sometimes explained by the statement that "Republicans just don't know how to talk to the man on the street." And that brings up an ambition I had for Rockne almost from the time I first knew him—to get him in politics. He laughed but he would have loved it. He would have been something in the Senate; he could have talked to the common man—and told Joe Stalin plenty too.

XVII

There was considerable comment in college circles when Harvard established the House System; but Notre Dame has always been organized along these lines through its residence halls, where the boys live by classes and compete against each other in intramural athletics. It was the existence of these interhall teams as well as the presence of minim and prep students on the campus, which led to one of the earliest misconceptions of the unusual success of Notre Dame football. It was conveniently explained that "Rockne had them from the first grade on."

Actually, the only varsity player who spent all his school life on the campus was Norman Barry, now a Chicago lawyer. Interhall was always more of a dumping than a feeding ground, a Battalion of Forgotten High School Stars not good enough for college competition. The interhall teams, wartime casualties but now restored, are interesting to watch on Sunday afternoons; they give the discards another chance to come through and now and then one of them does.

Rockne himself might never have played football for Notre Dame if it hadn't been for the interhall catch-all. He was a track man, small for football, since he weighed only 145 and was only five-feet, eight inches tall; but as he wrote, "a fellow wasn't much thought of unless he went out to try to make his hall team for football." So he tried; and Joe Collins, the varsity squad man who coached Brownson, recommended him for a chance with the big boys.

Shorty Longman, the power-minded coach, saw nothing but nuisance in the Norwegian shrimp and used him at fullback, of all places, in just one scrimmage session against the varsity. "I was a dud, a washout, not even good enough for the scrubs," Rock wrote, "and Shorty sent me back to Brownson." It may have been Shorty's purpose to discourage, for coaches have been known to do that with unpromising material; but he just didn't know Rockne who was back the next year, fortified by the prestige of a track letter.

This time he tried out at end, his high school and sandlot position—and thus began the most spectacular career in football history.

Rock was a regular for three seasons; he never knew defeat in his playing career, which included twenty victories and two ties; in his senior year he captained the squad which began the Army series with a 35-13 upset; and he made Walter Camp's third eleven, a rare distinction for a Notre Dame player in those days.

He served as assistant under Jess Harper for the next four seasons which saw 26 wins, 5 losses and one tie.

In thirteen years as head coach he won 105, lost 12 and tied 5—a record which includes his first year, the informal wartime season of 1918, when Notre Dame won three, lost one and tied two.

He never had a losing season. His total record, as player and coach, was 151 victories, 17 defeats and 8 ties; if you throw out the ties, he won nine of every ten games in which he had a part; and if you include the ties, he lost only one of twenty. His twenty years in football saw seven perfect seasons and one more in which the team was undefeated but had one tie.

That spells *competitor*—and that, more than any other one word, spells Rockne. He fought to live and he hated to lose—at anything or under any conditions. I twice saw him stake his life to win big football games. And I saw something else which was even more convincing.

The old gym at Notre Dame was used for many things—among others, when nothing more important was scheduled, as a tennis court. I walked by there one afternoon and through the door happened to see Rockne, red-faced and grim, with a tennis racket. I hadn't known that he played tennis because he used to scoff at such sissy sports.

At that time we had a Chinese student who was popularly supposed to be worth $40,000,000. Probably all he had in the American world, outside his measly forty million bucks, was his tennis. Somehow, Rock, in his rambles, had met up with him on the court; and he never fought harder to beat Army before 80,000 than he was fighting to beat that tennis player before no audience at all. I didn't stay to see how it came out; it looked like Rock might be losing and I never like to have to see a hard fighter lose.

Don't die gamely—*fight to live.*

That was his motto; and I've often thought of this man, who always fought to live, in his last moments, caged in that diving, flaming plane. All that we know is that he finally did surrender—to God. His rosaries were in his hand.

In his book Rock didn't tell too much about his playing days except that, in his first game, against Ohio Northern, he was tense as any other beginner; but he did give enough of his experiences to indicate that he was pretty much as he always was—learning things about people and about gridiron technique; emphasizing the simple things, the ABC's, the two-and-two-makes-four which the hardheaded person recognizes as truth and never tries to change.

Throughout his career, at football and in all other things, Rock was never a sensationalist, though he was sometimes sensational in performance. He was not so much an inventor of plays as a superb adaptor. He built upon solid fundamentals, such as blocking, tackling and rushing the passer. He accepted basic facts as worked out and proven up to his time, then added his own refinements; he could pick up a variation from another coach and beat him at his own game the next time they played—as he took the spinner from Wally Steffen and beat him with it.

His system was the most successful of his day, the most widely used, by his own pupils at other schools and those who always follow the leader. Therefore it was always the most thoroughly scouted. Rock played the part of the wily fox—when the hounds got close he changed directions. When the rules committee legislated against his shift, penalizing speed by slowing it up, he went for a heavier type of player.

The T of today is a return to speed and cleverness—so it is easy to imagine Rockne having adopted its modern breakthroughs. His basic formation was a T which shifted into the single wing—which is exactly the move of the moment. The platoon system of offensive and defensive teams? Rockne had that in 1921 when he introduced his shock troop idea. Faking, feinting and acting in the backfield? The Four Horsemen were experts.

Take a good look at any new look in football and you will see an old look recolored and refined. Rockne was the style leader of his day, and all of us who knew him well believe that he would always have been a step or two ahead of his field; that Leahy football is not much different than Rockne football would have been if the master were still around—based on sound fundamentals, framed by sound human experience, plastered with imagination, painted by the calculated daring with which Rockne casually dismissed his own success: "When the breaks came my way I had sense enough to take advantage of them."

Rockne's football was his way of life. His basic strategy was to play the percentage; and if now and then he seemed to be daring, it was only because he figured that particular play had the best chance of succeeding at that particular time. **Opportunity** didn't have to knock more than once to impress his alert mind; but in his book the *new thing had to be good.*

That's the book of Notre Dame, the basic philosophy behind its success in all things. Fundamentals: work; fight; think; pray. Daring when it is indicated by solid thinking—but no razzle dazzle for itself alone, no quick success leading to inevitable failure, no one step forward and three steps backward, no jumping in until you can swim, no skating on thin ice. Feet on the ground, shoulder to the wheel, heads up, eyes open, mind working and humble prayer for guidance from the Architect of All.

That has also been the book of America, the book America will do well to remember, will forget at its peril. In these days of economic and ideological experiments, our national coaches can learn much from football, as all of us can in our private lives. Adapt, refine, improve—yes; but never forget the facts of fundamentals, never be propagandized into razzle dazzle for itself alone. Hitler found that out. Stalin will find it out. History has seen many systems; ours has been the most successful of our day, not because it was new but because it is based upon fundamentals as old as man and part of his essential being—the liberty and dignity of the individual, his right to free choice, his will to fight for all of this.

If you think I have overemphasized, that this detour doesn't belong, I ask that you re-read the last few pages, take time out to think again.

See if you can't see what I have long seen—one of those buried little truths that come up after long digging and patient application: Sport is one of the clearest reflections of our basic national life; it has the great advantage of being frequently tested and examined; the score is up there for everybody to see and no alibi can change it; the defeated coach, if he is smart, takes a fresh look at his system; he determines whether his basic vehicle has somewhere missed a road sign; and if it hasn't he will

104

usually find his answer in the motion pictures of the game—a missed block, a missed tackle, a failure to rush the passer or to cover a receiver. So, if he's practical, he goes back to fundamen-this.

Isn't that exactly what you do, or what you should do, if you have lost a big game in your own business or profession? Isn't that what the Republican party tried to do after the last election? Football people had a ready answer for that too: Dewey was overconfident; he was lulled by the experts; he looked at the spot sheets, saw he was favored by nineteen points, and tried to win without getting his hair mussed or his uniform dirty. And so he was upset by the underdog who knew he had to fight for his life.

A few years ago a name coach came to a Big Nine school to lift it from the doldrums; he had a new system and was an expert salesman. The alumni came out for the launching full of hope and enthusiasm but, unfortunately, the home team lost by two touchdowns. That night the coach had a party; and in the manner of the slick propagandist, he made a lot of X's and O's on the tablecloth, explained very cleverly just what had gone wrong. But a cynical sports writer interrupted:

"Don't show me them plays on the tablecloth, Coach—show me them plays on the field."

XVIII

The popular legend has it that modern Notre Dame football began with Jess Harper—that he introduced the forward pass in the Army game in 1913; that Notre Dame was unknown in the East until that game; that Rockne invented the Notre Dame system; and that Notre Dame was forced to become a national power by the Big Freeze of 1910—compared to which the present schedule pressure is a mild frost.

In the main current, these things are true enough; but as usual, there are important tributaries.

Jack Marks, the Dartmouth man who preceded Harper in 1911-12, picked up the pass after it had been used by others; Harper's distinctive contribution was the backfield shift he had learned under Stagg at Chicago; Rockne perfected both maneuvers.

Notre Dame would have become a national gridiron power in any event since it was a national school; the Conference action merely accelerated a movement eastward which had already begun. Notre Dame's first Eastern football opponent was not Army but Pitt—which it had defeated in 1909, tied in 1911 and defeated again in 1912. But even before these games, the athletic prowess of Notre Dame was known and respected in the East.

In the same year—1887—that football began at Notre Dame,

baseball was introduced by a student who was to become one of the diamond immortals, Adrian "Pop" Anson of the Chicago Cubs. The first contest with another school was not played until 1892 against—guess who?—Michigan. Notre Dame won 6-4. The Irish became known for baseball long before football, and it was the diamond stars who actually blazed the national trail which the gridders were to follow and preempt.

Notre Dame has sent forty-eight players to the big leagues, including Anson, Roger Bresnahan, Bob Bescher, George Cutshaw, Bert Daniels, John Dubuc, Red Murray, Alex McCarthy, Ed Ruelbach, Art Schaefer, Frank Shaughnessy, Cy Williams, Red Smith and two sons of a famous big league battery, Ed Walsh and Billy Sullivan. You could pick a pretty fair all-time team from those names and challenge any other college to try and match it.

Notre Dame still has good baseball teams, as it has good teams in every sport—including such non-commercials as fencing and golf—because the campus climate is just naturally salubrious for athletics. It sends few men to the big leagues now for the same reason that other colleges have fallen off in this respect, for the same reason that other sources of major league talent are drying up: Athletes who might become baseball stars are more attracted to the glamour of high school and college football; and more than a few others become golfers after serving apprenticeships as caddies. Professional baseball magnates, a conservative and stuffy group, have finally begun to do something about that on the high school and sandlot level.

Notre Dame baseball began to attract national attention in the period from 1906 to 1908 when the record was sixty victories against nine defeats; and the 1908 squad, which won twenty and lost only one, had ventured eastward as far as Dartmouth and Vermont—two years before the football schedule break with the Big Nine. During the next three seasons, the team remained in its own territory but entertained such nomads as Arkansas, West

107

Virginia and Penn State. In 1912 they played a ten-game Eastern trip; and followed this in 1913 with a five-game junket against Penn, Navy, Catholic University, Fordham—and Army.

The young men who lost to Army 3-0 on May 24 had not the slightest idea they had just broken ground in which a milestone of football history would be sunk the next fall. But that was exactly what they had done, for when Jess Harper came up from Wabash to Notre Dame and, as he recently told me, "sat down to write a few letters," he was following the trail of the baseball squad—a fact confirmed by William Cotter, now a New York industrialist but then the Notre Dame Graduate Manager who signed the contract for the first Army football game.

In fairness to the great institution on the Hudson which guards our national safety, it should now be apparent that it knew it was not scheduling a pushover but an outfit which had been tough enough to beat Michigan and incur the wrath of the Western Conference. Not then being concerned with the athletic problems of other sections, Army wanted a team good enough to give it a stiff workout; and Notre Dame also fitted into the West Point policy of giving occasional recognition to other parts of the country; one of the reasons, ironically, Army also gave for finally cancelling the Notre Dame series.

It was not so much the 35-13 Notre Dame victory that stunned the East as the manner in which it was accomplished— the fact that a "little team" from the Midwest had made devastating use of a weapon which everybody had known about for years but nobody *important* had considered worth doing anything about.

By 1906 football had developed into such a push-and-pull brutality, with mounting injuries and deaths, that the President of the United States, Theodore Roosevelt, had called for remedial action. The Rules Committee then adopted the forward pass to open up the game and soften it up; but the established masters in the East were so conventionally satisfied with what had brought

108

them success, that they gave little attention to the new idea—which is another typical illustration of how sport mirrors our national thinking in all fields.

Rockne himself, in making plain that Notre Dame had never claimed the patent on the pass, gave credit to Eddie Cochems, coach at St. Louis University in 1907, for its first effective use. He also wrote that Pop Warner of Carlisle and A. A. Stagg of Chicago had experimented with it but that "the pass complicated matters too much for most old-fashioned technicians who preferred to rely on Bull Strength and Lady Luck."

Where the Army espionage fell down in 1913 was not in its failure to learn that Notre Dame used the pass, which it must have known, but in its failure to assay properly the essential Notre Dame attitude—the alertness to see, willingness to adopt and courage to use, after they have been proven in laboratory, the *new things which are also good*. But Army could not reasonably be expected to have known that; nor to have been much impressed if it had known what Rockne and Dorais had been doing in the leisure hours of their summer employment on the sands of Cedar Point; not even if they had been told, as Mrs. Rockne told me, that "those devils said they were going to beat Army with the forward pass."

Army could not have been expected to know that it was going to serve as a springboard for genius, to be engulfed by the gridiron wave of the future, or be called upon to face a fanatical band for whom this game had social significance of a sort. Nor would Army have been disturbed had it known then what Rockne later wrote: "While the game was not all-important to Army it was the supreme test of our playing careers. We went to play them like crusaders, believing that we represented not only our own school but the whole aspiring Middle West." But canny crusaders they were, with the secret weapon primed and polished in the first three games of the season.

Army, with three all-Americans in its lineup—McEwen at

109

center, Merrilat at end and Pritchard at quarterback—was not seriously impressed by Notre Dame's victories over minor opponents, probably did not even take the trouble to scout, for scouting had not been developed in those days. (In fact I remember that Rockne did not even bother to scout Army in 1921. He told his team: "They'll hit here—and here—and here." And sure enough, that was what they did—exactly as they had done in the preceding year's game.)

The Notre Dame student body was excited, too, and got up long before breakfast to see the team to the day coach they occupied as far as Buffalo (from there the luxury of sleeping car accommodations to West Point). They were treated most hospitably, given the freedom of the Officer's Club and fed in the mess hall with the Cadets. And I can appreciate the thrill of all this for I went through the same routine on my first Army trip in 1921—the beginning of my longest and most satisfying football relationship outside of that with Notre Dame. Army has always been "good people"; and it will take a lot more than a schedule break to cancel that feeling among Notre Dame old-timers.

The game was played, as were all of Army's home games, on an open field which, I believe, is now used as the football practice field. There were no gate receipts but only a "fair crowd and the second-string New York football reporters." But one among the crowd was a young fellow named James A. Farley from nearby Haverstraw who never missed an Army-Notre Dame game and was always "neutral for the Irish." Notre Dame received a $1,000 guarantee—which was all it ever received, and all the Army budget could afford until the game was moved to New York.

These were the highlights of the game, with the quotations by Rockne himself:

"The Cadet body and most of the other spectators seemed to regard the engagement as a quiet, friendly workout for Army; and for the first part of the first quarter it looked that way. An Army line outweighing us by about 15 pounds to the man

110

pushed us all over the place before we overcame the tingling realization that we were actually playing Army."

After that the contest began to take on certain aspects which became traditional. It was always a "kidding" game with plenty of repartee. Rockne may have started that too. In a lull he heard an Army man say: "Let's lick these Hoosiers." So Rock explained to him how the term originated: "After every game at South Bend our coach goes on the field, picks up what he finds and asks: 'Whose ear is this?' "

It has always been a rough game. In this first one an official happened to observe an Army player teeing off on an Irish proboscis. The culprit was about to be banished but Rockne, as captain, explained that there might have been reasonable provocation and suggested that the boys not be restricted in what was only good fun. So nobody went out and the tradition of "clean hard football" was established. Football players have a code of their own about such things; certain enthusiastic gestures are acceptable but no smart coach encourages frankly dirty or cruel play—if only because it encourages reprisals and loses games.

Army, tumbling in to stop line charges, suddenly began to find Dorais fading back from his position (similar to that which the T quarterback of today occupies, though not so close to the center) to pass. But after three straight first down passes to halfbacks, Army began to cover all the eligible men.

Now Rockne, the campus actor, went into a football routine which is still effective. He pretended to be hurt, affected a limp, until "the Army halfback covering me almost yawned in my face. Suddenly I left him flat-footed, raced across the goal line as Dorais whipped the ball to complete a 40-yard touchdown pass. Everybody seemed astonished. There had been no tackling, no plunging, no crushing of fiber and sinew. Just a long-distance touchdown by rapid transit. At the moment I touched that ball, life for me was complete."

That was just what Rockne probably did feel as he made that first touchdown against Army.

"We proceeded to make it more complete."

Little did he or anybody else realize just how complete life was to become for Notre Dame; but it was later to be expressed in the "Hike Song":

> The march is on
> No brain or brawn
> Can stop the charge of fighting men.

Men are remembered for what they *do;* great names are linked with *events.* What happened on The Plains of historic West Point November 1, 1913, developed into one of those miracles of publicity no press agent could plan.

N-o-t-r-e D-a-m-e was writ in the football skies by the pass. In the press it became Little David, Lochinvar, things like that. It captured the respect and the imagination of the country. The 14 passes Dorais threw for over 200 yards proved that the *new* weapon was also *good,* could be an integral part of offense and not merely a threat.

Notre Dame proved it twice again later in that same season against Penn State and Texas—for Harper had written many letters.

The Irish were out of the Big Nine's box.

XIX

Poets, historians and philosophers have always been fascinated by the study of how much man is affected by conscious decisions. One school holds that things were meant to be, that he is a helpless bark on the stream of predestination. The opposite belief is that he controls his own destinies.

I believe in the doctrine of free will, that any of us at any given time, is, generally, and barring outright acidents, the sum of himself to that moment—of his judgments, beliefs, instincts and actions; that when we seem to get caught in currents over which we have no apparent control, we were drawn into these currents by instincts stronger than our conscious judgments or desires.

Rockne's life offers a good example. He was killed in a plane accident. Since there were no survivors it has never been established just what did happen to that plane; it may have been a mechanical failure over which Rockne obviously had no control; the weather was bad for flying, so there may have been a mistake in judgment by the man who allowed the plane to go up—or on the part of Rockne himself for going up in it. From almost every such disaster comes the story of the person whose life was saved because his judgment or his instinct (in which case an unconscious judgment) made him refuse to take the chance.

Regardless of that, Rockne did take that plane because he was following his career as the Notre Dame coach; and he was the Notre Dame coach mostly because of decisions he had made at decisive periods in his career; but not entirely. He had made two attempts to break away from Notre Dame before he became a coach; and later there were many times when he seemed about to break away. But the instinctive current always brought him back, as if Notre Dame had thrown a chain about him which he could not bring himself to break.

There was the first link which had brought him there, suddenly, after he had planned to enter Illinois.

In his junior year his father died; and, as the only son, he decided to quit school, look after his mother and sisters; but he was talked out of that by the same sister who had talked him into college originally.

He graduated with honors in chemistry, but like most football men he was not quite ready to break contact with the game. There was a coaching job open at a small Catholic college in Dubuque, Iowa, then known as St. Joseph's, later Columbia and now Loras. Rockne and Dorais, the inseparables and of equal football reputation, were the final candidates for the job—and decided to settle it by the friendly toss of a coin.

Dorais won the toss and the job.

But Notre Dame had not won Rockne. It was only recently that I heard, for the first time, the story of his attempt to become a doctor. Since Notre Dame had no medical school he decided to enroll at St. Louis University, and had arranged to coach a nearby high school team to pay his expenses. But somebody in authority, who saw as little in the little Norse as Shorty Longman had first seen, decided he couldn't keep up with medical studies if he also tried to coach.

So, after he had tried to flee her into the corridors of Illinois, Iowa and Missouri, Notre Dame brought Rockne back, as she was

114

always to bring him back—in humility and triumph and finally in death.

In 1914 he had compromised between football and science by assisting Jess Harper on the gridiron and Father Nieuwland in the classroom. I've often wondered how Nieuwland felt when he saw football winning. And I'm not too sure what the answer would have been had I ever thought to ask him. The Rubber Man was as human a little fellow as I've ever met. He would always give me a cheery hello when I passed him on the campus as a student. The only time I ever did have a long talk with him later, he kept me busy answering questions about Babe Ruth—which may tell you something about genius and Notre Dame priests.

Harper had got the break of a coaching lifetime in that first Army game; but many a man gets such a break and doesn't know what to do about it. Old Jess did and his method was very simple. He just sat down, wrote himself a lot more letters and the post-man brought him back quite a bag for 1914: Army, Carlisle, Syracuse—and Yale.

The Elis were to be met in the second game and the cocky Irish were going down to New Haven to show the Yales how the game should be played, just as they had shown Army. There was some justification for this confidence, as the only other loss of importance, apart from Rockne and Dorais, was the center, Al Feeney, now the mayor of Indianapolis. Ready to chew that Bull-dog up were such terrific guys as Eichenlaub, Elward, Bergman, Jones, Finnegan, Fitzgerald, Keefe and Pliska, supported by new men like Stan Cofall and Harry Baujan. Notre Dame was unde-feated for three years, had the secret weapon—shucks, the only question was the score!

Yale 28, Notre Dame 0!

"Humility," Rock later wrote, "is the lesson every athlete must learn in secret commune with his soul or he gets it in big doses on the field as thousands roar. Everybody but Harper, and including myself, was suffering from a bad case of fathead. Yale,

115

captained by Bud Talbot and led by a crack halfback, Harry Legore, lateral-passed us out of the park."

That defeat, not even yet quite forgotten, must have been the biggest disaster on the campus since the '79 fire. The students moaned and the coach decided something drastic should be done—which is the usual reaction at Notre Dame when the team loses a football game. And is that bad? In this case Harper added the backfield shift; and he always gave Rock credit for an important wrinkle of end play which was distinctive at Notre Dame—a "crow's hop" which enabled the smaller end to block a big tackle, instead of using two men for this job, as was customary elsewhere.

Army got even that year, 20-7, invited the Irish back in '15 for the rubber game; and when Notre Dame won that one, Army just naturally had to get even again. Which it did; but it kept on trying to win that odd game, was never quite able to do it—and that's probably as good an explanation as any as to why little Notre Dame remained on the Army schedule until it got big itself—and finally, too big.

Motion pictures would slide over the remaining three years of Harper's successful regime by showing Jess sitting down writing letters, while these scores flashed in a montage effect on the screen revealing the new schools added to the schedule:

1915	Notre Dame	7	Army	0
	Nebraska	20	Notre Dame	19
	Notre Dame	37	Texas	7
	Notre Dame	55	Rice	2
1916	Army	30	Notre Dame	10
	Notre Dame	20	Nebraska	0
1917	Notre Dame	0	Wisconsin	0
	Nebraska	7	Notre Dame	0
	Notre Dame	7	Army	2
	Notre Dame	3	W & J	0

Most of us are inclined to believe that we do more for other people than they do for us; but now and then a Blessed Stranger pops in, pops out and leaves us in his debt. Jess Harper was such a Good Samaritan to Notre Dame—and another Protestant to boot. He came along when the going was rough and friends were few. In five years he won thirty-three games, lost only five and tied one. He set up the Notre Dame system, gave the schedule its Army keystone and added Nebraska which, for many years, was to be the midwestern anchor. He developed Rockne, offered him to the University as its first home-bred coach. And he had George Gipp as a freshman.

In case you missed the significance of that 0-0 Wisconsin score, Harper also broke through the solid Western Conference front for the first time since 1910. And then, as if his job had been done, and perhaps because World War I was on and prospects for any football at all the next year were uncertain, he retired, like Cincinnatus of old, to the soil of his Kansas ranch. He came back once again, briefly, when the school called him after Rockne's death. He was also there for the end of the Army series at South Bend, sadder than any, perhaps.

Harper was the transition between the old and the new; and before leaving the old, let's call the roll of some of the other great football men of those days, not previously mentioned, with apologies to those my limited knowledge may omit. You can't know everything but let's scan the lists and see who pops out:

The Cartiers of Ludington, Michigan, for whom old Cartier Field was named; Jacob Rosenthal, three-year letterman; Rev. John F. "King" Farley, later hall rector and familiar campus figure for generations; Judge Eggeman of Fort Wayne; Rev. Dominick O'Malley; Frank Shaughnessy, now president of the International Baseball League; Nathan Silver, four-year letterman; Patrick Beacom, four-year letterman; Howard "Cap" Edwards, one of Rock's closest friends; Don Hamilton, great quarterback; Luke Kelly; Charles Crowley, later coach at Columbia; Alfred Bergman, first of three famous brothers from Peru, Ind.; Charles Bachman, later coach at Michigan State; and James Phelan, great quarterback, later president of the Coaches' Association and now professional coach.

Rockne's first year, 1918, was informal. The players were drawn from the S.A.T.C. group on the campus; only six games were played, at intervals during the season; and of these, three were won, one lost and two tied.

The war ended and the boys came trooping back.

The stage was set and the curtain was going up on Scott Fitzgerald's Flappers and Sad Young Men (none of whom were at Notre Dame), Pegler's Era of Wonderful Nonsense, Grant Rice's Golden Age of Sport.

And the Twelve Wonderful Years of Rockne—during which, and behind the spectacular football façade, the academic engineers achieved an even more remarkable and amazingly efficient expansion of the educational factory by the simple use of the simple formula of the Founder—work, think, fight and pray.

The second phase in the physical and academic building of a university was completed during Rockne's time. But the statue of Sorin remained; the basement chapel in the church and the outdoor chapel of the Grotto were unchanged; and Our Lady was ever brighter in the sky.

At Notre Dame the fundamentals never change; but Notre Dame grows ever stronger in this era of change.

XX

In the literature of rain there should be some brief mention of South Bend, which gets its share. The town never got into me much and I still get the points of the compass mixed up when I'm there. It always seemed like an in-law; but I wonder if that isn't about the way the average college student feels about the town; and South Bend is not a college town in the sense of Ann Arbor, New Haven or even Columbus, because Notre Dame is also a geographical lone wolf and lives alone, two miles to the north, ringed by its golf course, cemetery, forest and parking lots from the creeping suburbs of the city.

Before the Chamber of Commerce gets after me I hasten to report that South Bend has many good days and that the Notre Dame coaches insist that I bring the rain with me. But it was raining when I first arrived in 1919 and it was raining a week later when I stood with a group of other lonesome freshmen, waiting near the college post office for the old Hill Street trolley which already has its place in the literature of Ring Lardner, J. P McEvoy and others who have also waited there, probably in the rain.

It was dark, the trolley was taking its usual leisure and we were under the partial shelter of the trees. An automobile stopped and we ran to get in, thankful for the ride to town.

Rockne was driving.

119

A lot of rain has fallen since that night, thirty years ago, but that first impression still remains. Rock's personality was like the engine of his car—a charged dynamo, a compressed force, restrained with difficulty and always near the explosion point. I felt it then within the narrow enclosure of the dark car. I feel it now in the room where I write. There are several pictures of him here on the wall, some in his mellow years, plump with success and confidence. The body was shinier, the motor smoother—but the explosive power was always just below the hood.

That first meeting makes it easy to believe in symbolic patterns. Rock was always stopping to give a lift to boys. And I saw him last, twelve years later, in a car as we were both leaving the Hialeah race track. He waved a cheery good-bye.

Now, you may think I've been making a lot of this man, who, despite all of the things he might have been, was, after all, only a football coach, a teacher of games. So let's stop to try that case and for my first witness I would like to call Major-General Maxwell D. Taylor, one of the authentic heroes of the last war, who has just concluded a term as superintendent at West Point. In criticizing the 1948 report of President Truman's commission on higher education he said: "Education is far more than a matter of developing the intellect. . . . Character training and physical training should be introduced in proper proportion. The Grecian ideal of the importance of the whole man tends to disappear too easily in this age where technology and specialization count for so much. . . . Health and mental adjustment are surely as essential to the well-being of our nation as intellectual discipline."

General Taylor was making the case for the importance of sport in educational institutions. I would like to extend that to our national life. I believe that our sports program, particularly football, has had a distinct effect in inculcating our native philosophy into youth and maintaining it in adults; that it faithfully *reflects* our national character; that through the years, from the kids on the sandlots to the stars in the stadium, it has been a

120

powerful and subtle force in emphasizing the qualities which have made us great as a people: *incentive, competition, initiative, sportsmanship, loyalty, courage* and *democracy;* that it insists on a *score* instead of alibis and evasive propaganda; and it pays off on hard work, hard-hitting, superior thinking, physical training, mental discipline, the will to win and the execution of sound fundamentals.

There is an old gag that goes: "When a coach wins, he wins; when he loses, he builds character." But character building is not a gag. It is the primary goal of all the agencies which have to do with the training of youth—the home, the church, the schools—and the training of youth should rank close to the top obligation of any intelligent government. The practical truth, and I'm sure the parents of high school boys will agree, is that the football coach, if he is a man of character as well as talent, has more prestige and influence with the youth of his community than any parent, minister or teacher.

The successful college coach is a campus demigod; and when he becomes a national figure, his influence reaches to the youth of the nation. I quote from Alan Gould, now a top-ranking Associated Press executive but then its sports editor, at the time of Rockne's death:

"There has been no greater tribute to any figure in all the history of American sport than the spontaneous and heartfelt character of expressions all over the country following Knute Rockne's death. Walter Camp . . . and others have passed on in recent years leaving records of remarkable achievement and leadership. Beyond these factors Rockne left the effect of his astounding personality in the hearts of boys and men he knew, while also asserting a mass influence felt by those who knew him only through what they read or saw."

This, from a calm and disinterested Cornell man, may help you to understand my reactions about nine years later in an office at the MGM studio in Culver City where I sat with Scott Fitzgerald, Donald Ogden Stewart, Grover Jones and a few others, listening to the voice of Adolph Hitler as he was exorcizing himself and his followers for the invasion of Czechoslovakia. It was the ghastly voice of madness and it paralyzed us into silence because we knew what that voice was going to do to the world.

As I listened to Hitler I remembered Rockne—who had been even better at this sort of thing, but who had had the God-given graces of humor, humanity and intelligence which are the retreats from madness; whose message had always been: "Give them footballs instead of guns."

I was thinking: How fortunate for America that the explosive forces of its youth have been directed and detonated by our Rocknes instead of our Hitlers. How much better they fight with guns, *when they have to,* after they have been brought up as Americans, with footballs, bats and boxing gloves.

Healthy boys like to play. Play helps keep boys healthy and wholesome. Teach them to play and pray, to think and work, to love victory and hate defeat, to fight for what they love and believe in, above all things to *fight to live* with the confidence born of victory.

That's the case for college sport, for all sport in America.

Do you still think, perhaps, that sport is just a pleasant recreation; that men who devote their lives to teaching it to boys have wasted their lives?

Do you think Army and Navy will turn out better or worse officers after that 21-21 tie of '48?

Or that Michigan-Ohio State, Penn-Cornell, Harvard-Yale, Texas-SMU, Notre Dame-Southern Cal, Georgia-Georgia Tech, Stanford-California and all the others would do a better job of education if they just forgot those "classics" on the gridiron and concentrated on those classics in the classrooms?

Or that Notre Dame is wrong in teaching its boys to win honorably in all fields—even if it is taking a chance of winning itself right out of the football league and out of opponents?

122

The Rockne victory era divides naturally into four periods:

1919-21—The World War I returnees who won nineteen games in two undefeated seasons, lost only one, by three points.

1922-24—The Four Horsemen and Seven Mules who won twenty-seven, lost two and tied one.

1925-28—The Forgotten Men who, due chiefly to his one bad season in 1928, had the comparatively poor record (for Rockne, that is) of twenty-eight won, eight lost and two tied.

1929-30—The National Champions who won nineteen games in two undefeated seasons against the absolute best in the land.

Rockne never saw himself as anything but a football coach who wanted to win games and build up his schedule. He had no great design. He became the greatest figure in the history of American sports because of the little day-by-day things he did in his own way among the people he worked with and the boys he coached.

Let's watch him at that work. And see if we can go a step beyond the usual treatment of sports figures in print and motion pictures—the popping of colorful corn—and get into the laboratory where the human kernels are separated and analyzed.

Up to now you've met people mostly dug from musty archives and mouldy memories, into whom I've tried to pump living blood. From now on, you will begin to meet people I've known and lived with, and of whose names and deeds you may also have some knowledge and recollection.

And let's begin with Gipp (pronounced with a hard *G* as in *give,* which he did), a most peculiar sort of athletic saint whose canonization was hastened, as was that of Lou Gehrig, and Rockne himself, because he died at Glory Peak.

XXI

The legend has had Gipp turning up at Notre Dame as a blob of unsuspected athletic clay which Rockne discovered and shaped into a flawless football masterpiece called Gridiron Superman.

As always with a legend—yes and no.

George was born in Laurium, Michigan, up in the iron peninsula, the son of a Congregationalist minister. He had every natural gift of body, mind and spirit except the one which, more than anything else, made Rockne what he was—driving ambition. George just didn't seem to care much about things, including fame when it came. He was like a sleek and beautiful car which ordinarily ambled along with most cylinders idling, but which, now and then, would put on a burst of amazing speed. The power was there; but the spark had to be unusual to reach it.

Though he was to become a gridiron immortal, Gipp never made first string on his high school football eleven. He was better at basketball and later played on the town YMCA team. He was good enough in baseball to have been signed by the Chicago White Sox just before he died—but he never won either a baseball or basketball monogram at Notre Dame nor seriously tried for them.

Lazy? I would call it a superb indifference. Things came easy and he took things easy. After high school he was content to

124

drive a taxicab in his home town; and from some of the accomplishments he revealed in extra-curricular hours around South Bend, he probably knew his way around the seamier side of his home town, where police and hackies penetrate.

He came to Notre Dame as a baseball player, three years after he had finished high school, on the recommendation of Wilbur T. "Dolly" Gray, a former Irish diamond star who had gone up to the White Sox and whose home was in Calumet, near Laurium. So mark up another assist to baseball and happy accident in the Notre Dame football tradition.

Rockne used to tell a story about the man who visited Notre Dame and found that everybody he met carried a football and "hipped" into the backfield shift, including the president. "The funniest part of that story," Rock would conclude, "is that a lot of people believe it." But it is true that before almost every hall at Notre Dame there is a small campus where the students kick footballs back and forth in their leisure time, as on the vacant lots, and too often on the streets, in towns.

That's where Rock first saw Gipp—dropkicking—and hustled him into a football suit. That fall, in the freshman game against Western State Normal varsity, George found himself in a situation which appealed to him. The score was tied with three minutes to go, fourth down with the ball on Notre Dame's 38-yard line, and big yardage needed. George wanted to try a dropkick, was ridiculed, and sent back to punt. So he dropkicked—62 yards to win the game and put his name in the record book with what is still the second longest dropkick of all time.

The next week the varsity was going to play Army. Rock had Gipp out with the scrubs to impersonate Elmer Oliphant, the Army star. The varsity was primed to cool off the frosh wonderman, as the varsity always loves to do. "Gipp," Rockne related, "gave a perfect imitation of Oliphant—but unfortunately in the actual game, Oliphant gave a perfect imitation of

Gipp." (Army won that one 30-10 but was the only team to score against the Irish in the 8-1 season.)

In the spring George was out for baseball and violated instructions again. Ordered to bunt, he hit a home run instead, explained it was "too hot to run bases."

Rock's policy was always to give his older men every possible chance so he usually held the youngsters under a strong leash while they learned the finer points from observation. This was probably all right with Gipp; but he was, nevertheless, in the 1917 lineup against Army in the fading minutes when the Cadets, trailing 7-2, had fourth down on the Notre Dame 8-yard line. They lined up for a placekick; and if you are a little slow in catching the significance of that, Gipp wasn't. The first man to realize that three points would do Army no good, he alerted the backfield which promptly knocked down the attempted pass—and Rock was happy to know that Gipp could think under pressure, too.

That quality of poise was the gloss on the Gipp masterpiece. When everything else was stopped he was an expert at improvising on the field and was so successful at this that Rockne gave him a carte blanche which few football players have ever enjoyed —and which George utilized with sardonic humor.

In the 1919 Nebraska game, which Rock described as "the most gruelling game Notre Dame ever played with its toughest Western opponent," Notre Dame entered with several crippled stars who were promptly rendered out of service for the rest of the afternoon. With 12 minutes to go Notre Dame had a 14-9 lead but no more available substitutes against a Nebraska that was roaring with vitality. This situation also appealed to Gipp who conceived and directed a gem of scientific stalling that finally beat the clock and, quite naturally, exasperated the Nebraska coach who, after the final whistle, asked Gipp:

"What course do you take at Notre Dame?"

"Plumbing," Gipp laughed. He was taking law, as little as

possible, a fact which was to become widely known soon after.

He had been elected captain for his senior year, a rare honor for a Notre Dame backfield man. But when we returned in the fall of 1920 the campus was hit by the news that Gipp had been kicked out of school and that all efforts to get him back had failed.

All but one. I had troubles of my own that fall, and with the blessed brass of youth, had come to put the matter up to the President. I was next in line when Rockne came into the ante-room with Gipp. They took my priority, which was not the first time Gipp had done that. The preceding spring I had won my spurs as rightfielder for the Day-Dodger interhall baseball team and one day was already in the outfield when Father Cunningham, our philosopher-coach, held up the game. Gipp was coming across the campus and when he finally arrived, I came out and he went in. I choose to think that Gipp was my substitute; but he didn't bother me again; and I've often wondered how they got him out that day, the only time I ever saw him on the baseball field.

So he had substituted for me again, in the presidential ap-pointment line-up—and it turned out all right for all concerned. Gipp, perhaps through his mouthpiece, Rockne, asked to take an immediate oral examination without benefit of cramming. That sporting proposition must have appealed to Father Burns, who had been a varsity baseball catcher in his time, so he gave George his chance. And since this was one of those situations which called for a little extra effort, George made good. And if you think the President leaned a little backwards to help the football star that day, he also leaned to help the unknown sophomore, practically made a job for me where there was none before.

The thing I like best to remember about George is that though he did not have his captaincy restored and could have gone to many other colleges which were beckoning him in those loose days, he ate the humble pie and went on to bring to Notre Dame the greatest athletic renown it had yet known.

Marvellous in every game, the bright star of a constellation, he hit three unusually dramatic peaks during the 1920 season. The first was at Army on October 6. This was before radio and we got the returns in the gym on a board called the Grid-Graph, which showed the runner scampering up and down the field by electric lights. George *was* electric that day as he engaged in a personal duel with Walter French, the Army star who later played baseball for Connie Mack. George did everything there was to do on a football field and got so sensationally aroused about it that once, when he probably felt Army was becoming too effusive in its personal hospitality, he tore off his headgear and challenged the entire Cadet eleven.

This would seem to have been a situation which had finally hit all cylinders of the Cadillac personality that was content to move like a modest four-cylinder job on most occasions; or it may merely have been one of George's histrionic efforts calculated to do something to Army's human mechanism. But it was Gipp—Gipp—Gipp all afternoon and the first-string sports writers were there to see and properly evaluate one of the great individual gridiron performances of all time.

That night we marched in the streets of South Bend to the chant: Gipp, Gipp—Gipp, Gipp, Gipp.

The next week George got the hero's welcome back at Notre Dame, made an 84-yard wheeling run I can still see, without a Purdue hand touching him, which meant ten other guys blocking, too.

Then the team went to play Indiana at the ball park in Indianapolis. We were at the Grid-Graph again, ready for the feast.

Third period score: Indiana 10, Notre Dame 0.

Gipp was out of the game—something about his shoulder.

Norm Barry was in his place—the one boy in Notre Dame athletic history who had come up through the minims and the prep school to make varsity second string. And this day he played as if he were another man the years had carefully prepared for this drastic emergency.

Barry ran wild at left half . . . Mohardt at right half. Bang. Bang. One touchdown . . . 10-7.

Back they came—Barry and Mohardt, unfriendly rivals before this game but now forgetting all that—to the five-yard line.

There the march seemed to stop. Time was running out and Indiana was smelling the headlines: INDIANA WINS FIRST GAME OVER NOTRE DAME IN 30 YEARS!

Time out—and Gipp in again.

Tempest in the gym. Undefeated season riding on the next two plays. Gipp would do it! Gipp—Gipp—Gipp—

The electric ball wavered—stopped. Gipp was stopped.

Silence. That shoulder must be bad.

GIPP SCORES.

Notre Dame 13, Indiana 10.

That shoulder *was* bad. There was no doctor on the bench in those days. Rock didn't know how bad it really was and Gipp wasn't telling.

The open-field runner had made himself a battering ram to go that last five yards with a broken collarbone!

The next week was Northwestern at Evanston, the resumption of the series which was to go almost continuously for the next twenty-nine years and become the Army-Notre Dame of the Midwest—until the "schedule situation" finally got that one, too.

Gipp was there in uniform with his shoulder heavily padded. He was through with football but he could still dropkick—and before the game, he gave an exhibition from the 50-yard line.

Notre Dame didn't need him. The score was 27-7 in the late stages of the fourth period.

The game was in the bag and the crowd forgot the score.

GIPP! GIPP!

The crowd wanted to see Superman, the player of the year—the all-time player, they seemed to sense, even then.

Gipp wanted to play. He had crawled out on the grass to Rockne's shoulder. Gipp, who never cared much about things, was pleading to get into *his last game.*

It was a crazy idea and Rock shook him off.

GIPP . . . GIPP . . . GIPP . . . GIPP . . . GIPP . . .

The crowd chant became a roar.

Rock was a dramatist. He had been a player. He was a human. Gipp was like his brother.

Gipp ran out on the field.

Notre Dame was on the defense and George had his orders. He was to show himself, that was all. He was to play safety man but let the punt roll.

He did let the first punt roll.

Notre Dame on offense. Gipp back . . . Gipp passing— TOUCHDOWN!

Notre Dame on defense again. Gipp playing safety. Northwestern had to punt. Let it roll, George.

Let it roll, hell! George picked it up, started running, big shoulder and all.

Then came the finest thing I have ever seen on a football field. Two Northwestern ends met George, seemed to lay soft hands on him, to set him down gently as a baby, to say: "Now look, George, after all."

Rock got him out of there—quick!

Portrait (with apologies to Bill Stern) of the Swan Song of a Hero!

Corn? Sure. Tall corn. Good old Notre Dame corn—then and now. You should go to one of those current pep meetings and hear 5,000 young throats rip it out with the team listening.

Notre Dame believes. So does Navy. So does Army. So do all the winning football schools.

Good old American corn. Victory corn. Let's don't ever lose it, folks—unless you think the flag-raising at Iwo Jima was also corn.

130

XXII

When Gipp first came to Notre Dame he was on campus and worked as a "hasher" or table-waiter, a favorite occupation for athletes then and now at schools which operate the Job Plan. In his last two years, he lived downtown at the Oliver Hotel where, it is now generally accepted, he paid his expenses by certain skills around the green tables, skills he had probably developed during his taxi days in the old home town. What is not true is that he educated students in such indoor sports. I once heard Hunk Anderson, his pal and fellow townsman, say with some indignation: "George wouldn't play cards with the college boys."

He was billiard champion of the town and did play 15-or-no-count pool; but he never played with students for much more than fun—and I qualify as an expert witness here because I was the guy who racked up the balls at the Oliver. What probably is true is that he matched his poker proficiency with town hotshots and hotel transients with no more than reasonable success, because he lived simply; and it's just as well for football history that he operated quietly because Notre Dame considers a nickel crap game cause for expulsion.

Should the University have known that George played poker? That would have taken a lot of detection. It certainly wasn't common knowledge at the time because I never heard of it until years later and I worked at the hotel where George lived. I'm bringing it up here because it's one of those things that has crept into the legend and I'm giving what I think are the facts.

Personally he was a nice guy. I first met him socially in the spring of my freshman year at an evening party at one of the many lake resorts in northern Indiana—which might also have been against the campus law for all I know, though all of us lived in town. There was some necking which impaired nobody's amateur standing; and George's attitude toward such goings-on was consistent with his attitude toward the rest of life. He could take it or leave it alone; and in this case he must have left it alone.

The girls were all townies, nice girls, too, with cars, which is the nicest attribute a girl can have in a college town. Coming back I was in the car with George and his girl was driving. One of her friends, who evidently considered that George had not been properly attentive, pointedly remarked that plenty of other young men were interested in his companion.

Gipp promptly intercepted that very forward pass and ran it back for a quick touchdown. "Whenever the competition gets too tough for me," he said, "I just drop out." Which seemed to settle that though it was obviously a big lie because George never really started to work until the competition began to get too tough for the rest of the team.

I was moving up in the hotel business by an unorthodox method I do not recommend, had been fired from the billiard parlor for talking back to the big boss but had bobbed up again behind the desk as mail clerk. On my first evening there, while waiting for the big boss to catch up with me (which, of course, he eventually did) Gipp came over and shook hands. I was about as unimportant a freshman as you could find on the campus but the big star had come over to shake hands with me. That was Gipp.

It is also Notre Dame, where any man of distinction seems at pains to hide the fact, to go out of his way to avoid taking bows. It may stem from the goofing tradition which respects no position; but it does carry over. I still think the high spot of our football achievement was reached during the Penn game in 1930 when the squad rambled at will against the Quakers the week after having done the same thing against Pitt—both representative Eastern teams. That evening the squad had a private dinner at the Penn A. C.—just the gang and Connie Mack—but nobody, not even Rockne, would sit at the head of the table.

Gipp had to be aware of his position on the campus but he went to an extreme length to hide it—wore his monogram sweater inside out, a fashion adopted by other athletes at the time. Two weeks after the end of his last season the annual football dinner was held at the Oliver. Gipp was there to receive his letter; but when he was called upon, he was not there. We chuckled at that, figured George had ducked out to avoid making a speech. But two days later we learned that this had not been a simple case of modesty.

George was confined to his hotel room with tonsilitis. A few more days and he was in the hospital with pneumonia—which didn't worry anybody because a little thing like pneumonia didn't figure to bother Superman. But his condition quickly became critical. There was gloom on the campus as we waited; and daily bulletins in the press of the country about the fight for life by the Player of the Year.

Every so often sport produces an off-the-field situation much more gripping than anything on the field. This was one. A young man was dying. People who didn't care much about football prayed for his right to live.

The drama mounted when Walter Camp picked him on his all-American eleven—the first Notre Dame man who had ever made Camp's first team. And it was announced that he had been signed by the White Sox.

In a quiet hospital room two things happened which have become firmly rooted in the Notre Dame tradition. Gipp made a request which has been confirmed by the hospital chaplain who was in the room at the time. And he became a Catholic. Somewhere along the line of battle the spirit of this worldly young man had also been touched.

One of the finest things about the Notre Dame football tradition is the deep respect non-Catholic boys have for the spiritual feeling of their teammates. Some of them become Catholics later on, as Gipp and Rockne did; and the others get something out of it which they never lose. At our twenty-fifth class reunion, the first night had the customary masculine alcoholic tinge; but the next morning there was a mass for the deceased members of the class and everybody was in the chapel—including two Protestant ex-football players, who were also Masons.

George was buried from Sacred Heart Church on the campus. Father O'Hara said in his sermon: "To the eyes of the world it is deep tragedy as we contemplate the abrupt and painful close of the life of a young man, energetic, skillful, alert, keen-minded and resourceful—a life full of promise—snapped off in the moment of highest glory.

"But to the eyes of faith this death is a miracle; the passing from a life of transient joy and abiding sorrow to a life of happiness eternal. What wrought the miracle of this beautiful death? It was the reward of Notre Dame, the Blessed Mother, for a humble service which is dedicated to her honor; he strove in his own way to add luster to its tradition; and although we did not think of George as a deeply religious man, his inmost thoughts came to the surface when he faced death.

"He spoke, not of the honors he had received but of his death in the arms of God. May God grant us all the grace to view death in the same tranquil way. I commend him to your prayers."

He was to be buried at Laurium and business stopped in South Bend as we took him to the station in a snow storm. A platoon of police preceded the football eleven who marched in signal formation with the left half position vacant. The Monogram Club led the 1,500 students in a procession deathly silent by

134

comparison with the riotous march of a few weeks before, the night of the Army game. The faculty, then George, with six members of the squad as pall-bearers, including the three from George's home town who had followed him to Notre Dame—Hunk Anderson, Ojay Larson and Perce Wilcox. Then the family.

At the station we waited. The train came in and hats came off. We climbed telephone poles and baggage trucks as they put him in the baggage car. We were young and this was death. Most of us really found out about death that day.

The six pall-bearers followed him to the grave. The last six miles of the journey were made by sled. And the snows of Christmas powdered the grave of Thanksgiving's Hero.

Because he died so soon after going into the Northwestern game with a broken collarbone, it is sometimes said this led to his death. This is not true. We had all forgotten that injury before he was stricken. He had always had a chronic throat, as, strangely enough, had Rockne, both being caused by bad tonsils. A strep germ hit him and his resistance must have been low. There was no penicillin then; pneumonia reduced his vitality and the poison raced through him. George had been a magnificent physical specimen, had the perfect halfback physique—six feet, 185 pounds.

When he died he weighed eighty pounds. I did not go to see him dead. I did not want to remember George Gipp weighing eighty pounds.

Just how good a football player was he? What is his true stature in gridiron history?

There is no doubt but that his final season and tragic death have dramatized his memory, helped to place him among the immortals, frequently, and by Rockne himself, on all-time backfields along with Jim Thorpe. Nobody really knows about such things because nobody has seen them all. I have watched most of the publicized stars since 1919, and my judgment may be colored because I knew and liked him; but for what it is worth, I believe he has as much right as any I've known to rank at the top.

George was one of the first to be known as a triple-threat back. He has that dropkick in the record book and was a fine punter, though not as long as some I've seen. They didn't shoot much for the coffin-corner in those days but he would have had the poise and skill for that.

He was the best passer of his time, threw an arching ball with a flick of the wrist, that was easy to catch. The bullet pass had not yet come in but he had a baseball arm and could have done it. He was not a sensational open-field runner of the Red Grange type, but he was fast enough, could do the hundred in 10.1. His favorite play was off-tackle; he was a smart runner, could drive and hit hard, cut fast or change pace in the open, turn it off and on, outsmart tacklers and was a joy to watch in setting up his blockers.

He handled the ball on almost every play and was not called upon to do much blocking but could do that too. He would have made a great quarterback, occasionally did take over such chores —and, as previously said, was expert at improvising and executing spot strategy.

He was the defensive captain, a sharp tackler; and Rock wrote that he was the one player he ever saw about whom it could truly be said that "nobody ever completed a pass against him."

Above all the ordinary mechanical factors was his ideal playing temperament. Rock said that no matter how aroused George seemed to be in his purple moments, he was ice-cold inside. The fact seems to have been that no matter who was captain or quarterback, Gipp was the leader at all times. And he had that hallmark of the champion: He was at his best when his best was needed; he had a quiet confidence in his ability to do the right thing at the right time; and he seemed to have had a good idea when he was going to have to shoot the works. A few years ago I came upon a telegram he sent to a friend at school from Lincoln, the night before a Nebraska game: "They'll be tough but brains will win . . . Gipp."

It all seems to add up to the best—a *specialist at everything*. The moderns who remind me most of Gipp are Johnny Lujack and Doak Walker; but he could do more things better than either of them, had more hidden fire and maturity.

There was one thing more about George. I was vaguely conscious of it while he lived but the thought recurs whenever I see one of his rare photographs. He had sad eyes, seemed always to be waiting. Perhaps that was why he was not too much concerned with the commonplace.

A most peculiar kind of a saint.

XXIII

When Rockne began his schedule-building job he faced the staggering handicap of a home seating capacity of only 2,500—almost farcical for a school aggressively trying to break into the big time.

Yet, despite that handicap, he won the Midwestern championship in 1919.

By 1924 the stands had been enlarged to about 20,000—and in that year Rockne won an undisputed national championship with a truly national card that included Army, Princeton, Northwestern, Wisconsin, Georgia Tech, Carnegie Tech, Nebraska and a Rose Bowl victory over Pop Warner's Stanford—the only time, incidentally, that Notre Dame has ever played in a bowl game.

Rockne was aided, of course, by the fact that schools like to play as many games as possible at home—and colorful, crowd-pleasing, itinerant Notre Dame fitted nicely into this picture. But permanent schedules are built on a home-and-home basis and big-stadium schools like to play in big stadiums when they go visiting. With his customary astuteness Rock solved that problem in 1926 when "the school without a stadium" suddenly came up with the biggest stadium of all—Soldier's Field in Chicago, where the "home" games were played until the 54,000-capacity Notre Dame Stadium was completed on the campus in 1930.

There was a further difficulty, intangible but positive—the same which is now threatening the Notre Dame schedule structure—*prestige*. As Notre Dame became all-conquering, other coaches and schools began to question the wisdom of trading almost certain defeat year after year for sure-fire gate receipts and a shot at the honor that began to accrue to a school that *beat Notre Dame*.

Rockne met that by personal magnetism and a policy that was not only cagy but sound. His teams played open and clean football that took as little toll as possible of opposing manpower; when he got a safe lead—two touchdowns in his day—he got his regulars out of there, kept them fresh for the next game, gave his reserves the experience they would need when they would be the regulars. As a result he seldom humiliated a rival or threatened another coach's job. That was one reason he could beat them and make them like him.

His basic objective was to get back on the list of the major Conference schools because it is the more natural and economical arrangement to have a schedule imbedded in home territory. He accomplished this by vaulting them, by becoming so important in the national picture that they were eventually glad to have him back; and he made this easier for them as well as himself by playing the cards dealt to him with consummate skill and captivating charm.

It was a pleasure and an education in human relations to watch him work. He handled Stagg with kid gloves, Yost with boxing gloves, Zuppke with wit and most of the others with a disarming deference. They all must have known what he was doing but they seemed to admire and to be intrigued by the way he was doing it. And when the day finally came that Notre Dame began to overshadow the Conference in its own section, he still seemed to defer to the important people, and even to some, less important, who came to him seeking games. He was always an exciting man to be around—and that, I believe, more than any other one quality, explained his personal success with people. He was a leader, he made Notre Dame a leader—and people just naturally follow a leader.

This is the way he built the schedule, year by year, with the more important games listed and the significant additions italicized:

1918—*Purdue, Great Lakes,* Nebraska. (Army out—war year.)

1919—*Indiana,* Purdue, Army, Nebraska.

1920—*Northwestern,* Army, Purdue, Indiana, Nebraska.

1921—*Iowa, Rutgers,* Army, Purdue, Indiana, Nebraska.

1922—*Georgia Tech, Carnegie Tech,* Army, Purdue, Indiana, Nebraska.

1923—*Princeton,* Army, Georgia Tech, Carnegie Tech, Purdue, Nebraska.

1924—*Stanford, Wisconsin,* Army, Princeton, Georgia Tech, Northwestern, Nebraska, Carnegie Tech.

1925—*Minnesota, Penn State,* Army, Georgia Tech, Northwestern, Nebraska, Carnegie Tech.

1926—*Southern Cal,* Army, Georgia Tech, Northwestern, Carnegie Tech, Indiana, Minnesota, Penn State. (Nebraska out.)

1927—*Navy,* Army, Southern Cal, Minnesota, Georgia Tech, Indiana.

1928—Army, Navy, Southern Cal, Wisconsin, Georgia Tech, Carnegie Tech, Penn State.

1929—Army, Navy, Southern Cal, Wisconsin, Georgia Tech, Carnegie Tech, Northwestern, Indiana.

1930—*Southern Methodist, Pitt, Pennsylvania,* Army, Navy, Southern Cal, Northwestern, Indiana, Carnegie Tech.

There is the Rockne monument, and it tells its own eloquent story. He went out at the top, with them coming to him—all but the die-hard Big Three of the Conference; but they were also on the way—Ohio State in '35; Illinois in '37; and finally, in '42, good old Michigan.

It's quite a story from almost any angle you look at it—sporting, business or personal. And the story behind the story is that the football teams were unconsciously clearing the path for the expansion of a university which would have come along anyhow, but hardly so quickly. Rock and his boys went out and sold Notre Dame so fast that the educational engineers had to step up the pace to fill the orders.

It has frequently been said in recent years that there is nothing wrong with the Notre Dame schedule situation that a few defeats wouldn't cure.

The United States could probably make a lot of friends, too, if it should decide to start losing wars.

The preceding schedule story explains many things in the Notre Dame football picture: Why the Army game was always played in the East until it became such a fixture there that it could not be moved; why the teams were referred to as Ramblers and Nomads—nickelodeon nicknames the school never liked but to which it could not logically object as long as there was real basis for them; and why the "football factory" label was attached —it was assumed that a small school which played most of its big games away from home must specialize in football at the expense of scholastic work; that no squad which spent every weekend on the road could find time for studying.

This is, of course, a fallacy. The football season covers only a small part of the academic year; any school which goes only a small distance to play away from home, usually gives Friday and Saturday to the trip; and there is the further fact that football trips have educational values all their own, particularly for boys whose social and travel advantages have been previously limited, which is true of most college football players.

The "Irish" nickname of the squads, though a natural, also took on a derogatory aspect in the days when Notre Dame was a rank outsider fighting for recognition. It finally became so em-

141

barrassing that University authorities tried to play it down; but it would not die, partly because no compensating substitute was offered, and because opponents seemed to enjoy keeping it alive, with such references as appeared in a Lincoln, Nebraska paper in 1922: THE HORRIBLE HIBERNIANS COME TO TOWN TODAY.

This was too much, even for Rockne, who was neither Irish nor Catholic but who always preferred the "Irish" nickname and referred to himself and other boys in the line-up with foreign-sounding names as "Irish by environment."

After I left school and started writing sports for the Associated Press in New York, I referred to Notre Dame as "the Irish" but was informed this was taboo—and at the request of Notre Dame authorities at some earlier date. Since, like most other Notre Dame people, I disliked the "Rambler" tag, I tried to label them "the Blue Comets" because of their air game and blue jerseys. Like most synthetics it didn't catch on.

In 1925 I went to the *Evening Post*, which did not know about the ancient restriction; so I began to use "Fighting Irish"; and since I was pretty much the authority on Notre Dame athletics in New York at that time, other writers picked it up. Later I went to the *Daily News*; and its tremendous circulation so popularized "the Irish" that even the AP finally began to use it.

So now Notre Dame bandmen have shamrocks on their caps and feature Irish tunes; the squad wears green jerseys instead of the traditional blue and the mascot is an Irish terrier; other students bodies use the Irish motif in planning stunts and the game of football is the more colorful because Notre Dame has a nickname coming out of characterization instead of some synthetic tag that avoids an honest situation.

Every so often Notre Dame does catch a whiff of intolerance; there may even be a slight aroma, in the present schedule situation, of the old days when advertisements for help carried the restrictions: "No Irish" and "No Catholics." The Football Issue

142

of *The Scholastic* in 1948 recognized this possibility with an editorial which concluded:

"A slur became a symbol. It amuses some, annoys others. It stands for the fidelity and courage of everyone who suffers discrimination from any cause. It inspires respect for the basic Christian origins of our country. The tradition of 'Irish' at Notre Dame does not mean race as such; it is the memory of a long, uphill fight for equal rights in a free land, and for recognition under the code of sportsmanship."

That's hot-blooded student thought. For myself, and I think the average older Irish alumnus, I've never felt like one of an oppressed minority. The nation that made a holiday of St. Patrick's Day has easily absorbed one Irish football team among all the Tigers, Bulldogs, Wildcats, Golds, Trojans and such. There is ample evidence that the Notre Dame Idea is being honestly assayed.

Before the Illinois game in 1946, Ralph Cannon, sports columnist of the Chicago *Herald-American,* visited the Notre Dame campus and wrote this:

"Everything is so clean, almost religious. You never hear a foul word here. They have welded together the earth and the sky in football at Notre Dame and it is a wonderful thing. . . . They are out to win; there never has been a school where so many were ready to give so much to win. But superimposed upon that keen-edged determination and drive to win, is this saving grace of gentility, this mystic touch that all the genuine zealots have— the very thing that distinguishes men from brutes.

"These Notre Dame boys play football as hard as any team that ever existed; yet they are not brutal. They play with a sense of responsibility to a grand tradition, to the great ones who remain only in the intangible atmosphere all around them. That is something you don't get today, or tomorrow, but only with the years—with innumerable men playing hard, yet with a genuine, manly and courtly attitude.

"There are people—people who have never been a part of anything like this, who are color-blind to all of these exquisite overtones of human relations, who are deaf to just such harmonies as these—who insist that all of this is wrong, needless, savage. Such people are weaklings, who would in time bring an end to our type of civilization.

"All of us who believe in manliness, and the competition that is required for existence in this world, owe much to Notre Dame for keeping alive, by example, the things that we believe in and know positively to be RIGHT."

I have referred, previously, to little gems that appear now and then on the sports pages, where the literary detectives never seem to think of looking for them. I offer this bit from Ralph Cannon, believe there is in it a message for every American. If you don't get what I mean, go back and read it again.

Between halves of the game at Champaign later that week, the Illinois band lined up before the Notre Dame stands. All present expected the customary rendition of the Notre Dame "Victory March." Instead, the band began the solemn strains of the "Ave Maria" while a tenor sang the Latin words of the Hail Mary. And for that little while the stadium of one of the most powerful of the Conference schools also became an outdoor cathedral.

Nice country, isn't it?

144

XXIV

At an Ohio State-Michigan game I was introduced to a group by Oscar Thomas, the Buckeye ticket manager, as "the first of the college athletic publicity directors." That was news to me, but it might just be true; and if it is, the major credit goes to Rockne for this, as for so many other logical innovations in the transition of football into big business.

Because it played no big games at home in the early days, Notre Dame was seldom visited by big-time writers. A "write-up" by Walter Eckersall or a mention in *The Wake* was major news on the campus; a visit from a Chicago writer, a major event; and as for New York—even in my time, which included the first two years of the Four Horsemen, the only reporters who honored us with visits were Lawrence Perry and Ray McCarthy.

The school had a good journalism department but, as yet, no organized public relations and the publicity that did go out was haphazard. Athletic news was dispensed by men on the two downtown newspapers; and since these were paid space rates by the metropolitan journals, the boys, or so Rockne thought, sometimes buzzed their imaginations. Rock always enjoyed a fine press because he was good copy and personally entertaining; he liked reporters and they liked him. But he was skating on thin ice in his relations with other schools and was sometimes embarrassed by what he called the "back room fiction writers."

He solved this problem by direct and simple action—he created the post of official Notre Dame athletic correspondent who would be responsible directly to him for the veracity of his output, and he advised the metropolitan papers to accept stories only from this man. This they were glad to do because newspapers don't like to be embarrassed by wildcat stories either. They were to pay for the service, as previously; so Rock, in a typical maneuver, had not only relieved himself of an irritating situation but had acquired a press agent who was paid by the newspapers.

To the job he appointed Arch, then Archie, Ward, a student who had done sports writing at Rockford, Illinois, and had been recommended by Gus Dorais. Arch held the position for one full year, 1919, and the football season of 1920—after which he departed for the Chicago *Tribune* where he has for many years been the most influential sports editor in the country. He originated the major league All Star Game and the annual football classic between college stars and the professional champions. He built up International Golden Gloves; and after twice declining to be commissioner of the National Professional Football League, he became the guiding spirit behind the formation of the All-American Conference.

But from my selfish viewpoint the greatest thing Arch Ward ever did—and I once told him this on a coast-to-coast hookup—was when he left Notre Dame and I got his job. I held it for three years; and where Arch, to the best of my knowledge, merely wrote stories for the press, I began to send out publicity releases—on my own, incidentally, for the dear old *Universitatis* was not sufficiently interested to buy me stamps. I also travelled with the football team, as the guest of our nation's railroads and some of our best hotels, though these were not aware of their kind hospitality.

Since these were the days before jerseys were numbered and printed information was passed around the press boxes, I was much in demand by sports writers because I was the only guy around who knew the Notre Dame players without a scorecard. And once, in 1923, Rock even paid my way to New York where I stayed the full week between the Army and Princeton games— the only time in three years and 12,000 Pullman miles I was ever able to look a conductor squarely in the eye and be among those present when the passengers were counted.

I was a newspaper correspondent by appointment of Rockne but an athletic publicity director by my own personal appointment, and over the objection of the Master, who would have much preferred that I stay home and build up the gate for the next game at Cartier Field. But I was also a student and regardless of the instructions he gave me before the team left the campus, I always bobbed up on the train at Elkhart. I was strictly on my own and he made this plain by coldly ignoring me on the trip *to* the game; but coming back was something else. I was very popular with him then because he always wanted to know what the big-shot writers had to say about his team—and him—in the press box.

So I may have been the first college athletic press agent; I don't remember any others in my time and I got around wherever Notre Dame teams went, which was considerable. It was an inevitable development and now represents quite an industry—a group of clever and efficient men at every school whose real value to the college, I suspect, is as weakly appreciated as was mine at the time.

When Rock first appointed Arch Ward, he even arranged for him to cover Notre Dame for both downtown papers, the *News-Times,* which had morning and afternoon editions, and the *Tribune,* which published only in the afternoon. This was a tough spot and Arch tried to split up the news breaks; but since the *News-Times* had a morning paper and normally would have first crack at most news, it pulled out of the arrangement after the first year, gave Ward his choice of writing for it or the *Trib.* Rock, who was never quite happy unless he had some small feud going on, which he would conduct as though it were a world war, took umbrage at the *News-Times* for upsetting his cozy little arrangement; he advised Ward to stay with the *Tribune* and said he would give him all the news, which he did with gusto.

It was into this situation that Father Burns unknowingly dropped me in 1920, for my job, also on space rates, was to cover campus happenings and interhall football for the *News-Times*. Rock watched the games on Sunday afternoons and undoubtedly knew who the *News-Times* reporter was; but he was not in my orbit and, under the glacial conditions, I was happy to stay out of his.

But after the football season ended, the *News-Times* turned the varsity athletics over to me and now I had to try to establish some sort of relations with the ogre. It was a short and painful interview. Rock told me in so many words I wore the enemy uniform, was on my own, would get nothing from him. And I didn't. I covered the basketball games and practices and quoted myself in the *News-Times* while Arch Ward quoted Rockne in the *Tribune*. Then came one of those fictional breaks without which no ambitious young man can really get along in this world.

I had a 1:15 Spanish class in a room in the Administration Building just around the corner from Rock's office—the single room which then housed all the Athletic Department because Rockne was it. And there one day I saw on the blackboard, in Rock's own scrawling hand—typical of high-strung people—the *1921 football schedule*. The Athletic Board had met at noon, Rock had written the schedule for them and forgotten to erase it. I copied, erased it—and probably wasn't much good in Spanish that day.

I had a delicate and important decision to make. The football schedule was the biggest athletic news of any year outside of the actual playing of the games. I could print it the next morning, thereby scooping not only my friendly rival, Arch Ward, and the opposition paper, but the great Rockne himself. But I knew that if I did that, the Master would be after my hide for keeps.

That afternoon I went to him, told him I had his football schedule.

He reacted on all sixteen cylinders, refused to admit even the possibility; and when I quoted it to him, looked as if I had picked his pockets or rifled his desk.

I told him how I had got it; said I *could* print it the next morning before he could give it to Arch, but I would make him a proposition: I would hold it till afternoon, at which time the *Tribune* could also use it—on the condition that hereafter he give me an even break.

He agreed. And kept his word.

A month or so later I was at a dance in the hall of St. Patrick's Church downtown. Rock and his wife were there as chaperones. He told me Arch Ward was leaving to go to the Chicago *Tribune* and would I like the job?

I would. It was like getting out of a coal mine and into a bank. It meant security and just about every other nice thing I could imagine at the time—and all sorts of things I couldn't imagine at that moment. Would I had always been so smart and clever!

But I was soon to pass another test—and so was Rock. He was also track coach at this time; and since he had no assistants and the system of student managers had not yet been installed, all the details of running home meets were in his hands. Part of my job was to act as official scorer at all varsity events; and shortly after I took over, there was an indoor meet with Illinois. We were not doing so well, as was usual against the Illini trackmen, and Rock was a whirring dynamo. All of a sudden and for no good reason, I found myself taking a sharp dressing down before what seemed like an awful lot of people.

The next day was a holiday. I took a long walk—then came to Rock's office, told him I needed this job very badly—but not enough to be publicly humiliated as I had been the night before.

I realized the chance I was taking on losing a good thing, that he could tell me if I didn't like it he could get somebody else. A small man would have done just that.

But Rock seemed to like what I had done. He said he had an unfortunate habit, when he got very mad, of letting go on the nearest person whether that person had it coming or not. He was sorry about what had happened the night before, promised that if I would stay on the job it would not happen again. And it never did, even though, on at least two occasions, my writings embarrassed him tremendously.

The first was more amusing than serious. The Conference backed the Drake Relays which were held on the same day as the Penn Relays in Philadelphia. There was always keen competition for top stars; and as Notre Dame had a bevy of such this year, the Big Ten moguls made Rock referee of their meet, assuming that he would bring his best men with him. He did bring all but Johnny Murphy, the national champion high-jumper. Innocent of the political ramifications, I sent a squib to the press which said that Murphy was going to the Penn Relays "because there would be no competition for him at Drake." Quite naturally, the Conference ribbers brought this around for the referee to read. Also quite naturally, Rock later called this to my attention, in such an explosive mood that I couldn't help but laugh. So he walked out of his own office. I always figured it was either that or punch me on the nose.

Later I really put him in a tough spot. When I had taken over the correspondent's job I also wrote for both downtown papers; but once again the *News-Times* rebelled, gave me the same choice it had given Ward—and Rockne gave me the same advice, which I took. I wrote for the *Tribune* and got all the inside stuff. Well, we had a merry war for a year; and it so happened that on the day in 1923 that I was leaving South Bend for good, the *News-Times* lads decided to drop Purdue. I called Rock, who exploded; when I asked if I could quote him, he said I could quote him on anything, and the stronger I made it, the better.

I shouldn't have done that—but I did.

That afternoon's *Tribune* carried this banner across the sports page: ROCKNE RAPS BACK ROOM FICTION WRITERS ON LOCAL MORNING NEWSPAPER.

Since there was only one local morning newspaper, the *News-Times* boys established a new local record for the running high jump. Three of them landed on me in the hotel lobby that evening as I was preparing to leave with the team for Carnegie Tech. They said Rockne had denied my extensive quotes and they were going to murder me in print the next day. So we went looking for Rockne, who had been in the lobby just before the indignant delegation arrived, but was now nowhere around.

We reached a compromise. The *News-Times* sports editor was also going to make the trip; we were to see Rockne on the train; if he backed me, they were going to climb all over him; if he discredited me, they were going to hang me out to dry as a journalistic skunk; and since I wasn't going to be there any more, that wouldn't have been good for the reputation of a reporter about to invade New York.

The *News-Times* sports editor, a man named Hughes, was okay, even checked my trunk to Pittsburgh on his ticket, since I was travelling incognito, as usual. On the train we started the hunt for Rockne, finally located him in a smoker next to the baggage car. The dialogue went about like this:

"Rock, did you say I misquoted you?"

"No, I said that I would deny anything you said that I hadn't said."

"Didn't you call them back room fiction writers?"

"I did."

"Didn't you say I could quote you as strong as I liked?"

"I did."

"Did I write anything you haven't said to me at one time or another?"

"No—you could have made it stronger."

I turned the witness over to Hughes who made the mistake of speaking harshly—after which the roof fell in on him. He hadn't been around long and had been caught in the middle of this thing; but he had to answer for all the sins the *News-Times* had ever committed against K. K. Rockne.

That was typically Rock as I always found him. He could be wrong and he could be cute—but when the showdown came he was always a standup guy.

He handled his boys as he found them, rode the ones who needed riding, as some always do, but was gentle with the well-meaning, sensitive kids who couldn't take a riding. He usually had a patsy on every squad, as a foil for his wit, because he liked to keep his practice sessions and lectures entertaining. He was fairly accurate at estimating people; but when he misfired, blew up, or "let the nearest guy have it," he had the grace to come around later and try to square it.

He was interested in boys as human beings as well as football players and his interest continued after they left school. He liked to be consulted and he liked to do things for people. As long as he lived he was the patriarch of the Notre Dame athletic clan; and if somebody picked on one of his boys, that somebody heard from Rock.

Shortly after I took the job under him, he told me: "The one thing nobody can ever take away from you is your own integrity." He was interested in the newspaper business, picked up bits of gossip and information from the big-timers in New York, passed these on to me when he returned with something of a professorial manner; and he once demanded that I admit that I had learned more journalism from him than I had from the Journalism Department, with which he was also conducting a feud at the time. I wouldn't admit it then because I liked to needle him, too; but I'm sorry now that I didn't—and the additional fact that I learned more about practical living from his football lectures than from any other class at the University.

152

XXV

It was my good fortune to begin my professional career as a college sophomore; to be in on the ground floor with a rising star, to have had opportunity to study and learn from one of the most interesting minds of the era. I graduated when information about Rockne and Notre Dame were in demand and when I had almost exclusive knowledge of them. They helped me to make the broad leap from the campus to New York, were the crutches I used to get into the magazine, book and motion picture fields.

I learned a lot from Rock, but the important thing was that his football strategy, which boiled down to playing the percentage, was a good system to think and live by, the next best thing to the Ten Commandments. That's what all of his boys learned and why so many of them became successful coaches; for the Rockne system was not so much a matter of technical football—almost any coach can teach that adequately—as the human philosophy behind it. I repeat, because I think there's food for everybody in the thought: All else being equal, every football team, over a reasonable period of time, reflects the personality of the coach. And that goes for all organizations, including business and government.

It was impossible to be around Rockne without absorbing the essence of his personality and methods; and the publicity job became an excellent springboard for at least two others who followed Arch Ward and myself: George Strickler, who built Grant Rice's paragraph about the Four Horseman into the most enduring publicity phrase in football history, later became publicity director of the National Football League; and Joe Petritz, who succeeded Strickler, took over the same job for the All-American Conference.

Rock was proud of his newspaper boys, too, though he never missed a chance to let us have the needle. In 1930, Ward and I were in his office with a group of other sports writers before the Carnegie Tech game. Joe Petritz was new on the job; and thinking to give him a deserved plug, I said: "That's a good boy you have there, Rock. Don't you think so, Arch?" Arch did.

But Rockne said: "You're telling me? He's the best I ever had."

But he could laugh at himself, too. On the trip to the Southern Cal game in 1930, we were sitting with Warren Brown, the sardonic Chicago sports editor, and J. P. McEvoy, an old Notre Damer who once characterized himself as "the lowest form of student life—a student waiter who waited on the student waiters." This day, wisecracking in his best form, Rock was telling a story about somebody who had compared him with Mencken.

"Can you imagine me comparing myself to Mencken?"

"Yes." McEvoy said. Rock enjoyed it.

Notre Dame has produced other big name sports writers who were not directly trained by Rockne but who must have been affected by the athletic climate. These include Bill Fox of the Indianapolis *News,* the acknowledged fashion plate of our profession; Bill Fay, brilliant young magazine star, who worked under Arch Ward on the Chicago *Tribune* and was tennis captain at Notre Dame; Jim Gallagher, general manager of the Chicago Cubs; Jim Kearns and Bill Moloney, also Chicago men; and that ex-editor of *The Dome* who is now the hottest of the sports columnists, Red Smith of the New York *Herald Tribune.* I have never heard of any of them giving their alma mater the worst of it, either.

Sports writers are as fair and objective a group as you will find. They are fans and have their private loves; but they are reporters whose first loyalty is to their readers. They resent fawning, resent incivility, appreciate courteous treatment and good working conditions. Notre Dame gives them what they want, neither asks nor offers unusual favors. Its publicity men play a good game, too; and that, also, is according to the gospel as laid down by Rockne.

As every experienced college press agent knows, it is good policy to pick a candidate for all-American early and to bear down on him. After Gipp had made such honors in 1920, Notre Dame was in the spotlight and I put the emphasis in '21 on Johnny Mohardt, who made Camp's second team. At the beginning of the '22 season, the first year of the Four Horsemen, I asked Rock to pick a man among the sophomores but he would not do it—said that was my job. He was always very conscientious about playing favorites; and for that matter, so are sports writers, because such things are very important to the players.

I learned about that in '21. There was no complaint about Mohardt in the backfield for he was the logical choice; but I had also picked a spectacular junior lineman for major attention. In midseason, one of the regular backs came to me. "We've been talking. We don't want to tell you how to do your job, but we'd like you to do one thing this Saturday. Take a good look at the *other* tackle."

I did, saw what they meant, and switched the emphasis in midseason to the other tackle who got a lot of all-American mention. He was, and is, one of those quietly efficient operators—Buck Shaw, now coach of the San Francisco Forty-Niners in the All-American Conference. And ever since I have been more impressed by the testimony of players than by any others. The

155

writers do the best they can; the coaches sometimes have their little angles; but the players are in there getting hit.

For such a cold perfectionist and hot explosionist, Rock was easy to work for. After he had decided I could be trusted not to go haywire, he gave me my head, seldom criticized or complimented, acted almost as if he never read my stuff—though I knew full well that he never missed a line.

Once we did a good job together. He came into his office, pink-faced with outrage, because somebody had suggested that varsity letters be awarded to debaters. There even seemed to be some faculty support for the idea and Rock decided the way to scotch it was by ridicule. So we sat down, like a couple of Hollywood hams, kicked out a story line, dressed the debaters up in ruffles and laces, had them go at each other in fierce formations, used the football analogy and wound up giving them varsity letters—and that seemed to take care of that.

He was a mortal enemy of any such sissifying influence that bobbed up on the campus, and had a wonderful story about two teams of "tea-hounds," as they were then called, who would be playing football for Northwestern and Notre Dame in 1930. They were led by T. Pickerdyke, III, of Northwestern and Two-Lump Oolong of Notre Dame. Pickerdyke got loose and was en route for a t.d. (no Notre Dame man having *tagged* him) but Two-Lump was a quick thinker.

"Yoohoo, Pickerdyke," he yelled, "you've got a *run* in your *stocking*." Whereupon the chagrined Pickerdyke forgot the game and ran for the dressing room to repair the damage.

The best laugh about that story was that when Notre Dame and Northwestern did play in 1930, the Wildcats had won the Conference title, Notre Dame was finishing its second consecutive season without defeat and the game was a recognized national championship affair. It was typical of all the meetings between these two old rivals, a rough session, and even-Stephen until midway in the final period when Marchy Schwartz, the

156

present Stanford coach and one of the undersung men in Irish history, broke through for one of his copyrighted off-tackle runs.

I spent hours with Rock every day, at the practices and lectures and in his office. I usually knew what he was shooting for and tried to follow the party line in my daily stories. He built me up as an authority in the lectures, just as he did his quarterbacks, and for the same reason—he wanted the squad to know that he respected our judgment so they would do the same. Rock, at least, encouraged my philosophical wanderings because they fitted into his coaching pattern. After awhile I became an unofficial member of the coaching staff, the vice-president in charge of squad psychology. But once I let him down badly.

I had promoted myself a column on the *Tribune* called "Quad Wrangles" which featured all the campus activities, including the goofings and other gags. Eventually I began to bring the downtown girls into it, to stress dances and parties. This was good for circulation and it also got me invited to a lot of parties; but Rock made it very plain he considered the column a subversive influence.

These were the days of Rudolph Valentino; and following his picture *The Sheik*, what we now call a "wolf" became known as a "sheik." So I got one of those brilliant ideas, started a contest which was to elect an official Sheik for each Hall and finally the Grand Sheik of Notre Dame; and to start it off I nominated the better known campus characters, who happened to be mostly athletes.

I got a lot of letters signed by girls; and while many were from legitimate dolls, it was quite obvious that a lot of guys were being nominated by their roommates; and the nominees then spilled the dirt on the pals they thought had nominated them. It was one of those things that caught the mood of the moment; the column began to be read by the adults of the town and Mc-Cready Huston, editor of the *Tribune* and a nationally known short story writer, helped out with an editorial in which he

157

viewed with some alarm the tendency of modern youth to en-
shrine the wrong type of hero.

To Rock this was all pure treason to the athletic department. So one day, among the mail, I found a letter which I knew
had come from the Great Man himself, because it included certain
of his favorite phrases. He laid the entire foolishness to the inferiority complex of the tea-hound type who, lacking certain
essential manly qualities, tried to soothe his ego by showing off
among the weaker sex.

I printed the letter—and since I was not supposed to know
who had written it, answered it with some patronizing references
to the "superiority complex" of old folks who missed the boat on
what the younger people were really thinking.

That night, in the Oliver Cafeteria, where everybody gathered, Rock sat at one end of the room and I carefully took a position at the other end. He watched me steadily as if he were trying to make up his mind as to whether I really knew he had
written that letter—and what he might do about it if he were
sure that I had. I took no chances, kept my distance for a week or
so until the contest was over.

Later, in a group discussing other things, Rock made a casual
reference to the "inferiority complex." Then he grinned at me
and said: "Okay, now I'll give you an idea for a real contest."

"What?"

"A *He-Man* contest."

He began to give me nominees from the various halls, practically all athletes.

I exercised the editorial prerogative by turning down his idea
—and that really burned him. I may really have been exercising
that human trait of enjoying saying No to the boss. But it was a
mistake. I tried a new contest, something about Bohemians,
which flopped. A He-Man contest, especially one suggested and
vigorously promoted by Rockne, would have been a natural.

Rock was a great teacher but he also had a feud with the professors. "If they know so much," he would say, "why aren't they out making some money instead of staying here telling boys how to do it for $4,000 a year?" I never took his feuds seriously, nor, I suspect, did most of the people he feuded with; but in the case of the teachers, it was probably the old story of the professors objecting to the prestige and the salary of the football coach.

About that there would seem to be only one logical answer: The coach earns what he gets because if he doesn't produce he doesn't get it for long. The professors don't have to take those weekly examinations, have the alumni on their necks—or the students organizing Good-bye Harry Clubs.

Rock was expert at using scorn and satire to needle his squads. It was part of his technique during the practice sessions, during his lectures to the squad—and in print. Shortly after I left school there began to appear in the *Tribune* an occasional column written by a certain Bearskin, who was obviously an insider because of the cracks he took at the players. The boys were fairly certain Rock was back of it; but not entirely certain because Bearskin also took the hide off Rockne now and then. It was Rock, of course, and the column was used by other coaches for years after his death.

In one of my first stories for him in 1921 I did some boasting about the number of lettermen we had returning. Rock checked me on that: "Never tell them how many you've got coming back —tell them how many you *lost*."

That was the basis of his, as of most coaching psychology, which explains the tradition of the Crying Coach. Overconfidence is the deadly enemy, as even Lachrymose Leahy learned anew in the '48 Southern Cal game. Coaches jockey for the position of underdog on the theory that a team fighting for its life fights harder.

And it's sound psychology. I learned that at Iowa City in 1921—in a game which has become a milestone of football history.

159

XXVI

There have been many celebrated players in gridiron history but few famous units; and while names tend to become absorbed in the unit, some live longer because the units are remembered—the Vow Boys of Stanford, the Iron Men of Brown, Fordham's Seven Blocks of Granite. Every so often these tombstones are located and the ghosts bow briefly.

The Four Horsemen will probably live longest in Notre Dame tradition because their unit has a name; but Rockne had two other groups which matched them—his first and his last—and none of the three will concede superiority.

Notre Dame loves them all, in the manner of fond parents. You would never catch Rock ranking the three. Nor will you catch me. Each was the best according to the *rules* and *conditions* of its time and that should be enough.

All had superb backfields. The Four Horsemen were comparative lightweights, but played in a day when speed and cleverness were at the highest premium. Crowley, Layden, Stuhldreher and Miller—averaging 165 pounds—might not have been so effective in '30 as Carideo, Savoldi, Schwartz and Brill—averaging 190—proved to be; but these heavier men might also have been less efficient in '24

The 1920 backfield—Gipp, Mohardt, Wynne and Brandy,

averaging 170—operated when the shift was unimpeded but had not yet reached its highest development; but they were also heavy enough to have held their own in 1930. Gipp weighed 185, Wynne 180, Mohardt 165 and Brandy 150; each was a specialist but, as all Rockne backs, an all-round football player. Mohardt could not kick with Gipp but was almost as good a passer, a faster and more elusive runner. Wynne had the combination of speed and weight a great fullback needs; Brandy was the perfect Rockne quarterback—a brainy gamecock. All four were exceptional competitors—full of fire and spirit.

Paradoxically, the earliest of the three lines is still the best remembered. They played in a day when the first eleven stayed in there until the game was won; when almost all passes were thrown to the ends. Their later activities have also kept their names in the news.

The center was Harry Mehre who coached at Georgia and Mississippi. The guards were Hunk Anderson, who succeeded Rockne at Notre Dame and has long been line coach of the Chicago Bears—and Clipper Smith, of Santa Clara, Villanova, the Boston Yanks and now of Lafayette. The tackles were Buck Shaw of Santa Clara and the Forty-Niners; and Frank Coughlin. The ends were Dr. Eddie Anderson of Holy Cross and now at Iowa; and Rodge Kiley. Coughlin, captain of the '20 team has been prominent in Indiana politics; Kiley, now a Chicago judge, earned enduring fame as one of the great pass-receivers of college history and favorite target of Gipp and Mohardt.

Kiley, Shaw, Mohardt, Hunk and Eddie Anderson played three years, were the nucleus of the group and so good individually that old-timers will still give you an argument if you try to move any of them from the all-time Notre Dame eleven. In their two undefeated years, '19 and '20, they had, in addition to Gipp and others already named, such teammates as Slip Madigan, Paul Castner, George Trafton, Arthur "Little Dutch" Bergman, Leonard "Pete" Bahan, Cy and Ed Degree, Jim Dooley, Dave

Hayes, Bernie Kirk, Norm Barry, Walter Miller, Fritz Slackford, Glenn "Judge" Carberry, Arthur "Hector" Garvey, Chet Grant, Fred "Ojay" Larson, Frank Thomas, Earl Walsh, Grover Malone, and Bob Phelan—mostly seasoned veterans of World War I.

In 1921 the first eleven had Mohardt, Wynne, Grant and Danny Coughlin as regular backs with Thomas, Castner and Tom Lieb as chief replacements; Mehre at center; Kiley and Eddie Anderson at ends; Shaw and Garvey at tackles; Hunk Anderson and Jim Dooley at guards. These were backed by the experienced leftovers and newcomers like Gus Desch, Mike Seyfrit, Harvey Brown and Fod Cotton. It was a power-packed squad which everybody expected to go on through a third consecutive unde- feated season; and after home warmups against Kalamazoo and DePauw, the boys proceeded with absolute confidence toward the first Iowa game in Notre Dame history. A lot of history was to be made at Iowa City.

Howard Jones, the Hawkeye coach, had backs like Aubrey Devine, his brother Glenn, and Gordon Locke; an end named Belding and the great Negro tackle, Duke Slater. Iowa was good but we were Notre Dame; and we hadn't lost for so long we had forgotten how.

The squad made the eight-hour daylight trip from Chicago by day coach, which will give you an idea of football finances at that time; but that was no unusual hardship and everybody had a lot of fun. Nor was the holiday mood disturbed when we arrived at Iowa City. They had that "Notre Dame—Notre Game" sign up but didn't seem to take it literally. I was carrying $125 of student money—in small denominations it made quite a roll—but could only get five bucks up. I was fearful that my clients would suspect me of holding out on them when I returned their money—as I had suspected a chap who had returned $50 I had sent down to West Point the year before to bet on the Army game.

Johnny Mohardt and I had a philosophy class together and

were quite friendly. I walked to the stadium with him, waved a blithe farewell, said I would see him after the game—just like that—and went to the press box where, among other duties, I was to send the Western Union play-by-play account back to the students in the gym, since this was before radio.

The first period was quite a shock. The Iowa line outcharged our boys and Aubrey Devine sliced through for short but consecutive gains which accounted for a field goal and a touchdown. Bothersome but not too worrisome. Our team had gone in cold and cocky; this had happened before; they would wake up and show these Conference guys who was boss.

They did wake up, got a touchdown in the second period; took charge again after the next kickoff—and soon Eddie Anderson caught one of Mohardt's passes and was on his way. He was caught at the five-yard line but that meant nothing.

Except it did. We forgot to score.

Football players remember such incidents vividly; and twenty years later Chet Grant, our quarterback, went over every detail of that series of plays for me. It seems that the Iowa center, name unknown to me now but no doubt enshrined in Hawkeye tradition, had been shifting before the ball was passed. Grant, small but smart, planned to take advantage of that; but the cussed Iowa center persisted in shifting to the *right* spot each time—and added insult to injury by grinning at Grant. On such little incidents, in the little theater of the line, big games are won and lost, history and tradition are made.

The Iowa line was just too much brain and brawn at that moment so Chet called a pass. It was well conceived and the end was loose—but again the line! Somebody broke through, hustled Mohardt—and Aubrey Devine intercepted on the goal line, danced back along the side-strip for 40 yards. The score at half-time was 10-7; we were surprised but not dismayed. I sent a message to the students back in the gym not to worry.

But the third period found the teams marching up and down

between the 30-yard lines; and now I was really shocked because Iowa seemed as good as we were. Our boys had long since got the foolishness out of their system, had been playing their game; but time was passing, their game wasn't quite good enough—so they reached into the bag for the spiritual reserve.

Something comparable had also happened to Iowa. The Hawkeyes had also begun to smell those headlines. The underdog had tasted blood and was hanging on. How he was hanging on!

Four times in that final period Notre Dame had first down inside the 10-yard line. Always it was just *about* to happen but never quite did!

Something else was happening. It was getting dark. Iowa wore black sweaters, Notre Dame dark blue and it was hard to tell them apart in the gloom. Belding, the Iowa end, was almost a physical double for Kiley, our glue-fingered pass-catcher; and Belding was *dropping back to defend against passes*—the first time an end had ever done that against Notre Dame. Slater was breaking through to rush Mohardt; Johnny was doing a great job dancing away from him, fighting him off, getting the passes away —but *Belding* was either catching them or knocking them down.

I have suffered and died many times since in the press box, when Notre Dame was losing; but this was the first time and I had been completely unprepared for it. As I sent each heartbreak back to the kids in the gym, I knew what was happening back there, how they were pulling and praying for that one line of good news which would "shake down the thunder from the sky." But the good news didn't come. I was a reporter—Pagliacci style. I sent some of my youth back with that final score.

Iowa 10, Notre Dame 7.

There's a terrible finality about a final score—on a field or a deathbed—wherever it is posted.

I went to the dressing room. Rockne had not yet come in. Nobody had come in. Notre Dame had lost. The players were alone.

164

They were stunned. Some of those big tough fellows who had gone through a world war were crying. An awful thing had happened. Notre Dame had lost a football game. They were the culprits.

Rockne came in. He was strong and tough. He had never lost as a player, either; but he had seen defeat as a coach.

"There will be no alibi." Then he went among the boys inspecting their bruises.

If somebody loses, somebody wins. Iowa had won and this was Iowa. They hadn't expected it but here it was and it was glorious, ecstatic. It was a small town and every stranger on the streets was automatically a Notre Dame man. We were probably easy to identify at that. They let us have it and there was nothing to do but take it. Our train wasn't scheduled to leave until midnight. We talked to ourselves: They wouldn't bet but they could celebrate! That didn't help much.

We were going back in style—one Pullman car was on the siding, waiting for the train to come in, waiting for the long trip home—home to the students we had let down. There were about thirty in the official party but fifty people climbed on—and nobody got off. We had come by various methods—freight, hitchhiking, even by Pullman, which was the way I had come, using another student's pass. But somebody else was to use it going back; so I stayed on the squad car, too.

Rock had the drawing room, had gone to bed early. Now, just before the train was to leave, somebody knocked on his door. "You'd better come and get—" (let's call him Clarence).

"Where is he?"

"The cops have him."

Rock went and got Clarence. It had been a long evening in town. Clarence wasn't feeling very good, had got himself a few beers and stopped at the lunchroom near the station. After the train had started and everybody who had a bed had gone to it, I sat in the washroom as Clarence described his adventure.

"I didn't mind when they called me an Irish Catholic; even when they called me an Irish Catholic soandso; but when they called me an Irish Catholic suchandsuch soandso, that was too much. So I cleaned out the joint."

Clarence was neither Irish, Catholic, nor any sort of a soandso.

I began to feel conspicuous and climbed in an upper with Pete Smith, a Texan, who had generously invited me to share his quarters. All was quiet for awhile as the train rolled along with its sad cargo; but some stinker at the station had noted that a lot of people got on and nobody got off. The conductor had again roused Rock, to find out who was who, and Rock was giving a fine imitation of an indignant man who was learning for the first time that people who didn't have tickets travelled with football teams.

Trapped, I waited my turn. My roommate had the old college spirit. He rolled over to the edge of the berth, tried to make a barrier behind which I could hide. He pretended to be asleep when the curtains parted.

"Two in upper seven," the conductor said.

"Wallace—what the hell are you doing up there?" Rock asked, as if he didn't know.

"Got a ticket?" the conductor asked.

"No. How much is it?"

"Nine sixty-five."

"I'll see you in the morning."

"You'll see me now—nine sixty-five."

I reached for my pants, took out the roll of student money, peeled off ten bucks. The conductor gave me the thirty-five cents change and a dirty look which plainly said that here was really a heel—with all that dough!

Sleep comes, even to the vanquished and harassed, when they're young. The next morning, as I piled off the car, Rock got off the other end. I walked hurriedly, heard him stepping up his

166

pace. It was like one of those scenes in a movie thriller. Finally he called to me. Now I was going to get it but good.

"The next time, Frank—not upstairs."

He told me how to do it next time.

Rock surely knew all there was to know about football; and for the rest of my tenure I followed his wise counsel with such success that I became President of the Road Scholars. We even had our picture in *The Dome* one year.

What happened next you may hesitate to believe. It was eight o'clock on a Sunday morning in Chicago; but the word was passed around and we split up into small groups as we walked along the streets. We didn't want people to identify us as that Notre Dame team which had lost a football game.

XXVII

We were free to spend the day as we pleased. A few took earlier trains but the main body was on the New York Central that left Chicago at eleven that night. Again we were split up, though this time not purposely, and I was sitting alone in the smoking car.

Rock came up and joined me. He was depressed, had things on his mind, wanted somebody to listen. He could no longer carry on as coach, trainer, student manager, business manager and everything else for the football squad. (In his spare time he also distributed tickets at the newsstands and cigar counters throughout northern Indiana.) He did have one assistant, Walter Halas; but Walter scouted on Saturdays and spent most of his time during the week giving the plays of the next opponent to the freshmen, preparing them for scrimmage.

Rock said he had to have more help. This would have to be done and that would have to be done.

You see, he had lost a football game. He had lost it to the coming Big Ten champions and after his team had outgained Iowa three to one; he had lost after winning twenty straight and that was intolerable. I listened and agreed but mostly I listened because that was what he wanted. I was not conscious that the train was approaching South Bend until it began to slow up. Then we heard a familiar sound—the yell known as the "Sky Rocket"—an afternoon sound in the night.

It was one o'clock in the morning but the student body had come three miles to meet the team.

They were looking for Rock, who had sneaked out the door on the opposite side. I told the boys where he was; and when the train pulled away they spied him, caught him, picked him up and started to carry him.

Rock was mad, actually fighting them, swinging at them. People didn't do things like this to Rockne. Nobody made Rockne do a thing he didn't want to do. But these kids did. They planted him on a baggage truck and a thousand students gathered round, cheering him.

He stood on the truck, perhaps the same which had carried the body of Gipp less than a year before, perhaps the same which was to carry Rockne's body ten years later.

He stood there crying—and you can bet he would have given anything not to have appeared that way before the student body—or anybody. Now they really shook down the thunder from the sky. He said a few appropriate things and then he said:

"After this I will never leave Notre Dame as long as they want to keep me here." He could have said: "Until I die."

He meant it and he proved it. As I have said before, he was tempted many times; he would seem to make agreements; but he always left himself a verbal "out," which usually was: "I owe Notre Dame a lot and I'll leave only if they are satisfied to let me go."

After he had made the Columbia deal, with this verbal qualification, he did not even ask Notre Dame to let him go—he told me this himself. When Columbia tried to pressure him by making the matter public, Notre Dame blandly said it would not stand in his way—which put the decision squarely up to her sorely tempted son.

Even then he didn't leave. I think that, whenever these

things came up, his mind always went back to that scene at the station; I believe he always knew that when the showdown came, he couldn't quite bring himself up to breaking away. But he was also cute enough to take full advantage of such situations to strengthen his position at Notre Dame.

One of the schools which wanted Rock and thought it had him was Ohio State. It was looking for a man to replace Dr. Wilce and, according to the story I got from Hub Atkinson, chairman of the Buckeye Athletic Board at that time and who was in on the negotiations, a call came from John Griffiths, Conference Commissioner, that he had a man in his office who was interested in the job. L. W. St. John, the athletic director, was very much interested in that man. He was recently quoted: "Rockne was the only man I would ever have signed without first consulting other people." The inference was that he knew everybody would have been happy about the selection.

The contact was made. The two principal reasons Rock gave for wanting to come to Columbus were: (1) By getting into the Conference he could get a crack at Yost of Michigan and Zuppke of Illinois, neither of whom would schedule Notre Dame in football; and (2) he wanted a stadium built at Notre Dame but the authorities were using the football profits to erect residence and academic buildings.

There would seem to be honor for everybody in that second reason. As a coach Rock would naturally be interested in getting that stadium he so badly needed; if he used his offers from other places as a pressure argument, that's done right along. But the Notre Dame authorities were certainly entitled to give the over-all needs of the University priority over the stadium. It is possible that the school might have been bringing this situation to a head when it seemed to embarrass Rockne by telling him he was perfectly free to go to Columbia. The authorities also must have felt quite sure that he wouldn't go.

The fact is, Rock didn't go to Columbia, or Ohio or anywhere. He was an impetuous man, inclined to be possessed by the

170

mood of the moment; but when that passed, he could see the other fellow's side of the argument and reach a fair conclusion. The stadium did come, in due time; just as, in the present projected building program at Notre Dame, a new field house will also come—but it's well down on the list.

All this may give you a fresh slant on the importance of athletics in the general scheme at Notre Dame; and a further insight into the manner in which the football business is twined throughout the entire collegiate structure. It was only a year or so ago that the newspapers carried reports that a major athletic figure in a Big Ten State school was threatening to accept another offer because "University officials were putting money into academic buildings instead of into the athletic program." He didn't leave either.

Leahy has also said that he would never leave Notre Dame as long as the school wanted him to stay. I believe that he has that same deep devotion to the place that Rockne had. I think he has also given some thought to the callous suggestion, which sometimes breaks into print, that the schedule heat might be taken off Notre Dame if Leahy were to be kind enough to remove himself.

Recently he indicated to me that he might have to give up coaching after a year or so. I told him that his health should come first; but that if he had any thought about leaving just to take the heat off Notre Dame, he should forget it; that the school was not going to throw him to any wolves, regardless of what happened to the schedule. I think that's what he wanted me to say because twice later he thanked me for saying it. A very peculiar man, Leahy, an enigma, hard to understand, maybe because he's a simple, a loyal man who says what he means and means what he says—a throwback.

But when you begin to add up all this corn and sentiment—Rockne crying, Leahy being noble, Gipp's deathbed request, Masons getting up to go to Mass, Hering suggesting Mother's Day, all this sort of stuff—you begin to add up Notre Dame. Not just football but Notre Dame. You begin to get the picture of an old-fashioned sort of place that seems out of this world—but still seems to do better than most in this world. You might also begin to get an idea that maybe this world could do with a little more of the Notre Dame Idea.

If they erected stones on the sites of football landmarks, the 1921 Iowa-Notre Dame tablet would read something like this:

> Here, on October 8, 1921, Iowa defeated Notre Dame 10-7 for the championship of the Midwest. It was Notre Dame's first loss after having won 20 straight and going undefeated in 22 games. It established an Iowa "jinx" over Notre Dame which was to result in three straight "upset" victories (the others in '39 and '40.) It began the clashes between Rockne and Howard Jones, later to be continued at Southern California in a pioneering intersectional series that frequently decided the national championship.

And this footnote might also be added, for whatever bearing it might possibly have on the schedule freeze: "It marked Notre Dame's fourth successive failure since 1898 to defeat a team which won the Conference title—but also its last failure; for, beginning in 1926 and continuing through 1946, Notre Dame won eight and tied one of its nine games with teams that had either won or shared the Conference crown. Three of these victories were over Northwestern ('26, '30, '36); two over Minnesota ('37, '38); one each over Ohio State ('35), Michigan ('43) and Illinois ('46). The tie was with Northwestern ('30)." (Information quoted from the Des Moines *Register* and *Tribune*.)

Aubrey Devine became all-American quarterback as a result of the '21 Iowa victory, and for many years scouted Notre Dame for Jones at Southern California. He was in the press box at Columbus in 1935 when the Irish made their sensational last-period

172

comeback to defeat Ohio State; and the next day he completely agreed with my fear that Notre Dame might be upset the very next week by Northwestern, as happened. We both remembered Iowa City.

One of the nice things about football is that great men from other schools can live in a college tradition. Ohio State will never forget Andy Pilney as Army will never forget Rockne and Gipp, as Notre Dame will never forget Aubrey Devine and Duke Slater. Only last year Judge Kiley grinned and said: "I passed a ghost in the Hall of Records the other day—Duke Slater came by and I instinctively moved over to let him go through." Duke, incidentally, played the full sixty minutes that day, was in there after most of our tough guys had gone out—perhaps because he played it like a gentleman. Once he came down under a punt and could have annihilated 132-pound Chet Grant as he caught the ball, but Duke just sat him down gently. If I were picking an all-time team, I'd give quite a thought to Slater at tackle.

A significant by-product of that Iowa game was the green playing jersey which Notre Dame now wears, though the school's colors are gold and blue. Because of what had happened in the dusky fourth period, Rock decided to have a contrasting color available when the other team wore dark blue or black. Green was the logical color and was so popular that it is now used permanently. Contrasting jerseys are now compulsory, with the visiting team required to make the change. But Rockne was twenty-six years ahead of the Rules Committee.

Mention of playing jerseys brings up another innovation in football—the numbered jersey—which Rock resisted but for which he was nevertheless responsible for bringing along faster than it otherwise might have come. As early as 1920 he had begun to experiment with his "shock troop" idea. He would start his second string to take the first shock of the enemy strength. Substitutions were confined to quarters then; so at the beginning of the second period he would send in his regulars, who played until the beginning of the fourth period when, if the game was in hand, as it usually was, the shock troopers would come back.

This was something new in those days, one of the colorful tactics which helped to popularize Rockne football; it was sound football and it also had the psychological effect of eleven fresh men warming up on the sidelines and then dashing in en masse. The crowds loved it but the press box hated it. Numbers had been used here and there but most big-time coaches were against them because they didn't want opponents to know who was going in and out of the game. Rock was particularly cool to the idea because of the confusion caused on opposing benches by his mass substitutions. But the press hollered and the numbers came. Rock was much too smart to jeopardize his otherwise excellent relations with the sport writers.

There's a lot of squawk today about the platoon system used by Army, Michigan and others, but to my mind, this is just another of those things in the book which is neither very new nor very good. What's the difference whether they substitute eleven at a time or three at a time? Look at the box score after the game and you'll find one team has had about as many subs as the other. The important thing to remember—and this has been generally overlooked in the arguments—is that free substitution was put in the rules as a safety measure for the players, to prevent serious injury by making it easy for a coach to take a boy out, let him get his bearings and check on his injuries.

From the technical standpoint, I think the coaches hurt their own teams when they quarterback the game from the bench; and reduce the efficiency of their players by running them in and out too often, instead of letting them get warmed up to the business at hand. While the offensive-and-defensive unit idea is showy and might make coaching easier for the short-term pull, I think it will prove harmful over the long run because it will not produce all-round football players. I'll take eleven Doak Walkers and Chuck Bednariks, with eleven other all-round men in reserve, and you can have the offensive and defensive specialists.

XXVIII

The 1948 season developed considerable speculation in the press about the Notre Dame schedule freeze; and as reporters probed for explanations, the delicate matter of religion came more and more to the surface. An article in *Life* magazine brought the charge from an anonymous Conference source that Notre Dame used religion to attract football talent; and Grantland Rice, a fair and competent observer, quoted "the head of a Western Conference school" in this fashion:

"We have nothing against Notre Dame University or the football team. But the answer is this: When we play Michigan or others in our city, 80 percent of the spectators are for us. When we go to their cities, 80 percent of the crowd are for them. But when any of us play Notre Dame, 70 percent of the spectators are for Notre Dame. Why? It's a matter of religion."

That would seem to be reminiscent of the 1910 situation when Father Crumley charged that "the question was decided on theological rather than on athletic grounds."

Notre Dame would much rather leave racial and religious implications out of its football situation; but since these have been brought in, answers would seem to be in order and here they are:

Somebody wrote that "half the boys in big-time college

football are Catholics"; there may not be that many but there undoubtedly are a lot, since so many players are of foreign and probably Catholic extraction. Quite obviously Notre Dame could absorb only a minute fraction of them; and to assume that it gets the absolute best would be cutting it rather thickly. Actually, Notre Dame meets many Catholic boys in every opposing lineup; Howard Jones had an ambition to defeat the Irish with eleven Catholics and once almost did it. My authority for this statement is a former Trojan captain and devout Catholic who has for years been an enthusiastic bird dog for his alma mater.

Pitt, under Jock Sutherland, had so many Catholic boys that it adopted the Notre Dame custom of having the boys go to Mass on the morning of a game; and the man who promoted the idea was the late Bill McClintock, a Catholic, who had attended Notre Dame. I think it can fairly be said that nobody ever plays with more spirit against Notre Dame, nor enjoys beating it more, than the Catholics in the other camp, including now and then such Notre Dame stalwarts as Eddie Anderson, whose Iowa squads twice upset the Irish, and Jack Chevigny, whose Texas squad ruined Elmer Layden's debut as a coach.

There are many other Catholic colleges in big-time football, with the same religious advantages, but there is only one Notre Dame; there are many other major colleges with sectarian backgrounds but nobody drags religion into their football situations. And as to crowds: They follow the winner. I've seen a lot of Notre Dame games and have never noticed any great lack of enthusiasm on those occasions when Notre Dame was being beaten —including the day in the Notre Dame Stadium when a boy named Art Murakowski ran 91 yards with an intercepted pass to give Northwestern a temporary 7-6 lead.

Notre Dame does have enthusiastic support from non-alumni wherever it plays. I will now give you various opinions about these people and the reasons they exist. The first came during a sermon delivered by Monsignor Shannon at the time John O'Hara,

176

a former Notre Dame president, was consecrated a bishop: "We here assembled testify to the leaven of Notre Dame, already fermenting the whole Catholic life of America. . . . Some wit has chiseled out a synthesis which he might have thought a clever gibe. But it is not beyond the larger fact that there is an alumni which has never entered the portals of Notre Dame. Millions call it their own who have never seen it, nor will ever see it. But they have a holy nostalgia for it. And the heart of the multitude always rings true. Many hearts thrill today over this event, sharing in every emotion that grows out of the ceremonies. They see the real spirit of Notre Dame loosed on another field, one that is even dearer to them than that which crowds the pages of the daily press. In some deep and mystic way this institution responds to the high cravings of the lowly multitudes. And this is a rich asset, not the less real because intangible. . . ."

Paul Gallico, in the New York News in 1934: "The annual visit of the football team of the great University of Notre Dame to New York City for the football game with West Point brings about a phenomenon, one of the strangest and most curious in all this country, and therefore probably in the world, since it could happen no place but in this mad, grand land. This is the annual gathering of that amazing clan of self-appointed Notre Dame alumni which will whoop and rage and rant and roar through our town from sunup until long after sundown tomorrow in honor of a school to which they never went. The West Point supporters at the Yankee Stadium tomorrow will be numerous and vociferous, but of the 78,000 spectators, three-quarters will be bawling at the top of their lungs for Notre Dame du Lac. . . . And this business is a phenomenon purely for this one game. There are no self-appointed Colgate or St. Mary's or Tulane or Purdue alumni when those teams come to visit our town. But there is some sweet magic about the name of Notre Dame that annually draws the damnedest rabble out of its warrens. There is nothing that the proud old University can do about these boorish sons."

I fear that my old sports editor protested a bit too much about our synthetics. I never saw them quite that way and neither does Notre Dame; and where did they get the tickets, since Notre Dame always had less than half at its disposal and quite a few of these must have gone to civilized people?

After the 1932 season Lawrence Perry, syndicated writer for the New York Sun, wrote: "One of the phases of the football season just passed that has interested the public generally and in particular has amazed our economists, is the enormous drawing power of the Notre Dame eleven in a period of national depression. . . . Aside from its alumni and the pride that Catholics throughout the nation take in its position among the football playing institutions of the country, Notre Dame has almost, if not quite as heavy, a following among those without collegiate affiliations and varied, if any, religious adherences; who know a good football team when they see one; who love football as a game and whose enjoyment of it is heightened by the fact of having some university team to tie to. So they tie to Notre Dame as to no other college team in the country. . . . Finally there's the sporting crowd which likes to feel the vicarious thrill of competition. These hard-boiled gentry know that whenever the Irish are involved in a football game, that game will be a contest—if the other team is qualified to make it so. . . .

"General sentiment, even in the case of representatives of other colleges, exists for Notre Dame. Perhaps this is due to the lovable and genial atmosphere with which the late Knute Rockne invested Notre Dame football; this and the wholesome friendly atmosphere of the University itself which is carried out into the world by the men she graduates. In any case, Notre Dame football elevens are national favorites sentimentally as more frequently than not they are in the matter of sporting predictions."

Here's Arthur Daley, a Fordham man, writing in the New York *Times* about basketball: "The cold truth of the matter is that Notre Dame could move into the Garden, choose up sides for a practice match and the arena wouldn't be big enough to accommodate the clients. There is such magical appeal to the Fighting Irish that they hold an unparalleled attraction for the citizenry of our town, every one of whom is a violently loyal member of the famed subway alumni. . . . Nothing in sport bears even a foggy resemblance to this strange situation. A school that is hundreds of miles away from our bustling little village has caught the fancy of the usually blasé New Yorkers. What makes this even more extraordinary is that Notre Dame is a sectarian university which is fiercely proud of its sectarianism."

Joe Williams of the World-Telegram, before an Army-Notre Dame game: "This is by no means the biggest football game of the year or even of the day. Notre Dame has lost two games, Army has lost one. And yet it has the Big Town in something approaching a mild hysteria. It's bigger than the heavyweight fights, bigger than the world series. And it so happens, it always is. . . . The Big Town loves a show and the gray-coated Cadets, with their precise, breathless maneuvers, never fails to produce. But perhaps more important is that the Big Town has adopted Notre Dame.

"There is something very sentimental, almost maudlin, about the Big Town. It is so tremendous in size, so impersonal in its every day contacts that it searches around, quite pathetically, for some medium through which it can express its pent-up enthusiasms—something like a bachelor who always wanted a child. . . . There must be some explanation for the fact that this is one game the Big Town waits to see. . . . I'm pretty sure there are people who go to this contest who never see another game of football all year. To them, possibly, there are only two teams playing football—Army and Notre Dame.

"I have a feeling Knute Rockne contributed importantly to this unique situation. Rockne was the sort of fellow the Big Town goes for. He was an individualist, a leader and a showman. He was a legend even before he died. People around here talked of football in terms of Rockne. He was the high priest, the main works. . . . Somehow the Rockne heritage still lingers. There probably will be a number of people attending tomorrow's game who believe Rockne is still coaching. Unless you have been around here a number of years you can't appreciate the enduring imprint he left."

There's religion in it, yes; but there's something else that has nothing to do with religion. Rockne and Notre Dame just built one of those mousetraps. That has always paid off in America and fortunately it still does.

New York misses its "gridiron Oklahoma." Army probably does, too—the Cadets, the squad, the Athletic Association. Notre Dame certainly does. But those who miss it most of all are the Notre Dame players who would have taken part in it. I was close enough to the boys to know how they felt about the Army game in those early days when it was still being tried out as a road show on The Plains. I've made a lot of football trips in my time, visited a lot of colleges, but never a trip with the thrills of that first trip to West Point in 1921.

The Iowa frustration had come out in a 33-0 bolt against a good Purdue team; further victories over Nebraska and Indiana had launched a new seventeen-game winning streak, put our world back into focus, and we prepared for the Army game which was to have a trailer that year on Election Day with Rutgers at the Polo Grounds—the first Irish appearance, incidentally, in New York City.

A home-game with Haskell Institute the following Saturday would complete a three-game program in eight days. The Indians were not much of an attraction and I was supposed to stay home and build up the gate. Rock personally laid out the publicity campaign, told me with a straight face that fullback John Levi was a great-grandson of Sitting Bull; he traced the relationship of other Haskell players to Indian celebrities, might even have included Manitou. I listened; but when the train pulled out for the

180

East I was present and accounted for. Rock wasn't glad to see me.

I've read that there was a superstition about the Army game; that on the first trip there the Notre Dame squad had, by mistake, gone through the kitchen en route to the mess hall; that because it won that game, it always entered through the kitchen thereafter. I don't remember the kitchen but I'll never forget the greeting we got from the Cadet Corps as we filed to our places and had lunch with them. Army has had a special place with me ever since, as I think it must have for every boy who has ever gone to West Point with a visiting team.

We were given the freedom of the Post, particularly of the Officers' Club where we played billiards (I've just wondered if Gipp ever took on any of the sharks up there) but mostly we wrote letters to all of our girl friends, using West Point stationery, of course. There was no big hotel then and the squad was quartered in something called the Annex. There were four beds in our room, two against each wall, which left just enough space for me to lie on the floor between them, though I was comfortable enough, wearing four monogram sweaters. I didn't sleep much but neither did Paul Castner who was thrilled as a kid watching the boats go up and down the Hudson River. But he played a great game the next day, which seemed to prove Rock's theory that the important night's sleep was *two* nights before the game.

I was at the press box early, at my job of cultivating the New York reporters, identifying the players, particularly Mohardt and Shaw, my all-American candidates. And I evidently didn't do badly for myself either. George "Monitor" Daley, whom I was later to have as a traveling companion with the Yankees, gave me my first mention in a New York paper, called me "Brakebeam Bill" which was bad reporting since my brother's name is Bill and I was always a Pullman man.

We led 14-0 at the end of the first half—after which there developed quite a rhubarb, which is always an unusual event on a football field. Whenever you build a better mousetrap, you also

181

build antagonisms which sometimes take strange forms. Notre Dame has met, and is still meeting, a few of these. Rockne was then meeting the early criticisms about his backfield shift. This day Charles Daly, the Army coach, protested to the officials between the halves.

Rock had a superbly convincing answer. In the second half he told his boys to operate without the shift. Result? Two more touchdowns and a final score of 28-0.

Rock always had the answers. When opposing coaches who couldn't compete against his shift finally pulled its teeth by legislation which took away all the advantage for the fast, clever and imaginative type of player, the "boxer," he went to power, mixed it with the first of the modern deception—and beat them with that. He played the game they preferred, with whatever deck they gave him, was always out in front, running away and laughing. Crowds like that, too.

Rock was a great American; and after the game that night, in a New York theater, he met another great American. Joe Byrne had provided seats for the Follies. The fellow on the stage, twirling the rope, lassoed Rockne—and that's how the friendship with Will Rogers began that was to continue until Rock's death. They belonged to the same fraternity—By Gum We Gotta; they were great showmen, great human beings. They started at the bottom, went out at the top and in the skies.

Late that night at the Pennsylvania Hotel, I came upon a nice, clean, unoccupied bed—and was asleep in two minutes. An hour later, I was up out of there in a hurry. Rockne's bed! But this time he was in good humor, told me to go over and sleep with Gene Mayl in the next bed.

The next morning, after Mass, we went to the dining room. Breakfast appeared miraculously and a much better breakfast than usual, although we always ate well enough. We gave the credit to Joe Byrne's magic wand, and with equal magic, made the food disappear. On the way out we passed another group of young men who had been there ahead of us and were still waiting.

This was the Harvard squad returning from Princeton. The waiters had made a mistake and we had intercepted the Crimson food, with perhaps some poetic justice for we had beaten Army and they had lost to Princeton. Notre Dame has played Yale and Princeton but that was the closest it has ever got to a Harvard team.

The 1921 "Notre Dame" squad lost one other game in addition to Iowa, a very informal and sequestered 6-0 decision to "Illinois" which does not appear on the record books but is more remembered by old-timers than the eight victories and one tie in nine other games played since against the Illini—before that series also got to nipped by the frost.

XXIX

Taylorville and Carlinville, coal towns in southern Illinois, had one of those small town football rivalries which was to be climaxed with a game at the end of the season. The local gamblers tapped in and each gang figured they would put it in the bag by hiring a group of college players. The boys got $100 each, the standard price for such junkets which were not so unusual at that time; but each group thought they were going to mingle only with sandlotters until they stepped on the field. They decided to go through with it, were assured it could be kept quiet. "Illinois" won 6-0.

But tinhorns talk and gamblers squawk. The culprits from both schools were declared ineligible for further athletic competition, which didn't amount to much in our case since they were all seniors and nothing was lost but some track eligibility. But they were embarrassed and in disgrace. The Chicago *American* had carried a block headline: NOTRE DAME PLAYERS CONFESS.

Confess to what?

To breaking the law which said that while a college could make money out of the amateur sport of football, a player, even after he had concluded his eligibility, could not pick up some Christmas money he badly needed. Just a week before the game, I had walked three miles to school with one of the "culprits" in zero weather because neither of us could scrape up sixty cents taxi fare.

The law, as then in force, had been broken; there was nothing either Notre Dame or Illinois could do but enforce it; nor that any other school could have done, or could do today, when a law is broken. But this would seem to be the spot to include a warning, to players and school authorities alike, about the danger of any sort of association, no matter how innocent it may seem, with gamblers. Professional football has already been burned around the edges. The colleges and The Coaches Association have continuing committees to guard against it. The chief danger, these days, lies in the "spot sheets" whose operators attempt to get inside knowledge of what is going on inside every football camp. Sometimes they get under the tent under the guise of "helping the boys." Regardless of how well-intentioned these gentry seem or claim to be, they have elastic standards which are a menace to gullible young men. I recommend, with all possible emphasis, that all people concerned with college and high school football take a fresh look at their own recruiting organizations. Coaches who fool with known gamblers are really fools.

That phase of the amateur law has long since been abandoned; every year now, individual seniors play openly in bowl games and other exhibitions and get paid in one form or another; but the colleges still insist, and more emphatically than ever before through the N.C.A.A. Sanity Code, that it is all right for them to exploit the labor of football players but criminal for the players themselves to profit as long as they have college eligibility left.

The unfairness of this position first struck me back in 1921 when I saw how it crucified a group of my friends. No matter how it is washed up, justified or explained, I still think it unjust and hypocritical. I believe most of the working people in football agree with that conclusion; that most college presidents would also be relieved if a realistic and honorable solution were reached; but these seem powerless to break the spell of the evangels of the

185

holy religion of amateurism in the higher echelons of the N.C.A.A.

It would be a very simple matter really, for any college president to investigate his own athletic setup. All he would have to do would be to keep his ears open on his own campus; ask a few questions; inquire into the personal finances of each boy; see who is paying his bills, if his family is not in position to do so, which it seldom is; if he has a job—see how much work he actually does; if he has an honor scholarship—see what percentage of these are earmarked for the athletic department; get out in the field with the bird dogs, particularly during their frenzied hunts at summer high school all-star games, take a look at their efficiency charts on each prospect.

If one of the collegiate Reverend Davidsons ever did do all this, I think he would find precious little amateurism; and if he followed through according to his own gospel, he would wind up with the type of football squad Pitt had for so many years after Chancellor Bowman, against my advice, incidentally, did try to play a big-league schedule with the material the stork dropped on the Cathedral of Learning.

I think the practical and honest solution is to legalize what is being done and what, from all indications, will continue to be done. And I would like to make it clear, once again, that I see nothing wrong with any system, properly and realistically regulated, which gives deserving boys a chance to pay for an education with time and unique talents the university exploits for profit. I also believe that athletes, as a group, are more serious and successful students than the non-athletes—if you gauge success on how much they improve their state in life.

There are good reasons why athletes should be more successful. They are usually hungrier than the sons of the well-to-do, more alert and self-reliant because they know they have to be; the rugged qualities which make successful athletes also pay off in the battle of living; an athletic reputation is an advantage in business, professional, even social life; coaches want their boys

186

to do well after they leave school, help them get started and keep a fatherly eye on them.

It was no accident that most of the Rockne stars went into coaching. His pupils were in demand and he always had a list of jobs to be filled by his recommendations—another reason why boys with coaching ambitions came to Notre Dame in his time. Rock liked his work, liked to see his boys go into it; the average football player also likes the game, wants to have his own team to direct and is fascinated by the job of working with young boys and watching them develop. Rock's advice was to use the off-season to build up their other professions for the time when they might no longer want to coach, or—since this is the most precarious of professions—fall by the wayside.

Rock was fanatically against his boys going into professional football. He had played it himself, in the harum-scarum days, had seen too many men pick up the easy money during the season, then drift along on that, waiting for the next season. He thought pro ball made bums of college men, which was a legitimate criticism before the game had become established on a firm business basis. Few of his boys ever did go into pro ball; it has only been in the last few years, since the advent of the All-American Conference, added opportunities and big salaries, that Notre Dame players have veered toward the pro game.

One of the '21 group who did was Johnny Mohardt; but his was an exceptional case as Johnny has always been an exceptional man. In college he was a letterman in baseball, track and football; he took the difficult pre-medic course, with philosophical subjects as electives, and despite all this, graduated with a general average of 92 percent which would have made him eligible for Phi Beta Kappa if Notre Dame had had fraternities. He was good enough in baseball to be signed by the Detroit Tigers who farmed him to Atlanta; but it was always big-league or nothing with Johnny.

He entered Rush Medical College at Northwestern and paid

his way through by playing four years of pro ball with the Chicago Bears, where, for awhile, he was a teammate of Red Grange. He won a scholarship to the Mayo Clinic, left football behind, became a doctor in Chicago. During the last war he was a major in the Medical Corps and, according to report, left behind him a brilliant record in an Italian hospital.

Joe Brandy is a newspaper publisher in his home town of Ogdensburg, N. Y. After years of coaching, Chet Wynne went into business; so, with the luminous Gipp, there was a lot more than football talent in that 1920 backfield. Danny Coughlin is a newspaper publisher in Minnesota; Chet Grant combined sports writing with coaching, wrote an unusual novel and one day may crack through with a major opus. Slip Madigan did a Rockne job in putting St. Mary's of California on the football map, is now in the construction business. Dutch Bergman coached the Redskins for a spell and is established in Washington. I've seen most of the others at various times through the years and they all look well-fed and prosperous.

Then there is Hunk Anderson, who occupies a unique place in Notre Dame tradition and affection as a player, coach and personality. As Rockne's first assistant at the time of the latter's death, he took over the difficult stop gap job for three years; and while he ran into difficulties, he grew, as a man, in the estimation of Notre Dame which regards him as one of its most beloved and loyal sons.

Here's a column I wrote for the New York *News* in 1933 just before Hunk finished his tenure as head coach; I still think it says a lot about Hunk Anderson, the coaching business and football:

THE GENERAL

Three young men, just out of high school, left the iron peninsula of northern Michigan to come down into warmer country to look for gold. Had they remained at home they would have enjoyed the happy uncaroled ex-

188

istence of small town men. The accident of football ability changed the course of their lives. The colleges had begun to accept athletic ability as payment for education. The three young men joined the football gold rush.

One of them was brilliant, on the field and in the classroom. He became the greatest player of his time and remains an immortal for the ages. Life held for him its sweetest tokens—then pulled them away and closed his eyes forever. He died at the flush of glory—and an admiring nation became a mourning one. A campus was crushed in gloom. Feet which had rushed in unison to his name a few weeks before, marched in slow cadence behind his cortege. His two mates went home with him, back to the iron country. The last six miles were covered by sled. And the snows of Christmas powdered the grave of Thanksgiving's hero.

Then there were two. The second was just a neutral in the warfare of life. He was a good football player, had good health and good humor but no consuming or prodding ambition. After college he played professional football, got married, passed out of the big picture. He was not geared for glory; and when they pulled the mountain out from under his feet, he floated slowly back to earth, back to the iron earth.

Then there was one—and this one was tough; tough in body, tough in mind. People thought of him as tough; not viciously tough but humorously so. He had a squat, iron body with a sailor walk; a ringing iron voice and a wild, challenging eye. He didn't die and he didn't go back. He became top sergeant to the general at his own school. It was a perfect spot. He combined coaching with business. This was his niche—a good, tough job, nothing to worry about, no responsibilities.

Once he ventured forth. He tired of being a top sergeant and wanted to be a captain. He became head coach at a minor school. He was neither failure nor success. The General sent for him. He was needed back on the old campus. He came, somewhat quickly, back to the haven of home. His iron voice rang out again over the greensward. He was the same, good-natured, tough, iron fellow, as before. He was in his niche. He got his business job back. He was set for life.

The General died. There were majors and colonels in this football army, but they were at distant posts. The Top Sergeant was on the ground. He knew his stuff. He knew the boys. They liked him. He had been loyal and true. Why not give him the chance—temporarily at least? The chance was given to him. It was a fine, gracious gesture of sportsmanship by his university.

The Top Sergeant was now the general of the finest football army in America. Being a fighter and a good tough guy, he took hold, in a good, tough, fighting way. His iron voice rang out. His sailor walk was exaggerated. He did all right. The team did all right. It was a good, tough team. It hit hard and it rolled up scores. The reservation was removed. The Top Sergeant was now the top general. The camp followers rushed to get under his standard, anxious for those small flatteries a head coach of a big gridiron army can bestow, returning, in kind, larger flatteries to the general; and whispers of jealousy and envy.

The general of such a fine army is in the spotlight. Being a tough fellow, afraid of nothing, he stepped into the glare, did his job. Never having practiced too much the delicate arts of fancy speech, a little blinded by the glare, there was some fault to find with the nuances of his spoken and printed words. The newsreel and the radio preserved his hearty mistakes. Sophisticates, ever proving their strength by poking fun at hearty men, made jest of him.

A good tough guy wouldn't have bothered; but a good tough guy with brains did. He started to make himself over; to temper the iron tones to silver; to take more care with speech—and when he was not sure he took it easy, measured his questioner, his auditor, then himself.

The storm came. It blew his tents down. Enemies came from all sides. Bedlam. Liquid fire of criticism. Gas attack of hypocrisy. A little confused, trying harder than ever, unable to understand why nothing will go right any more, the Top Sergeant stands with his troops and takes it—like a good tough guy. That's his job.

Three young men came down from the iron country to look for gold. The neutral one was Ojay Larson. The snows of another Christmas will soon be powdering the grave of George Gipp—George, who would have been the ideal successor to Rockne. Hunk Anderson who lived to be the general, grows older with each day. Today Hunk is an impressive figure, a dual success. He coaches the Bears for three months and for the rest of the year is an executive of a Detroit steel firm—an outstanding example of what football can do for a man who has what it takes.

There was a fourth in the group who, though Gipp had been his substitute in high school football, was never quite hefty enough to make the collegiate big-time, though he played in all sports and was an exceptional hockey man. He is Perc Wilcox, one of those good, solid men who grow on you with the years.

There's another story which came to me from a non-Notre

Dame source, which I believe to be true but have not checked because I might be asked not to use it. But I think it belongs in the Notre Dame tradition.

One of Hunk's teammates had a small son who was dying. The last thing the boy was conscious of was the gold football on his father's watchchain and it was firmly clutched in his little fist when he passed away. The father could not take it from him, let it be buried with him. Later he wrote to Hunk about it. So our tough guy coach took the gold football from his own chain and sent it to his old teammate.

The father was Dave Hayes, called by his contemporaries, "The Typical Notre Dame Man." Dave had arrived from Connecticut by freight, washed dishes, made up with guts what he lacked in size; after time out for World War I, in which he was shot up some, he came back, washed more dishes, made a key block for the winning touchdown in an Army game. When he was graduated he had somehow saved $250; but the University had a drive on. Dave said to the President: "I came here by freight and broke. I'm leaving the same way. Here, Father—take this. There's a freight pulling out for Hartford tonight."

Portrait of a football factory! Take it away, Bill Stern.

XXX

College football squads of today are divided into three groups of men:

1. The tramps—of whom there are now relatively few. They bring too many headaches, are automatically screened out at the better institutions; and if they do get in, are usually caught up by the first examinations.

2. The "students"—who come in without recommendation, usually have difficulty hanging on because they are just not good enough, and seldom make the big-league grade.

3. The hand-picked high school stars—brought in, often after feverish competition, taken care of financially by the Job System, open or covert scholarships; but these men are also academically qualified and usually eager to capitalize on the fortunate accident of their athletic ability.

Realistic observers will readily admit that the average major-league squad is composed of a big majority, and sometimes almost exclusively, of boys in the third group. But these have their troubles, too, are usually in the position of the young genius arriving in New York. He knows he is good, the home folks know it, but they don't seem to know it yet in the big city.

A few do, of course; but the coach is busy with the varsity and the bird dogs are about the business of flushing out next year's covey. So nobody recognizes the all-state back who got such a rush all summer; and when he reports for practice he learns that most of the other freshmen were also all-state; that from now on he's on his own and will have to hustle to hold his own. And, too often, he discovers that the "arrangements" are not quite as the persuasive bird dogs had pictured them. Sometimes he can't take it; he goes back home—or jumps to one of the other schools which had courted him, if they still have room for him.

It is generally accepted now, even by its critics, that Notre Dame has more good boys knocking at its doors than it can possibly accept. The applicants, presumably, are screened; and the personal influence of the sponsor carries little, if any, weight. As an officer of the Alumni Association, I know that we have no group contact with the Athletic Department; and while I've done a little bird-dogging in my time, though seldom in recent years and not just for my alma mater, I've never placed a boy with Frank Leahy. That's okay; it saves me headaches.

Anyhow, Leahy seems to be doing all right, too well for some of the other bird-dog organizations who complain that he is entirely too aggressive. He seems to be a good salesman and there's nothing wrong with that as long as he stays within accepted bounds which, to the best of my knowledge, he does. He does have a lot to sell, and most of the boys who come to him have been sold on the idea for years.

The Four Horsemen, I think, offer a typical example of how athletes are "influenced" to come to Notre Dame. Harry Stuhldreher had an older brother, who was not an athlete, in school at the time he came, so I assume there was a reasonable predisposition in his case, although there was also some rumor that Harry had been thinking of Princeton. Jimmy Crowley was coached in high school and probably personally brought in by Curly Lambeau, the Green Bay Packer man, who had played for Rockne in Gipp's earlier days. Elmer Layden was a personal protégé of Walter Halas, Rock's only assistant coach at the time. There was some

194

fear that Elmer might, as a freshman, jump to Wisconsin, because there was a coed there in whom he was supposed to be romantically interested. This fear was so keen that I took it upon myself, when Elmer and I "bummed" to a track meet at Madison in his freshman year, to keep an eye on the young man.

Don Miller was Notre Dame bred, a member of the most famous football family in collegiate annals. His oldest brother, Harry, now a Dupont lawyer, was the famous Red, hero of the 1909 Michigan game and the model for the character of the same name in "The Potters," the J. P. McEvoy play which also ran as a comic strip for years. The second brother was Ray, later mayor of Cleveland, the Democratic leader in Ohio and primary candidate for governor. The third was Walter, regular fullback with Gipp's crew in 1919, and one of the most popular men of Notre Dame history, whose spectacular hats have been a feature of Irish gatherings.

The Miller clan comes to the big games en masse; and on one occasion the car in which Walter was riding was up-ended. Red and Ray, in a following car, pulled up in time to see Walter crawling into the flaming wreckage; horrified, they wondered what member of the family he was risking his life to save; but it was only his sack of spare hats.

Don and Gerry, the fourth and fifth brothers, played together in high school. Gerry, a scat back, had been the star and was also expected to be the college hotshot; but he was a little too small; and Don, bigger and very fast, was a surprise to everybody. I remember well the day in spring practice when Don first began to go and Rock knew he had another great player.

The second generation of Millers has already begun to produce. Red had two sons on the squad in Leahy's early days, Tom and Creighton; and the latter also starred, as had his father, against Michigan in the '43 Notre Dame victory, a rare family circumstance, indeed, considering the few opportunities. I know of no other father-and-son all-American duo in football history, though there may have been. Ray Miller also has a son on the present squad. Walter is still married to his hats.

Don, after four daughters, has a son. The Four Horsemen have remained close through the years. So after Don's son was born, in the manner of the proud father, he was telling how tough the kid was, how he had thrown a block through a window. Crowley quipped: "That's the first time I ever heard of a Miller throwing a block."

The Four Horsemen were fortunate, as individuals and a quartet, because they came along at a time when the backfield jobs were open—as other good backs were unlucky enough to come along with them and be compelled to play in the second fiddle section. The Seven Mules were an entity only in their last year; before that they had to serve their various apprenticeships as substitutes. Adam Walsh was the standout of the Mules because he was the '24 captain and had more playing time in his first two years.

Certainly nobody on the campus at that time suspected that from the '22-'24 group would come the most celebrated backfield of all time, a national champion and the only Rose Bowl team in Notre Dame history, a future Notre Dame coach, the commissioners of the two professional football leagues, head coaches for Fordham, North Carolina, Alabama, Purdue, Navy, Wisconsin, Villanova, South Carolina, Duquesne and several small schools; head coaches for Pittsburgh and the Chicago Rockets in the pro leagues; and assistants at Yale, Ohio State, Georgia, Georgia Tech and Vanderbilt.

Nobody could have guessed that a blight would strike the guards, that three of the first four, after promising early careers, would be dead within the decade, along with their coach; that one of these guards would become a member of Congress and die as an American officer in another World War; that a substitute back with the easy temperament of Gipp, would die while saving a woman from drowning.

Even less, except in mystic moments and dreams of destiny, did anybody see on the campus another squad, a black-robed squad, which in less than a decade would cause a new university to arise, whose spires would dwarf the old, with a backfield of four future presidents—Matthew Walsh, the historian; Charles O'Donnell, the poet; Pepper O'Donnell, the football player; and John O'Hara, the prefect of religion—who were to operate behind long lines of blockers.

But they were there; and they had come, as the athletes had come, because they had wanted to come; and they had come from the types of families which have built Notre Dame, and America —physically vigorous, mentally hungry, spiritually humble.

The time had come and the men, as always, were there.

In 1921 the Notre Dame endowment amounted to exactly $100,000. The University was actually $10,000 in debt. The post-war, and perhaps post-football influx of students had overflowed the campus of this tight little boarding school into the town, where more than 1,000 now lived, with an aggravation of the problems of morale and traditional discipline. There was the further financial fact that each new student was running the school deeper into debt because education is sold at a loss.

This was the acute administrative situation of which we on the campus, enthralled by the gridiron pyrotechnics, were blithely unaware; and if we had known, we probably would have been equally unconcerned. There had, in fact, been considerable grumbling because the traditional prep department was already in process of elimination to provide housing for college students.

In 1921 also came the first outside help. The Rockefeller Foundation offered $250,000 and the Carnegie Foundation $75,000—IF Notre Dame could raise $750,000. The drive got under way enthusiastically, and then stopped so suddenly that Father Burns, at the end of his first three-year presidential term, resigned to give all of his time to fund-raising. It was finally done, the hard way, tooth-by-tooth; for Notre Dame men were not rich.

197

Father Walsh was a younger and bolder man; he had been a chaplain in World War I, had seen more of how the world operated. He had an idea—which the more cautious Burns had shied away from—that residence halls could be built and would pay for themselves over a period of time. So he began to borrow and build. In six years he spent $1,650,000 for residence halls and a great dining hall which itself had cost $750,000. The day students were brought back on the campus, the buildings began paying for themselves.

Football profits, then averaging around $250,000 a year, also helped. Rockne wanted his stadium but Father Walsh insisted that the dining hall should come first—and now we have a better idea of the internal background at the time of the Columbia incident.

After the new residence halls and the dining hall were erected, Notre Dame was (and is) running one of the biggest hotels in the world. It evidently was a good idea Father Walsh had.

But no Notre Dame president can serve longer than six years; so in 1928 Matt Walsh went back to teaching history and Charles O'Donnell, the poet, took over. He had also been a war chaplain and he became an even bigger builder. During his six years he spent $2,800,000 for more residence halls, academic buildings, the Rockne Memorial—and the stadium. He also was bringing in prestige figures to illumine the growing academic program.

One of these, G. K. Chesterton, happened to be there the night the stadium was dedicated. The crowd recognized his massive figure as he took his place on the stand and 20,000 throats yelled out:

> He's a man
> Who's a man?
> He's a Notre Dame man
> CHESTERTON! CHESTERTON! CHESTERTON!

"My—they're angry," the distinguished Briton said.

Rockne had been startling the football world during the Twenties; but Notre Dame's bigger team had been doing the bigger job behind the spectacular facade of the football factory.

John F. Cushing came to Notre Dame as a poor boy. In 1905 he called on President Morrissey, told him he could not afford to return for his senior year. Father Morrissey said not to worry about that, that John was a good boy and a good student and the school would see him through. So John graduated as a civil engineer in 1906. In 1931 he wrote his old classmate, President O'Donnell:

"Because I find at Notre Dame the conditions that make for the two-fold training of great engineers, a technical training that ranks with the best and a training in character foundation nowhere excelled, and because I feel I owe Notre Dame a debt of gratitude I can never fully discharge, I ask you to accept from me a gift of three hundred thousand dollars toward the erection of a hall of engineering to serve the immediate needs of the College of Engineering and to meet the expectations of older men like me who confidently look back to Notre Dame to produce the men that are to carry on."

There have been other gifts like that from other men like that for other reasons like that.

Joe LaFortune's father worked for the University, in the old machine shop located on the present site of the dining hall. After graduation Joe went to Tulsa, Oklahoma, got into the oil business, prospered, became a member of the Board of Lay Trustees—and recently gave the University $100,000.

Other important gifts have come from men who were neither Notre Dame men nor college men but came to believe in Notre Dame as a training school for moral leadership and as a bulwark of the American idea of government. Help has come from industry for scientific research—the field in which the school now seems to be concentrating. The first item on the present program of John Cavanaugh is a $1,700,000 science building. The endowment of flesh-and-blood is now being supported by endowments from important outside sources, of money and ideas.

Here's a thought: Notre Dame put its bold building program through when costs were down, much of it in the very depths of the depression.

Providential?

XXXI

In addition to think-work-fight-pray there is another outstanding Notre Dame word—fun. Boys thrown together can be depended upon to make their own fun. Rock had been a fun-maker as a student, was a laugh-maker as a coach, knew the value of merriment to a squad, used it to relieve the tedious work of practice and to get his points across. Coaching dignity kept him from taking any part in squad horseplay; but the departing 1921 squad once "included him in."

Rock was then beginning to pioneer spring training. His sound idea was that this relaxed period of the year could be utilized to give the coaches an opportunity to get acquainted with the new material; to teach the fundamentals of blocking, tackling, pass defense and rudimentary offense; that, since the majority of injuries in the fall are due to carelessly executed fundamentals, spring training could become a valuable safety measure—a factor which should always be foremost in the minds of coaches and rules-makers.

To give it a little zip and relief from drudgery, he announced that the 1922 spring season would be climaxed by a regulation game in which the departing stars would be pitted against those who would form the next year's varsity, including the freshmen. And he provided an extra diversion by playing quarterback for the old-timers. He was thirty-five at the time and already carrying a well-developed spare tire around his middle but still fancied himself good enough to take it. So they let him have it.

His usual routine was to have the quarterback carry the ball on the first play, so the field general could get the feel of contact and, with that inhibition removed, clear his mental deck for thinking. On the first scrimmage play, when the pudgy bantam strutted his own signal, the old-timers did everything but issue engraved invitations to the lads on the other side of the line. Every hole became an open door and the defense was practically bowed in.

Eleven men swarmed on the coach—and I'm not too sure some of his own team were not also on the pile.

Rock got it. He snorted, glared, grunted: "Wise guys." He called his own signal again—but this time for a pass. He chugged down the field, caught the pass—then took himself out of the line-up; but only after he had looked good. That was part of his technique, too: He seldom took a man out after an obviously bad play because that would have been bad for individual and team morale.

Spring training met long opposition from the fuzz-heads who always object to anything new because it is new. Like intersectional games, which Rock also pioneered, it is now accepted; but like too many other good things in football it is also abused. I see no objection to the spring games which now climax most training periods, often for gate receipts and some charitable purpose; nor to occasional practice scrimmages with neighboring squads; but at too many schools spring training begins in January in the gym and carries over into summer under the guise of physical education classes. Where this occurs the football man is in harness for most of the year—which, is, however, another reason for giving the boys some financial return for all this labor.

The Rockne system used humor as a psychological weapon; his squads were always kidders and goat-getters.

Once the Gipp gang was playing a minor opponent in such bitter cold that the other team wore canvas gloves. Brandy called a huddle, then a play into the line. There was a lot of milling around; the Irish gained no ground but came up with all the gloves.

In a Nebraska game there was a strong silent Cornhusker guard, lethal in performance. Slip Madigan, who was taking the brunt of the fellow's charges, turned to Brandy and said; "Did you ever see a homelier-looking gorilla in your life than this guard?" The gorilla glared, which was the idea, and became less effective in performance; but he refused to talk back or do the bit of slugging—which might also have been Madigan's idea—that would get him out of the line-up. But when the final whistle had blown, he hauled off and let his tormentor have one on the nose.

The Army games were full of impolite repartee and "hard-clean" football; but it all came under the head of good fun and psychological warfare, without any running to teacher, which was something our boys always used to like about the manly Cadets. Rock once called it "the game in which nobody quits and nobody cries."

The 1921 squad had a screwball quartet of Hec Garvey, Mickey Kane, Ed Degree and Mike Seyfrit who kept things humming. Garvey could roar like a bull, Degree could bark like a dog, and gentle intellectuals walking along the campus were sometimes frightened by such noises coming from the trees; but their top performance was given in New York the day after an Army game. The squad attended Sunday Mass at St. Patrick's Cathedral and then boarded the regular buses. When these passed each other now and then in the traffic, Fifth Avenue was disturbed by the strange noises of Garvey bellowing at Degree and Degree barking at Garvey.

Kane, the baseball captain, was just a fair halfback; but when the lists were put up for road trips, Mickey was always down near the end. He seldom got in the big games but he was a lot of fun and that was why Rock brought him along. Notre Dame always has a morale man and one of the best was Ziggy Czarobski of the recent post-war group. He had an intellectual quality to his wit which was invaluable during games and on trips. Pep meetings always ended with a speech by "The Alderman"; and the supposedly humorless Leahy encouraged this sort of stuff.

Kane was still around in 1922 and immediately teamed up with sophomore Jimmy Crowley to form as fine a pair of end men as any football squad ever had. Regardless of what happened on the field—and it was usually good—we had fun going and coming. On the Georgia Tech trip in '22 the spirit really bubbled. This was in the early days of prohibition and Crowley was running for president on the Pro-HY-bition ticket with Kane as his campaign manager. We had a colored porter who had obviously never run into anything quite like this and, with one thing and another— including the Road Scholars—the boys kept him well confused.

They called him Battling Siki, after the fighter of that period and, since he was from Chicago, made him a member of the Notre Dame Chicago Club. On the return trip, after we had beaten Georgia Tech, he had been well indoctrinated. About three o'clock one morning the train stopped at Danville, Kentucky, home of Center College, which was then having its brief period of gridiron glory. Siki met another colored man on the station platform, did a little boasting about his Notre Dame team; and when the other scornfully said that Center could beat 'em, Siki challenged: "You gets your team and I gets mine and we plays right here."

One of the staunchest of Notre Dame's synthetics was Urban Turnquist, the first president of the Pullman Porters and Maids Protective Association. He made his maiden trip in 1926, was nicknamed "Tom" by Art "Bud" Boeringer, the all-American center of that year. From that time until his death in 1937, he was the personal porter of the squad, a friend of a generation of players and, in his Notre Dame sweatshirt, a familiar figure and most successful mascot on the sidelines from coast to coast.

After the '22 Army game, we were in an open-topped bus at the intersection of Broadway, Seventh Avenue and 47th Street, a busy sector on a Saturday evening. Joe Byrne had gone into the old Moulin Rouge to arrange for dinner, which nobody had gotten around to up to that time. Mickey Kane, who was to do well in Massachusetts politics later on, thought this an excellent opportunity for his candidate to make a pitch. So Jimmy Crowley, who had already forgotten his fumble on the three-yard line that day, gave them his Pro-HY-bition talk which anticipated current political technique by promising all things to all men.

Naturally he drew quite a crowd and jammed traffic. The irate cop on duty came over full of storm—until Joe Byrne explained that this was the Notre Dame team. He was an Irish cop.

Byrne, who went to college with Rock, and is now commissioner of the Port Authority and a few other such things, has been the all-time godfather of Notre Dame squads. Along about 1940 they gave him a big civic appreciation dinner in Newark and all the Notre Dame boys in the vicinity turned out. Coming back our driver made the fatal mistake of crossing the line in the Hudson Tube and the cops waved us over at the exit. When they learned Crowley and Madigan were in the group they said we really should be more careful in the future—and got some autographs for their kids.

Crowley got his fun out of "situation," was quick with the comeback (as even Rockne found out on occasions), was always his own man and became one of the great wits of football history. He was also a fine coach and a lot of us thought he was the man best fitted to succeed to the unique portfolio Rockne had created at Notre Dame. When, in 1933, the authorities began searching for a man to replace Hunk Anderson, I was one of those asked to submit recommendations. Crowley, then at his coaching peak at Fordham, was my first choice; but before I submitted his name I sounded him out. He said no Notre Dame man could turn down such an opportunity but that Fordham would have to be agreeable. I then put it up to Jack Coffey, the Ram athletic director, who said he understood and gave me the green light.

But at Notre Dame I ran into a surprising point of view: They liked Jimmy, agreed he was a fine coach but were inclined to fear he was not quite serious enough for the job. I reported that to him, thought he might change their opinion if he talked to them. But Jimmy said: "I've always lived my own life and think it would be a mistake if I tried to change."

To thine ownself be true. Jimmy always has been and to other men as well.

I had been asked to name my five leading choices. One was Buck Shaw who was, I believe, later approached and found reasons for regretfully declining. Another was Elmer Layden, who at that time was in the more obscure post at Duquesne but had done an excellent job in lifting that school into the big time despite important local opposition. I thought I had observed real interest when I mentioned Layden's name.

Returning to New York, I stopped off at Pittsburgh, went to Layden's house. His season had ended and I asked if he were coming to New York for the Army game the next weekend. He hadn't intended to. I suggested that he do it, told him what was in the wind and that, though my first choice was Crowley, I thought he had a real chance for the job. He came to New York, was introduced at the alumni dinner for the squad—and they tore down the house, for this was the first time most of them had seen Layden since his playing days.

After his appointment was announced, I learned that Layden's name had been among the first five nominated by every person who had been consulted. That had impressed the authorities— and the reception at the New York dinner certainly didn't hurt.

Layden did seem to change after he took over the job; he tightened up, as if he were conscious of the heavy responsibility and had made up his mind to do nothing which might throw him off keel; actually I think this was a development rather than a change; for Layden, though a pleasant person, had a much more intense personality than Crowley or Don Miller, who have remained boys at heart through the years. Stuhldreher was always cocky, assured and ambitious, which was why he was such a great quarterback.

Layden proved to be an excellent selection. He was a good businessman type of coach as his seven-year record of 47 won, 13 lost and 3 tied, proved. He won some great victories, including the 1935 Ohio State 18-13 comeback, which is one of the high spots of all Notre Dame history and, from all angles, probably the most dramatic contest in all gridiron history.

The present schedule situation has also pointed up the previously unappreciated fact that Layden was a great athletic director. He retained all the old relationships and added Ohio State, Illinois and finally Michigan. He was the highest type of Catholic gentleman; and though he seemed to withdraw somewhat from the inner circle of Notre Dame men, he was a sensational success at cultivating the people he wanted to improve the schedule— which has been Leahy's only weakness. Of course, they could also beat Layden about twice a year—and that might be a factor.

Layden not only got Michigan back but did something even more astounding to old Notre Damers—brought Fielding Yost to the Notre Dame campus.

Yost and Rockne had been deadly feudists. It probably stemmed from the 1910 situation when Rock was a freshman. Furthermore, as Rockne developed, he became a personal rival to Yost, who had long dominated the Midwestern scene—as Leahy later became a rival of Crisler's. This dormant situation came to a boil at Ann Arbor during an outdoor Big Ten track meet at which Notre Dame was represented. The athletic directors had reached an agreement that, in case of dispute, they would stay away from the officials and not attempt personal pressure.

The dispute came on the final event which was to decide the meet between Michigan and Illinois. Harry Gill, the Illinois mentor, stayed out of it—but Yost was out there with the officials. Rockne was not concerned in the thing; but he and Gill were very friendly while he and Yost were definitely not. So when Gill wouldn't do anything about it, Rock did. He went out and reminded Yost of the agreement.

I was in school at the time and I'm giving you Rockne's version of the rhubarb as he told it to me the next day. After that the war was really on. Mr. Yost was a tough guy, too; he held the better cards and he played them well—until Rockne finally dealt around him and made Notre Dame independent of the Conference.

So you can imagine my surprise, one day about 1939, to meet Yost in Layden's office. I accompanied them on a tour of the campus and we finally came to the Rockne Memorial. There's a bust of Rock in the foyer, a grim and fearsome face—and a wide miss on his personality.

But this was probably the Rockne that Yost had known.

Yost stood and looked at Rock for quite a little while. Rock glared back. Layden, Jack Lavelle and I said nothing. This was drama.

A few years later I spoke at the Heismann Memorial Dinner in New York when Tom Harmon received the award as Player of the Year. Yost and Crisler were also on the dais. I told the story of Yost at Notre Dame, said I thought it had ended the feud between two of football's greatest men. I didn't know how Yost would feel about that. But after the dinner he came to me and thanked me for saying it. So you see, there's quite a bit of Notre Dame-Michigan tradition even though we don't see each other so often. But when we do—sparks!

The Four Horsemen have, through the years, retained a fine

friendship and a pardonably prideful unity. I remember an evening after an Army victory in New York when Joe Byrne and I accompanied Layden on a round of cocktail parties, which I suspect was part of the coach's official duties—visiting people who might someday be inclined to buy us a new library or something. We wound up near Crowley's apartment and dropped in. Fordham had beaten Purdue that day and George Vergara and a few other close friends were helping the coach feel good about it.

This had also been one of the better days out in Madison, Wisconsin, where Stuhldreher had beaten Illinois. We called Harry who also seemed to be pleasantly relaxing—and the three Old Horsemen had a fine time congratulating each other. We kept the group together, had dinner at 21 (courtesy of Joe Byrne, as usual, who has never got over his early habits) and then went across the street to Club 18 where Jack White finally got Elmer and Jimmy up on the stage. They sang the "Victory March"—and cold sober.

It's about time I told you about that "Victory March." Very early in the football development, the need for a song worthy of the movement was realized—and the need again found its men, two of them this time. Johnny Shea had been captain and shortstop of the baseball team in 1905 and had come back to Holyoke, Massachusetts, to go into politics and become a brilliant speaker and writer. His brother Mike had become Rev. Michael J. Shea, S. J., and was at that time the organist at St. Patrick's Cathedral in New York.

Together the Shea brothers wrote the song and wanted to try it out on somebody. On the streets of Holyoke they met Prof. William C. Hammond, who had been Father Mike's music teacher. They told him about the song and the Professor invited them to try it out on his new church organ. So they went, accompanied by three other guys named Kelly, Doyle and Powers. While Father Mike played the song, a group of church deacons walked in to have a meeting, saw the Catholic priest at the organ and the strange but devout congregation.

In the best Sorin tradition, the Notre Dame "Victory March" had its tryout in a Protestant church. It has since been heard all over the world, including many barrooms, no doubt, for it is very catchy and a wonderful thing to sing and march by. Boys returning from the wars reported hearing it in foreign lands, sometimes in difficult situations, where it gave them the same lift it sometimes gives the boys on the field. Once it was played by Japanese, who thought it was one of our national anthems— which, in a sense, it is. Here, in case you have never sung them, are the words:

> Cheer, cheer, for Old Notre Dame
> Wake up the echoes cheering her name
> Send a volleyed cheer on high
> Shake down the thunder from the sky
> What though the odds be great or small
> Old Notre Dame will win over all
> While her loyal sons are marching
> Onward to victory.
> Rah! Rah! Rah!

XXXII

The dressing room speech is as old as football, part of the general hoorah of student rallies, bonfires, organized cheering and other psychological and emotional devices designed to fire up the squad. The coach gets the last shot at them, just before the game, tries to send them out there in a mood in which all things are subordinated to the desire to win. Some of football's best stories have come from the locker room.

Here's one I heard recently from a member of the squad, who was in the room when it happened many years ago, as Princeton was about to go out against Yale. The coach, one of the most famous of current football names, exhorting his boys in the most fervid tradition, wound up: "I want you to go out there and fight, FIGHT, FIGHT! And I want you to tell me, as you leave this room, that you ARE going out there to FIGHT." So he took his station at the door and, with tears streaming down his face, fervently shook the hands of his boys, most of whom, by now, were also crying.

But there's always the hard-bitten sophisticate who has seen all this before, who is apt to whisper to a mate: "He was much better last week, don't you think?" On this day the cynic waited until all the others had gone; he went to the coach, as the rest had done; but instead of taking the outstretched hand he patted the mentor on the shoulder, said: "Get hold of yourself, Toots."

The boys are getting too wise, have heard too much about this sort of stuff, so modern coaches mostly use the analytical approach. But Rockne was a master of the oratorical art and never fell flat—not just because of his own virtuosity but because he was a Notre Dame man talking to Notre Dame men about Notre Dame—and Notre Dame men believe in things. He might deliberately search for a theme, but it always had in it the substance of the occasion; and once into it he was a great actor in performance—believing himself, he could make his players believe.

His opponents, hearing of these dressing room dramas, accused him of unduly playing on the emotions of boys to win a football game. I confess I also had some such reservations until the day, at Pitt Stadium in 1929 when I was six years out of college, that he made me cry, and others much older than I.

The scene had a powerful background. In the first eight games of the 1926 season Notre Dame had gone undefeated, with only one touchdown scored against it, by Minnesota; and one of its victories had been over Northwestern, which shared the Big Ten title that year with Michigan. Then came one of the most shocking upsets in football history. Notre Dame was defeated at Pittsburgh 19-0 by Carnegie Tech—as Rockne sat in the press box at Soldier's Field watching Army and Navy!

It was accepted as a fact that he had thought the game such a setup that he had gone to Chicago in the interests of his newspaper syndicate. And the word got around that the squad, in his absence, had got out of hand under Hunk Anderson and broken training the night before the game. I've checked that rumor with Johnny Niemiec, one of the stars of the squad, who assures me there was nothing to it.

What happened was logical enough. Carnegie had an underrated team, led by the great Howard Harpster; but the Big Ten Schedule meetings were being held in Chicago on the Army-Navy weekend and Rock, who had his usual fish to fry, wanted badly to be there. Also, he had scheduled Navy for the next year and may have wanted to do a job of scouting. His absence had a two way effect at Pittsburgh. His team probably did have a psychological letdown; and can't you just hear Wally Steffen, the Carnegie coach, telling his boys in the dressing room that "the great Rockne didn't even think enough of you to make the trip here with his team?"

Rock took a chance—and became the laughingstock of football. Steffen, a Chicago judge, poured it on during the banquet season by referring to the game as "a setup—not an upset." Rock took the rap without attempting to alibi—but planned for the day when they were to meet again. But that day came in 1928— the year he had his only poor team; and Carnegie followed the famous Army game when the Irish cripples had scored their own greatest upset in Notre Dame history and had nothing much left.

Carnegie defeated them again, 27-7—the first time Notre Dame had lost at home in twenty-two years. Steffen now re- vived the "setup" gag and poured further acid by proclaiming that Carnegie had Notre Dame's number and would prove it again the next year at Pittsburgh.

You can imagine how Rockne prepared for that next year— but when *it* came he was on his back with phlebitis!

Tom Lieb did the active coaching for the first three games, won them all.

Carnegie was next—the jinx team. The doctors said Rockne couldn't go; but when the squad arrived in Pittsburgh Friday morning, he was with them. His personal physician had come along and immediately put him to bed; but he was in high good humor and held court through the morning with the New York re- porters for whom he always put on a show; and now the gags were about his leg.

Lieb took the boys to the stadium for a physical workout after which they came back to the Athletic Club for one of the strangest practice sessions ever held—on a handball court where they walked through their plays as the coach, now highly nervous, checked from a wheel chair.

It had been customary for Rockne to entertain a group of his closest friends the night before a game; and the session lasted long because he could never sleep much before a contest. Joe Byrne was usually the host and the rest of the group depended pretty much on what town we were in—in the East it would include Doctor Maurice Keady and Johnny Niesen; in the Midwest Al Feeney, Doctor Nigro, Cap Edwards, Senator Maypole, Byron Kanaley; in Los Angeles, Leo Ward, Gene Kennedy and the Scotts. In Pittsburgh this night it would have been Doctor Leo O'Donnell, Byrne, Keady, and Elmer Layden, who was then at Duquesne.

But there was no party this night. The word was passed around that Rock had collapsed in his room, that full rest was ordered, that nobody could see him at all. I made no effort and I assume that none of his other close friends did. I did not see him until fifteen minutes before game time, outside the Notre Dame dressing room.

The great stadium was already filled, waiting for this grudge game which had been so advertised from coast to coast. But there was a dramatic prologue which none of the seventy thousand people in the stands could have imagined.

An automobile drove through the stadium gates and to the entrance of the dressing room. Inside the team was ready and waiting, very quietly, wondering if their coach would come.

A call came for Tom Lieb. He went out to the car, picked Rockne up in his arms and carried him like a baby into the dressing room. Rock couldn't have written a better script but he was not writing scripts this day. The football fates had charge of this performance.

Lieb placed Rock on a table where he sat, back to the wall and legs stretched out. I remember that he wore tan shoes and black overshoes—and overshoes on Rockne seemed to be the sym-

214

bol of his weakness. His face was very sober and set—which was unusual for him. He sat there for several minutes, which can seem an awful long time in a football locker room when the boys are ready and waiting to go, when time is running out, when the crowd is waiting. But Rock looked at nobody, seemed hardly conscious of anything or anybody around him.

The boys looked at him, away from him, bit their lips, glanced at the floor, did other things to put in those minutes—boys who were to make football history by winning nineteen straight games and two successive national championships—tough fellows like Twomey, Carideo, Savoldi, Brill, Moynihan, Conley, Elder, O'Brien, O'Connor, Colrick, Culver, Donoghue, Kassis, Metzger, Nash, Yarr, Vezie, Schwartz—and Leahy.

There were only minutes left. He would have to say something soon. It would have been laughable if it had not been so serious—Rockne being carried into a locker room like a baby and sitting there with black overshoes on tan high-tops—and everybody waiting.

Byrne, Keady and I, with one or two others, all very close to Rockne, were back of the lockers, out of sight. This was something between the coach and his players.

You may laugh at this, think it overplayed or overdone, a very silly business to become so excited or tragic about, a mere football game. You may consider it maudlin or banal or other things—but this was twenty years ago, just a few days before the great market crash; this was Rockne and Notre Dame and that was Carnegie Tech, his jinx team, and Wally Steffen, his tormentor, who had to be beaten.

That, my friends, can be drama.

It could have been more than that. Behind the lockers, Doctor Keady whispered: "He has an even chance of not leaving this room alive. If that clot is loosened from excitement, it might hit his heart or his head and kill him. If he shoots the works—" We could hear Rock start talking, his voice strong. This is almost an actual record of the words he used:

"There has been a lot of water under the bridge since I first came to Notre Dame—but I don't know when I've ever wanted to win a game as badly as this one.

"I don't care what happens after today.

"Why do you think I'm taking a chance like this? To see you lose?"

(He was beginning to shout.)

"They'll be primed. They'll be tough. They think they have your number. *Are you going to let it happen again?*"

It was quiet. I don't know what the boys were doing—but all of us behind the lockers were crying.

"You can win *if you want to.*"

Now he shot the works. I watched his face through a space between the lockers. As he talked, it was distorted with an almost insane determination. His voice was strong and vibrant: "Go out there and crack 'em. Crack 'em. *Crack 'em.* Fight to live. Fight to win. Fight to live. *Fight to win*—WIN—WIN—WIN—"

He was shouting, pouring himself out, repeating the famous phrases of his battle cry. The squad was leaving with an angry roar. As the last of them left, Rock collapsed.

His eyes were shut; his face was in pain; he was sweating and the doctor was gently mopping the sweat from his face, feeling his pulse.

Rockne wanted to win more than he wanted to live—when the winning was important enough. He wanted his boys to feel that way. That's the Rockne spirit, the Notre Dame spirit, the American spirit—what Chevigny had at Yankee Stadium and at Iwo Jima.

Is that bad?

Is it bad to teach boys that what is worth believing in is worth fighting for—that some things in life are more precious than life? Or to play on emotions to rouse a man—or a nation—to fighting pitch? Isn't that exactly what we do in time of war with music, oratory, even prayer?

I think one of the finest things Notre Dame gives its boys is this tremendous will to win at all things they think worth doing.

It wasn't easy that day at Pittsburgh. Steffen had made a speech, too. He and his squad knew what they were up against, what they had asked for. There was no talk on the field this day. It was grim, hard, savage—but remarkably clean. I was on the bench, close up, could see and *hear* it. And that's football—when you can *hear them hit*.

Rock was calm and efficient on the bench in his wheel chair. There was no score in the first half. Between halves he was analytical, told them they had been too tight, to relax. "They'll pass this half."

In the third period Jack Elder ran back a punt 35 yards to the seven-yard line. There was no deception in the following plays. Notre Dame seemed to want to do it the hard way, to settle this thing man to man. Four times Savoldi hit the middle of the line— the last time from the one-yard line—and he made it for the only touchdown of the 7-0 victory.

Later in the season Elder was also to run 98 yards with an intercepted Cagle pass in eight-above-zero temperature for the only score against Army.

Once again that year Rockne was to shoot the works in a dressing room speech against Southern Cal. Notre Dame won that one 13-12. That night I took Alan Gould in to see Rockne who was in bed. His little son Jackie was with him—asleep, with his arms around his daddy's neck.

Later that night the clot did break loose—but passed through the heart safely, missed the brain and lodged in the other leg.

In that Southern Cal game a second-string right halfback was led from the game after the first scrimmage play. He had an egg on his eye and couldn't see. His name was Bucky O'Connor. Remember the name.

XXXIII

The first Rockne pep talk I heard much about was at Atlanta in 1922. The Four Horsemen had got over their first four games; Georgia Tech, with Red Barron as its star, was a major hurdle on a foreign field and Rock wanted his team to be "up." He stood before them in the dressing room; tears were in his eyes as he read a telegram he had received that morning from one of his sons whom all the boys knew.

"I want my daddy's team to win."

They won, 13-3. The story of the dressing room speech got around the campus. The old heads smiled. Rock had pulled a dandy.

But he hadn't. I'm not saying he wouldn't have pulled it if he had thought of it; nor that he would; for he had a fine feeling about his family. But a year later I had a date with a young lady who was a friend of the Rockne family. The night before that Georgia Tech game she and her boy friend had thought up that telegram.

There is a story for every game—pathos, drama, human interest, tragedy, humor. It would take another book to tell all the Notre Dame stories. I can only give you the highlights and the significant developments.

Against Purdue in 1922, Tom Lieb, who had been shifted

to tackle where he might have become all-American, broke a leg and his playing days were over. That was tough but Tom was a clown; and when he came down on crutches and wearing an old army shirt to see the squad off for Georgia Tech, the boys put him on the train and Rock took him along—without even a toothbrush.

The squad went to Indianapolis to play Indiana at the baseball park, for the Hoosiers had stadium trouble, too, and still have; but when they arrived, an Indiana student manager wouldn't let them in because they had no tickets. "What's the matter," Rockne barked, "weren't they expecting us?"

The Hoosiers, though defeated by a handy 27-0, seemed to have our plays exceptionally well scouted, including some very new ones devised for that game. A rumor spread that there was a traitor on the campus. Nobody really believed that; but when Rock learned that one of his varsity men, coaching an interhall team, had given his pet plays to the Sunday players, he took full advantage of the situation to drive home a lesson. His practice had never been secret, but on Monday afternoon the gate was closed and on it was a sign:

> Secret practice. Come and bring your notebooks.
> K. K. Rockne

We moved on, with the usual complete confidence, to what was going to be the last Army game to be played at West Point, though nobody knew it at the time. It turned out to be quite a toughie. Finally, in the last period, our youngsters put together a 64-yard drive that ended on the three-yard line where Crowley learned anew the answer to one of Rock's trick questions: "The first qualification of a halfback is to hold the ball." It was actually stolen from him, which is a legitimate action in football and one of the things a young player has to find out about the world.

The score was 0-0 and a moral victory for Army since it was

the first time in seven years they hadn't lost to us. They escorted us to the train, told us to "come back next year" and try again. We were not so happy about it and Rock sulked in his drawing room. The next afternoon on the train our youthful spirits had revived somewhat; four of us were harmonizing or making a stab at it.

Rockne came down the aisle looking forbidding. We hadn't won; and when you don't win at Notre Dame you're supposed to be doing penance until you redeem yourselves. We thought we would hear something like that now from the coach; but we kept singing, though consciously softer. He stopped, looked at us for awhile, sat down.

"I don't know that one," he said. "Let's sing 'Darling Nelly Gray.'" As I recall it, Rock wasn't much of a singer; but he thought he was good at everything and nobody was unkind enough to dispute with him about it—particularly that afternoon.

The next week was Butler, which was then having a football revival and had a "married-man's" team—something unusual in those days, particularly to us because a married man could not then even be a student at Notre Dame. This was also in the Klan era and there was supposed to be some of that feeling mixed up in the game, which was also played at Indianapolis. We won easily enough, 34-7; but they broke Paul Castner's pelvic bone.

That was a bitter shock. It may surprise you but Castner was the outstanding back in the sophomore year of the Four Horsemen. He was, in fact, a regular Frank Merriwell and one of the great, if somewhat forgotten now, all-round athletes of Notre Dame history. In baseball he was the star pitcher and hitter, once shutout Illinois without a hit or run—and won his own game with a home run. He spent part of the next year with the White Sox but gave up baseball for a business career. He was the best college hockey player I have ever seen and could have gone to the big league in that sport, too. In football he was a

220

long, left-footed kicker, a good passer, an exceptional runner for his size and never better than against Butler until he was cut down. That injury probably cost him an all-American selection.

It also put Rock in a tough spot. Carnegie and Nebraska were coming up and in Castner he had lost his key man and old head in the backfield. Bill Cerney, the second-string fullback, had had a lot of experience with the shock troops, was a rugged fellow but lacked the speed and finesse to which the Horsemen were geared. So Rock came up with one of the surprise moves which studded his career, one of those rabbits he so dearly loved to pull out of the hat; and this one was as big as Frank Fay's Harvey.

Don Miller was the only one of the Horsemen who had been a regular from the first game. Conforming to his usual procedure of giving the senior the break, Rock had been starting Frank Thomas at quarterback. The future Alabama mentor was a good man, an experienced signal caller and could really scamper back with those punts on his chubby legs; but Stuhldreher had been playing more and more and by now was acknowledged first-string quarterback.

Crowley and Layden, rivals from the beginning, as they were to continue to be, had been dividing the left-half job, with Crowley having a slight starting edge, though Rock had done a good job of making them seem equal. Both were fine all-round players without a weakness on offense or defense. Elmer, a track sprinter, had exceptional straight-away speed and was a long punter; but Crowley was a really great open-field runner and never better than in his sophomore year.

Rock may have had it in his mind to use Layden at fullback the next season; but with Castner out, he needed Elmer's punting. So, in one week he made a fullback out of Layden—and on November 25, against Carnegie at Pittsburgh, the Four Horsemen rode together for the first of their twenty-two games, of which they were to lose only two, both to Nebraska and each by one touchdown.

The first of these defeats came five days later. at Lincoln on Thanksgiving Day. Two trips and two tough games may have taken something out of the squad; but they had certainly taken toll of the Publicity Department. I had spent only two nights in my own bed in the last six when we arrived at Lincoln on Wednesday; so I made a radical departure from routine, told Rock to sign me up for a room and I would pay him the two bucks.

"Well, Frank," he said, "I don't like to see you have to do that. I've got a double bed—you can sleep with me."

I was in bed at nine, a new world's record. Rock came in at nine-thirty—with the Nebraska track coaches. They played penny-ante until five in the morning. I didn't get much sleep but I did learn something about poker. And in the morning I had another tough break. I had a $50 Chicago *Tribune* check I wanted to bet on the game, having no doubt about victory, and intended to ride back in style, look the conductor in the eye. But since it was a holiday nobody would cash the check—until just before the game when some false friend came through.

We lost 14-6. The Cornhuskers were just too good, outweighed us fifteen pounds to the man. But even so, in the second half, our kids took the play away, filled the air with footballs, scored one touchdown and almost another. Rock came around after the game, shook hands with all of them, said they would never play a game of which he would be more proud because they had given all they had.

It was after this game that Rock first used his battle cry: "I don't want a man to go in there to die gamely—I want a man to go in there fighting to live—like Bob Regan."

Regan was the 160-pound center who, time after time, had been swept backward by the huge Scarlet flood—but each time crawled back to that line on his hands and knees. Bob coached with Stuhldreher for many years but is now in the women's dress business in Madison, getting rich, too, and wanting to know

222

why somebody didn't tell him about women's dresses all those years he was in football.

As always, on the rare occasions when he lost a game, Rock went back to the laboratory of his mind. There had been no weakness in fundamentals in that Nebraska game, which had been played on a new field whose unusually loose sod had operated against our speed; but the passing game, excellent though it had been in execution, had shown him a weakness. Previously his left half, who was also his best open-field runner, had done all the passing and mostly to the ends; now Rock put in plays which had all of his backs but Miller passing, and all four of them also going down for passes. In those days, in fact until Marty Brill arrived in 1929, there was no such animal as a blocking back specialist in the Rockne system. Every back blocked or he wasn't in there long. I still like it.

Rock's nimble brain developed another typical psychological wrinkle about that time. We were adding Princeton to the 1923 schedule and he wanted the boys to be "up" for this first Ivy League encounter since the lamented Yale game; so he started getting them ready in spring practice at the noon lectures. He "played" the game in advance on the blackboard. This was his method:

He would state the position of the ball at each scrimmage, the other conditions such as wind and yardage; he would then ask some player to call the next play and he would estimate the result according to his judgment of the value of the play called. This gave him a chance to compliment the smart players and rib the dumb ones. All this was entertaining, instructive and intensely interesting. The normal crowd was there the day we "played" the first quarter. The next day, the stragglers had heard about it. The third, athletes from other sports crowded into the room. The score at the end of the third period was tied.

When we were to play the final quarter, there was an overflow in the hall and the entire campus was waiting for the result of the "Princeton game" because Rock was capable of having us lose for the chastening effect. He stretched it out until the last minute when Crowley got off to a long touchdown run behind expert blocking by the entire team. Cheers!

Later in his office Rock laughed, said it would have been bad psychology to have lost. He wanted to make the boys believe they could beat Princeton but only after a long struggle during which they would have to be heads up at all times. The actual game proved to be much easier. The score was 25-2; the following year we also won 12-0; and that's the last Notre Dame has seen of Old Nassau—which is also too bad because the schools have much in common and Notre Dame has been called the Princeton of the Midwest.

That old office of Rock's was really something. It was on the second floor rear of the Main Building, looking out on the bakery. It was never locked, nor was the ancient rolltop desk which Sorin might possibly have used. A table against the wall was piled high with correspondence. People were always walking in and out but I never saw anybody disturb the letters or the roll of currency that rested in a cubbyhole of the desk for months. Every so often Rock would bring in a stenographer and wade through the letters, with accompanying wisecracks. The rest of the room was what you might imagine—old records, footballs, piled up pictures, pieces of uniform and other impedimenta.

This was the sole headquarters of the Notre Dame Athletic Association at a time when the school had already reached the football pinnacle. It should be a shrine but now houses somebody in economics. When I left in 1923 Rock had still not made those changes which had seemed so imperative after the '21 Iowa game. He had picked up a "business manager" who was also a student; and an informal student manager who was something of a patsy because Rock was always complaining of "inefficient student managers." There was no squad doctor. He did have the luxury of a "rubber," but the rubber was Joe Bach who had transferred from St. Thomas and was ineligible to play that year. Rock had a fetish against babying the boys. He said: "We had a trainer one year—but everybody developed a lot of bruises and wanted attention. So we got rid of the trainer."

Later, of course, all of those things came—a suite of offices, an alumnus business manager, the corps of student managers, a squad doctor and a trainer. I remember the first time I came back as a New York reporter to find Rock lost in the middle of all this magnificence. He said: "I don't know what's going on around here any more."

XXXIV

John Francis O'Hara was born, of all places, at Ann Arbor, Michigan. Part of his youth was spent in South America where his father was in the consular service; young John also did various work for the government and for awhile was a cowpuncher. He entered Notre Dame at the age of twenty-one and, while there, decided to become a priest.

He was the founder of the Commerce Department and the force behind the Notre Dame Good Neighbor Policy with South America. In his term as president, 1934-39, he advanced the building program, developed the graduate school and brought to the campus many European scholars who had been driven out by the Hitler intolerance. His regime also welcomed two other distinguished visitors, President Franklin D. Roosevelt and Eugene Cardinal Pacelli, the present Pope Pius.

But Notre Dame students from 1918 to 1934 remember him as the prefect of religion who first fostered daily communion and later sold it by the *Religious Bulletin,* which he described as "an application of advertising to the spiritual life." The language of the *Bulletin* is seldom either pious or polished; the students called it "The Wit and Humor Department" in my time, knew that its form of expression was used to gain readers. It has been a tremen-

226

dous success, has attracted international attention. Notre Dame has its feet firmly on the religious ground, too.

Daily communion is a profoundly gentle experience that must be felt; its practical effect is a peace of mind that simplifies the complex business of living, for people at peace with God find it much easier to be at peace with each other. And in these days when all nations preach peace, but practice war, there might be a powerful lesson in that, expressed in the phrase: "Nations not ruled by God will be ruled by tyrants."

Bishop O'Hara is an excellent example of the Notre Dame which so successfully blends muscle and spirit, which hits hard and prays softly, renders to Caesar and to God. The daily communion program is more successful on the campus because the rugged athletes are devoted to it; the influence of the religious habits of the football squad on the outside world is described in this excerpt from a letter to Father Charles O'Donell from a Philadelphia attorney in 1930.

"I wish to thank Notre Dame, through you, for a great favor unconsciously done me by the football squad last Saturday morning, when my three boys, aged fourteen and one-half, thirteen and twelve, all attending non-Catholic schools, and all of whom play football on the lots, arose at 6:00 A.M. on their own initiative and trudged and trolleyed eight miles to St. Luke's Church in Glenside, to see the archangel of the Laity, Mr. Rockne, and his squad. The example of manly, matter-of-fact devotion to the Blessed Sacrament manifested by the Notre Dame squad and its coach impressed my boys so strongly that it is impossible to exaggerate its effects. Your men have done, unconsciously, more to back up parental example and suggestion than anybody else could possibly do.

"I now perceive the value and importance in this country, not necessarily of your remarkable football squad, but of the quiet influence of the manly religion of the members of so remarkable a squad. Be assured their influence and the effect of their example are influencing the citizens deeply. It is hard, indeed, under such circumstances, not to root for Notre Dame even if one is a University of Pennsylvania man."

That last sentence supports the contention of the anonymous Conference school head to Grantland Rice. But is it bad? Is this something for Notre Dame to eliminate in order to get football games?

It was, by his own testimony, this quiet example of manly religion by his football men that finally converted Rockne. It was not an overnight change, and it was not done lightly. He worked it out through mind, heart and soul. At the time of his death, a football coaching colleague, and probably a non-Catholic, wrote:

"Rockne, while a great josher and humorist, had a serious side in which belief in right and loyalty to that belief were paramount. It never was generally known but Rockne was a Scottish Rite Mason until he left that order to become a member of the Catholic Church and after that step no more loyal Catholic ever lived. It involved a side of Rockne with which few were conversant and one day when a question of religion was mentioned, I said:

"'Rock, it is so seldom a man takes such a step as you have, and one so seldom thinks of you in connection with such things, I wonder if you would mind telling me why you did that?'

"He hesitated just a moment and then answered quietly: 'Why should I mind telling you? You know, all this hurrying and battling we're going through is just an expression of our inner selves striving for something better. The way I look at it is that we're all here to try to find, each in his own way, the best road to our ultimate goal. I believe I've found my way and I shall travel it to the end.'"

He made his first communion on the morning of the Northwestern game in 1925 because that happened to be the day when his son, K. K. Junior, was making his and he wanted to surprise the little boy who did not know that his father had been baptized the day before. It was to be expected that his team would want to give him a victory that afternoon; but perhaps they were trying too hard. At half-time the score was 10-0 against them. Rock came to the dressing room door, made his shortest and one of his most effective speeches:

"Oh, pardon me—I thought this was the *Notre Dame* team."

He closed the door, went up into the stands for the third period—but was back on the bench in time to help them get across the second touchdown for a 13-10 victory, one of the most treasured in Irish annals. But the boy who made it possible was Rex Enright—a Protestant.

This spiritual aspect of Notre Dame football was shielded from publicity until photographers, meeting the squad at Albany in 1921 for routine pictures, followed them to Farrell Institute where they received communion at the Grotto of Lourdes. But there was much more to it, something even I, who lived with the squad, did not know until two years later when, on the morning we were to leave for the Army game, I stopped in Sacred Heart Church for a visit.

The football squad was there with Father O'Hara. There had been some publicity from the East that Elsie Janis, a musical comedy star, was going to "kick off" for Army. Father O'Hara said: "Elsie Janis will kick off for Army. Joan of Arc will kick off for Notre Dame." He gave each of us a Joan of Arc medal. It was then I learned that he had been giving medals before each game.

Elsie Janis was on the Army sidelines, sure enough; and she rode the Army mule. But Joan of Arc beat her 13-0. And in case there should be any doubt about it, nobody expected valiant Joan to make any tackles.

This game, the first played away from West Point, was to have been staged at one of the New York baseball parks but was shifted to Ebbets Field when the Giants and Yankees both got into the world series. Because of the series competition there was some worry about the crowd; but we just didn't know Brooklyn. The gates were closed an hour before the kickoff and mounted cops patrolled the thousands who were shut out. The press box was on the sidelines, which, with Elsie and her mule, made it a bit crowded for me and the four wires I was filing for Chicago and South Bend papers.

The rest of that season was a breeze—except for the villainous Cornhuskers who beat us again at Lincoln, 14-7. Nebraska was very good in those days, particularly against Notre Dame; and maybe they did have our number that afternoon because the team lacked its usual stretch-kick. It was in the sorrowful last period that Rock told Max Houser he was saving him "for the junior prom." But there's a sequel to that famous *bon mot*. Max finally did get in; and his clean uniform was greeted with a derisive: "Well, you Irish Catholic soandso, when is Rockne gonna send in the Pope?"

Max said to one of the other Cornhuskers: "Somebody ought to tell that silly soandso I'm a Presbyterian."

The 1924 Army game was played at the Polo Grounds, which was also too small for the crowd. It was moved the next year to the Yankee Stadium where it remained, except for the 1930 contest at Soldier's Field, until it got too big for the Stadium, too.

The Studebaker agency in New York furnished a fleet of cars to transport the team from the old Belmont Hotel to the Polo Grounds. I was in the first car with Rock and Walter Eckersall, who was to be one of the officials. We followed a motorcycle escort through the New York traffic. Rock got a big kick out of it, said, when we got out: "I've had my thrill—I don't care who wins the football game." Not much!

He got plenty more thrills during the game, a tight 13-7 victory in which Captain Adam Walsh started with one broken hand and came out with another. Another big and continuing thrill, that was to carry through football history, came out of that game; for, when it was over, Grantland Rice, searching for one of his colorful leads, came up with this:

"Outlined against a blue-gray October sky, the Four Horsemen rode again. In dramatic lore they are known as Famine, Pestilence, Destruction and Death. These are only aliases. Their real names are Stuhldreher, Miller, Crowley and Layden."

The next week George Strickler photographed them on horses and the boys have been riding ever since.

The order in which Rice listed the names is interesting to me. Maybe Stuhlie was first because he was the quarterback or maybe he had an unusually good day. I have never honestly been able to say one was better than the other. They were all good every day and each took turns running solo through their final year with only the 13-6 Northwestern game at all close. Their old nemesis Nebraska did give them a brief pause by scoring first —but the Horsemen rode over their jinx 34-6, and went all out in a final explosive burst in the 27-10 victory over Stanford in the 1925 Rose Bowl game that marked the only clash between the two great masters of the era—Rockne and Pop Warner. It was Layden's turn to star at Pasadena with three touchdowns and a punting average of fifty yards; but light-hearted Crowley played himself into exhaustion and a hospital bed; Stuhldreher finished with a broken bone in his foot; and Miller was in there all afternoon, too.

The Horsemen deserve their place in gridiron history as the most brilliant backfield of all time—and the fortuitous nickname preserves their fame. Among their other qualifications was an almost miraculous invulnerability. Their only "lost-time" accident came when Miller missed the final two games in 1923 with a broken rib—again by courtesy of Butler's Married Men.

The Horsemen had, obviously, efficient support from the Seven Mules in their senior year and the other stalwarts who were in front of them at various times; but in this case I believe it can be said that the backs were not only superlative on offense but

231

actually made the line look better because of their savvy, speed, diagnosis of plays and sharp true tackling. They all went into coaching, but Stuhldreher is the only member of the quartet still active in football. Miller is now United States Attorney in the Cleveland district; Layden and Crowley have successful business posts.

Of the Mules, Rip Miller is assistant athletic director at Navy, Adam Walsh is back coaching at Bowdoin after a pro stretch, and Joe Bach is in pro ball. Noble Kizer died in harness at Purdue and John Weible shortly after he had become a doctor. Vince Harrington, one of the second-string guards, served in Congress from Iowa, resigned to become a major in the Air Corps and died while on duty in England. Chuck Collins and Ed Huntzinger are in business after long coaching careers.

The shock-troop backfield men, who seldom got their names in the papers but would have been regulars under less monopolistic conditions, included Red "Snaky-Hips" Maher, "Young Dutch" Bergman, Bill Cerney, Rex Enright, Doc Connell, Frank Reese and Bernie Livergood.

Other linemen, who served as regulars or subs during the Horsemen's three years, included my old roommate Glenn "Judge" Carberry, the '22 captain; Dr. Harvey Brown, '23 captain; Clem Crowe, Gene Mayl, Tim Murphy, Fod Cotton, Ed Degree, George Vergara, Paul McNulty, Gene Oberst, John Flynn, Joe Boland, Wilbur Eaton, Joe Harmon, Joe Maxwell, John McMullan (the third-stringer who twice stopped Ernie Nevers on the two-yard line in the Rose Bowl game) and Gus Stange, who had a long black bearskin coat and also, reportedly, fifteen million bucks—which the boys never held against him because he was a nice guy and a first-string tackle.

No story of Notre Dame life would be complete without mentioning the Ghost of Washington Hall who, if he or she *was* a creation of rascals who lived there, was certainly a most convincing one. They had a special bed ready for those who wished to spend a night with the ghost. I once did, in the line of duty, with a philosopher named Schmidt, who was seriously investigating, and with Doc Connell, a football gay-boy, who was there for the hellofit. Our hosts told us all the stories and left us. Things were quiet for awhile but Doc got bored and yelled:

"Come on, you devils, come on."

Immediately there were three resounding cracks on the ceiling, which might have come from a pool cue in the hands of Clarence Manion, the present dean of the Law School and once a candidate for U. S. Senator. But we started praying—even Doc. The ghost was around for quite a spell and has never been adequately explained, at least not to me.

John "Black Horse" Flynn was one of those big guys with artistic urges. He was a good writer, did a school song, and a lot of other things I won't mention. He was in both wars, is a Cleveland lawyer but probably should have been an actor; and he left a monument at Notre Dame, the first of the annual Monogram Minstrel Shows. The cast was all-athlete and mostly football-players, with the exception of a specialty by a couple of guys who did well later on, Charles Butterworth of motion pictures and musical comedy; and Ralph Dumke of radio, one of the old Sisters of the Skillet. Walter O'Keefe was also a student in my time, served on the *Scholastic* and did specialties with the Glee Club.

Vincent Fagan's "Hike Song," which has endured, was presented in the first Monogram show. Gus Stange led the orchestra, Harry Stuhldreher did a specialty and Judge Kiley sang "My Buddy." Musical direction was by Rev. J. Hugh O'Donnell, the beloved Pepper.

And guess who was in the orchestra—with his lucky flute but probably bossing everything?

K. K. Rockne.

There was another young fellow on the campus then who was not an athlete but knew everything that went on in that field, as he does today. He was the campus leader, the first president of the Student Activities Committee, very smooth and so competent in all things, that, for a few days, he even wrote my column "Quad Wrangles" while I was on an Army trip. After graduation he started a promising career with Studebaker—but after two years of that joined the Order. His room, through the years, served as reunion headquarters for our class and we always knew he would grow up to be President, which he did and is. At the '48 commencement he invited his old boss, Paul Hoffman, the Marshall Plan man, to make the chief address.

John J. Cavanaugh's job is to coach Notre Dame to the national championship in scholarship, leadership and research. He is also getting the material but could use additional facilities. Can anybody spare twenty million bucks—or any part of it?

XXXV

In his first six seasons at Notre Dame Frank Leahy had 50 victories, 3 defeats and 5 ties, with one perfect season, '47, and three undefeated but once-tied, '41, '46 and '48—a record unapproached by his contemporaries.

Rockne, in his first six years of normal coaching (omitting the 1918 informal wartime), won 55, lost 3 and had one tie; three perfect seasons; his three defeats were by three, eight and seven points and in only one of these, against Nebraska in '23, was his team convincingly out-played and "upset."

Rockne had the advantage of continuous tenure and system and, in his earlier years, a few more pushovers; while Leahy faced three conditions usually rated as handicaps: In '41 he took over an unfamiliar squad; in '42 he changed systems; and in '46 he returned from two years in the service. But the pupil took over an established business and an efficient organization; whereas the master, in addition to his coaching job, built up the business as he went, pioneered so importantly that he influenced the development of the game on a national scale—and did all of this with practically no help.

For the first six years, and Leahy would be first to agree, Rockne did a job that stands alone in football; one that, in the foreseeable future, may never even be threatened.

But his record for the next four seasons, '25-'28, was a very ordinary 28 won, 8 lost and 2 tied. In perspective the reasons are apparent enough. After the '24 campaign his personnel losses went down into the third team; the schedules were getting tougher and travel handicaps increased; beating Rockne became a challenge and his teams were extensively scouted and pointed for; he had begun to give away his own secrets in summer coaching schools and opponents had begun to hire his men as assistants.

More important than any of this, however, was the fact that he had been abusing even such a powerhouse of talent and energy as his own by embarking on summer coaching, lecturing, newspaper, magazine and radio. He did this because he liked to do new things—and because he could use the money for his growing family needs. It is a curious fact that Rockne never drew a big salary at Notre Dame; the figures were never released but I doubt if he ever received more than $11,000 a year; and contrary to one of the rumors, he got no "cut" of the gates he was building up.

The University did permit him to engage in lucrative sidelines; but there is no thing like a sure thing. The Columbia offer, for instance, totalled $25,000, part of which would have been for teaching chemistry; and while he may have been somewhat restricted, he might have even made more outside money in the lush pasture of Manhattan. Ohio State was willing to agree to outside activities which, with his salary, Rock estimated would total $35,000 a year. Recently I heard from a reliable authority that one of his later offers, from Southern California and implemented by one of the oil fortunes, would have totalled a staggering annual $100,000.

Yet he stayed at Notre Dame; and at the time of his death he is reported to have signed motion picture contracts that would have brought his total yearly take to $100,000. Had he lived, so fruitful were his facets, he might eventually have had even a $200,000 year. He was snuffed out as he was reaching for

236

the jackpot; but part of it did come to his family from two motion pictures based largely on his career; and it might be added that the University was much more generous in these matters than Hollywood.

Rock was a wonderful businessman for Notre Dame and all of football; but like many another genius, a poor one for himself. He was a sucker for touches on his purse and, much more important, the personal treasure of his time and energies. I never knew a man more genuinely eager to help his fellowman, more generous with praise where he thought it would do most good, more flattered and pleased to be asked for help or advice. And I know of no bit of writing which better caught all these aspects of Rockne, than this column by Westbrook Pegler in 1930—to which Rock, incidentally, took violent objection.

NOBODY'S BUSINESS

NEW YORK, Dec. 13—At my first glimpse of him, close-up, Knute Rockne had the typical appearance of the old, punched-up preliminary fighter who becomes doortender in a speakeasy and sits at a shadowy table in a corner near the door at night, recalling the time he fought Billy Papke in Peoria for $50. His nose is a bit mashed and his skull is more nude than otherwise. Maybe he was a preliminary fighter. I have heard so, but never have thought to ask him about it.

On this night, several years ago, he was sitting at the head of a table in a small, compact and chummy gathering of New York alumni of the University of Notre Dame, nervously gulping draughts of smoke from a soggy cigar butt. Frank Wallace, then a recent alumnus of the university, who has lately written a football novel called *Huddle* about Rockne and the Notre Dame teams, was the master of such little ceremonies as there were.

237

He would cast an eye about the room and light on some cringing and apprehensive victim and say, "And now we are going to hear from Brother So-and-So."

Thereupon, Brother So-and-So would rise slowly and begin, "Well, fellows, I haven't got much to say. I didn't expect to be called on for any speech. I just came down here to see old Rock and some of the fellows and have a couple of drinks."

Then, after some more hemming and hawing, painful to all concerned, Brother So-and-So would allow his voice to die away in a blurry mumble and sit down, reaching for the quart to refresh his glass and to compose himself.

It was not until Brother Wallace—they were all brother to one another—called upon Brother Rockne for some remarks that Brother Rockne began to justify his reputation. He spoke in a jerky manner, as though he felt that it was all nonsense for him to try to enlighten or entertain those fellow alumni of his, but there was a light of humor in his eyes and a plain, frank intelligence in his comments and, altogether, it was like an old, battered oil can giving champagne.

I have mentioned the drinks at this meeting merely because drinks are customary at all alumni jollifications and at most reunions of the old athletes, including the coaches. There is belief that such occasions are enlivened by nothing more stimulating than tea, coffee, and buttermilk, but this is a mistake. However, I do not recall whether Mr. Rockne, himself, used to drink with the boys in his social moments or abstain. Nowadays, I suppose, he does abstain, because his health has not been good for a year and more.

But I am sure that any one who really wants to know whether Knute Rockne likes a drink or whether he used to take a few now and again can find out by asking him. On the morality of liquor he is a liberal, unlike Mr. Stagg and Mr. Yost, who take prohibition seriously and even testify to its fine effects.

I see Mr. Rockne as a modest man who does not think much of himself, who is constantly amazed to find himself a great national celebrity, and who therefore wants to make all the money he can while he can, lest the public suddenly get next to him. He has a certain kind of confidence, but not much assurance, as though always apprehensive that someone will put him to the necessity of proving that he is a great man. Sometimes, when he predicts that his team will lose a football game, he merely wants to tighten up his players, but I imagine that most times when he says such things he is actually low-rating his own as he privately low-rates himself.

If he were fully assured of his importance he would not burden himself with some of the obligations that he constantly assumes. Last winter, in Florida, for instance, some promoter imposed on Rockne's reputation to declare a "Knute Rockne Night" at a dog track, and Knute, not wishing to seem arrogant or ungrateful, was intending to be present, although the state of his health was pretty bad, just so the promoter and the promoter's customers would not think Rockne had snubbed them. On another day, although it was dangerous for him to be on his feet, some high school principal prevailed upon him to visit the school and address the students on sport. The compliment, he thought, deserved the sacrifice, and it was not long after this that he was on his way back home to see his doctor about a relapse.

Of course Knute now gets more good football players from whom to select his teams than any other coach in the land, but it is the success of the Rockne teams that brings them there. A young football player who wants to play with the best team in the country or none at all goes to Notre Dame.

Rockne is so good and draws such good players that he can afford to insist upon the strictest amateurism and he tells of calling up a business man in South Bend who had given a switchboard job to one of his stars to complain because the boy's pay was too high. A certain amount, about $10 a week, was all right. The boy needed the money and the work was worth it. But $25 was an indirect subsidy.

Gradually Mr. Rockne has developed into a showman and this has necessitated some little change in his natural character for his platform appearances. But there is money in this and there is no telling what work he will be induced to try in time, while his market is good, for he wants to be independent.

If the public insists on regarding him as one of the greatest Americans of his time and paying him a fortune for chattering the same sort of conversation that he normally gives away by the hour to his friends, far be it from Mr. Rockne to dispute the customers or refuse their money.

Brother Pegler fancied it up here and there, even in those days. This was an alumni smoker in the Roosevelt Hotel, about 1926, at which Rock spoke to a carefully selected group of sports writers on the attempt then being made to legislate against the shift; and though that eventually was done, this speech definitely delayed the action. Rock was already fluent in delivery—and the master of ceremonies also had a most excellent and polished diction, with none of them there Brothers; but the plug for *Huddle* was much appreciated.

There may have been a little of the amber fluid in the tumblers; and if so, Rock might have lubricated his vocals; but to answer Peg's query, Rock was never more than a one-or-two-drink man. I was with him as much as the next one under all sorts of conditions but I never saw him even tipsy. He had the fountain of energy and gayety within him, as children do, never needed the artificial stimulant. The only habit he had that is usually considered injurious was cigar-smoking; but he didn't smoke them so much as he spun them expertly in his fingers while impatiently waiting for the other guy to finish so Rock could demolish his argument with the next powerful point.

This was one of Pegler's kinder efforts and I thought he had caught some essential things that Rock probably had never even known about himself. But Rock just didn't like to have people probing into his private self; and while I never thought he considered himself a handsome devil, he definitely did not like that crack about the battered oil can, even if it did give off champagne.

Pegler had been an obsession with him ever since he had grouped Rock among the ghost-written morons. As a friend of both I tried to explain each to the other; once I even got them to shake hands; but Peg ruined that with the column he wrote the very next day, one he may have thought temperate but which had such an effect on Rock that, in our discussion about it, he left the table and walked away from me, for the second time in our experience.

Rock's head must have been a roaring cave, most of the time, of facts, feuds and fancies. I think he liked it that way, had to live that way, would have injured himself more if he had tried to dam it all up, for from such come psychoses—followed by psychiatrists. (It would have been interesting to have watched somebody try to psychoanalyze Rock—and see who ran out screaming.) In addition to everything else, he was working out his personal religious problem and fighting the University for his stadium. Finally, even his superb organisms could not carry the load; he began to show

241

the strain after the '25 season, which was also about the time of the Columbia episode, when he actually came to me for advice, seemed ready to lean on somebody else, looked weak and uncertain.

Faithful Joe Byrne stepped in, prescribed a trip to Europe and went along. Joe reports that the boat trip over proved so salutary that his patient proceeded to take the continent apart with the same zest with which he had attacked every new experience. This was probably the first and perhaps the only complete vacation Rockne ever had; it was also the most fortuitous timeout he ever called; for he came back with all his batteries charged and, except for the depressive moments of his illness with phlebitis, he never ran down again.

Even at home he was always buzzing. He was a devoted father of four children, gave them a full quota of his time; but his mind was never off his work; he used to practice his new stories on his three boys while giving them their baths. I once visited him with Tom Lieb while he was in bed with phlebitis; he was supposed to have his mind off football; but as soon as his wife left the room he reached under his pillow and came up with a new diagram for a triple-spinner. Mrs. Rockne told me recently that Cap Edwards was the only person who ever really slowed down the dynamo. She came into the sick room once to find Cap asleep in the chair and Rock asleep in the bed.

On the field he was engaged in one big game after another in these middle years. People expected him to pull "rabbits out of the hat"—his own phrase—so he did his best to oblige and was never happier than after he had pulled one out. Off the field there was little happening in football in which he was not involved. In 1927, for instance, after my first magazine article in *Scribner's*, I was asked by a Providence woman's club if I would debate the subject of subsidization with "a prominent coach" who was to appear on their lecture program. The coach turned out to be K. K. Rockne—who had helped me with the article. I put it up to him and he said: "Okay—we'll give them both sides of it, give them a good show." But it never came off, which was probably just as well for me; I might have been the show.

He was, among other things, leading the fight of the coaching profession for prestige and security—even to the point of threatened rebellion against the Rules Committee previously described. And he followed through on this by never making a colleague look any worse than he had to on the field—a refreshing contrast from some of the present mentors who drive victorious chariots over outclassed foes while pursuing bowl games, championship ratings and personal awards for themselves and their stars. Rock was a team man all the way.

Since he was mixed up in so much of football he sometimes became involved in delicate situations. One of these was the Army-Navy break in the late Twenties over the playing of graduates from other schools; both did it but Army had an advantage because its older entering age allowed boys to come in whom Navy couldn't take. I got the idea of doing a magazine article from the background of the Academies and Rock gave me a letter to Biff Jones, who arranged for me to live at West Point for a few days. Biff then gave me a note to Scrappy Kessing at Navy and I did the same down there. I came out without scratches but Rock did not.

Since he was playing both schools, and the feud had become bitter, he had to do some fancy skating. Pressure was put on and inevitably the ice began to crack. I was called to West Point, not as a sports writer but as a friend of Rockne and a Notre Dame insider. Army felt that Rock had sided with Navy on a point which I now forget; and Colonel Koehler, the grand old Master of the Sword, who had always been very fond of Rock, felt particularly let down. They had a publicity release prepared which would, in effect, have forced Notre Dame to choose between Army and Navy.

I asked them to hold off until I could get in touch with Rock, said that from what I knew of his feeling about Army, I was sure there had been a mistake. Rock was shocked when I called him, immediately got in touch with Army and squared the rap. Army later released the story, but probably as a tactical maneuver, because the sting was out of it; and nobody much read it because it came on the day in 1929 which Wall Street calls Black Friday— and which historians might some day refer to as the beginning of the end of an American era. Anyhow, sports wound up among the ads that day.

This is the first time I have ever told this story of what almost happened to Army-Notre Dame relations twenty years ago. Times do change. For at that time Army was the school under fire, as Notre Dame now is, because its teams were too good; too good even for Rockne for awhile. In '25, Army, with Lighthorse Harry Wilson, Tiny Hewitt and other imports, gave Rock a 27-0 licking—the worst he ever experienced. The next year Notre Dame won 7-0 because of a 62-yard dash known in football history as Flanagan's Run. In '27 Chris Cagle, who for my money was one of the great backs of history, led the Cadets to an 18-0 victory.

In those three years Army scored 45 points to Notre Dame's 7. That doesn't compare with the 107-0 edge Earl Blaik's great Blanchard-Davis wartime unit ran up on the Irish just before the series went bust; but it is by far the greatest margin ever scored against Rockne or against Notre Dame under normal peacetime conditions. The coach who holds that honor is Biff Jones; and from the Notre Dame viewpoint it couldn't have happened to a nicer guy. Notre Dame still considers Biff Jones as good a friend as it ever had in football.

XXXVI

When Rockne was killed Will Rogers wrote: "We are becoming so hardened by misfortune and bad luck that comes along that it takes a mighty big calamity to shock all this country at once. But, Knute, you did it, just as you have come from behind all your life and fooled 'em where they thought you didn't have a chance. We thought it would take a President or a great public man's death to make a whole nation, regardless of age, race or creed, shake their heads in real, sincere sorrow and say, 'Ain't it a shame he's gone?' Well, that's what this country did today, Knute, for you. You died one of our national heroes. Notre Dame was your address but every gridiron in America was your home."

Herbert Hoover, President of the United States, wired: "I know that every American grieves with you. Mr. Rockne so contributed to a cleanness and high purpose and sportsmanship in athletics that his passing is a national loss."

The Notre Dame *Alumnus* put out a special edition, thick enough for a book in itself, of such tributes from all over the country and from other parts of the world. There were telegrams, letters, news stories, editorials, columns and poems—from kings and presidents, pundits and critics, coaches and crippled children. Rockne would have been amazed as any reader of today, unfamiliar with his life and times, at this phenomenal reaction to the death of a football coach.

He was, of course, more than a football coach. He had become a modern myth, a great star of the living theater; but also a warm-hearted human being who could be mourned sincerely because he had excited none of the intense partisan feeling which even death does not seem to remove from the memory of a great man of political affairs. People who had never seen him felt that they knew him because he had lived continuously in the print and air waves that came into their homes. Whatever happened to him had become news; and things were always happening to him.

In his last three years, he had run the gamut from failure to exalted triumph—had gone out at the top, and those are the people remembered. I believe, if they had a choice, they might even prefer it that way. Rockne, certainly, would have been a most unhappy man if he had lived for that inevitable day when the parade would have passed him by. There were times when that day seemed to have come; and I saw him in those times.

1928 opened without a cloud in the sky.

Without warning the sky fell—stars, moons, clouds—the works. Rock had his "bad" season—a winning season, five wins and four losses, but very bad for him.

In the afterlight the picture is clear enough—an old familiar picture at the football schools which reveals why success moves in cycles, why teams go up and down, why coaches and their faithful bird dogs hunt from dawn to twilight, regardless of any ideas their own faculty men or the N.C.A.A. theorists may have on the subject. The coaches, hard-bitten by experience, know that if they are to play big-league football, draw the crowds, satisfy the alumni *and* the faculty, win—they've got to keep those boys coming in, the best boys, lots of them, never enough of them.

Rockne knew that; but in the hurly-burly of his outside activities he had become a little careless, taken the inflow for granted; and another subtle influence had been at work. Bird dogs from other schools had been using this effective argument with

246

prep school stars: "Why go to Notre Dame and sit on the bench? At our place you can be a regular."

In 1928 Rockne's first string was not physically sound— chiefly, his triple-threat star, Johnny Niemiec, whose leg injury, received the previous year, had not responded to treatment. Other key injuries came but the replacements were not adequate; he did have a fine group of sophomores but these could not be got ready in time. The greatest coach of all time learned anew the lesson that a squad with championship aspirations cannot depend upon sophomores but must have that backlog of seasoned upper-classmen to hold the fort while the sophomores are learning the ropes.

The tip-off came in the first game when the squad was held 12-6 by Loyola of New Orleans—a game originally scheduled only as a favor to coach Clark Shaughnessy. The next week the bad news was there for everybody to see: Wisconsin 22, Notre Dame 6. Fullback Collins broke a wrist—and worse, the team looked blundering and dumb! They only skimmed by Navy 7-0 as Niemiec passed to Colrick in the last period; for Notre Dame, a dull encounter.

Rock badly needed a fullback, so he went to work on the finest bundle of sophomore football flesh I have ever seen—a boy weighing two hundred pounds, with great speed and the physique of a hero of mythology, but who knew nothing but how to run. In one week Rock tried to do what he ordinarily would have done in two years—make a regular of Joe Savoldi; but on the first scrimmage play Georgia Tech passed over him for a touchdown and that was all for Big Joe that year. The team got back some confidence against Drake and then eased by a fair Penn State squad.

Undefeated Army was waiting, the team that had scored 45 points to Notre Dame's 7 in the three preceding years; waiting with Red Cagle at the top of his form.

George Gipp had said: "Some day, Rock, when the going is real tough, ask the boys to beat Army for me."

This was the day.

I had picked Notre Dame in my paper as a sentimental sort of a prayer but waited in the press box, prepared for the inevitable. They even looked like boys against men as they ran out on the field; but I didn't know what Rock had told them in the dressing room—or that a tall tackle had knocked himself out by running into a concrete overhead as he rushed blindly from the room.

I was pleasantly surprised when Army didn't seem to go anywhere at the start; when my little team began to punch-punch-punch like a drill press through that big and terrifying Army line; when they didn't stop short of the goal, when Collins, with his wrist in a cast, went over.

The ball popped out of his hands!

Army recovered and we lost that miracle touchdown. (The present automatic-touchdown rule was not then in the book.)

Now I waited for it to happen—for Army to roar and rush. But instead, my little guys came back like bicycles through heavy traffic, and this time Chevigny went over, held the ball, yelled: "There's one for the Gipper."

He did say that. I checked it with Niemiec, my home town boy whom I had personally bird dogged into Notre Dame, and who told me that, regardless of how I may have felt in the press box, there was never any doubt in the minds of the team on the field about their ability to win. He said they seemed very calm and workmanlike about it rather than emotional. They had prayed some at the beginning; but then Moynihan, the Chicago cowboy, said as how he 'lowed that by now the Lord knew what they wanted and would be just as well satisfied if they just went ahead and played football the best they knew how.

With the score at 6-all and three minutes to go, it was Notre Dame that was challenging, with Niemiec still in there on his one good leg, Collins with his wrist in a cast and Chevigny (nobody knows for how long) out of his head.

The ball was on the Army 20 with third down and five to

go. Chev had been running well all day "for the Gipper" and now was called to make the first down—but he missed the ball which bounced straight back with three Army linemen dashing for it—and in those days they could have picked it up and convoyed all the way, which was what they probably would have done; but Chev's instinct beat them to it. Then they asked him the usual questions: he didn't know what day it was and out he came, was replaced by Billy Dew. And in this confusion, for the crowd was turbulent and both benches fluid, the tall sophomore end came in. Carideo had already called the pass play and O'Brien's entrance confirmed it.

"It was a regular reverse pass," Niemiec said. "I got good blocking and had plenty of time to throw. I saw O'Brien was in the clear and knew the play would be good." Just like that, he said it and probably felt it—which gives you an idea of the poise of those young fellows on the field while the adult crowd goes mad.

"He juggled it for a second—and then fell over."

The boys replay those games years after; and once around a lunch table at the Paramount commissary in Hollywood, Moon Mullins told us what he had said to his pal O'Brien: "I told him if he hadn't caught it, he might as well have kept on going."

"I juggled it and fell," O'Brien chuckled, "and didn't know I was over the goal line."

Collins had quipped after his fumble on that same goal line: "Imagine my embarrassment—no ball."

That was what Army was up against that day, Notre Dame with all stops out—think, fight, pray, work, fun.

What happened after that score explains Rock's statement to the team before the 1930 Army game: "Army never quits."

Cagle got hold of the kickoff, which he was not supposed to have done, set sail with all his fury and speed behind the enraged Army blockers, passed midfield, hit the sidelines, seemed to be going all the way when Collins came across and knocked him out of

249

bounds with a shoulder block—the perfect play at the sidelines for Cagle was as hard to tackle as Blanchard or Davis in full flight.

The next two minutes were as riotous as I've ever seen at a football game, not excepting the finish at Ohio State in 1935. Cagle, on the optional pass and run, was a touchdown threat on every play, a wild man, carrying, passing, moving steadily ahead; but Army drew two five-yard penalties—and suddenly Cagle was taken out of the game and Hutchinson came in.

I was never so glad to be rid of any man. Later I asked Biff Jones why he had taken Cagle out. He said time was running short —there was no electric clock for the crowd to see in those days—and Hutchinson was a better passer. Ted Twomey and Moynihan, in there at the time, told me Cagle had also been arguing in the backfield.

Hutchinson threw a pass into a mass of men on the three-yard line—and Army came up with it!

It was getting dark and the crowd was crazy. There was an argument with the officials—and through my field glasses I saw an Army man throw his headguard disgustedly to the ground. That gave me the first tip that the game might be over. It was.

That night Rock sat quietly, benignly happy—which was about the only time he ever really was quiet. Years later I told him the team of that day was my favorite and, I suspected, his. He didn't say it in so many words but he agreed. I think that was the favorite team of all Notre Dame people because it did the most with the least. Hunk Anderson's 1933 "goat team" did almost as well with its 13-12 victory over Army, with Nick Lukats as the star and Bud Bonar, another of my home town boys, *dropkicking* the deciding point. (Bull Poliski, a regular tackle in '26-'27, was also from Bellaire, as was Jim Harris, all-American in '32. Joe Sheekeetski, present Nevada coach, comes from Shadyside, an adjoining town; Wally Fromhart and John Lautar from Moundsville, one of our West Virginia "suburbs.")

The next afternoon, after a few of us had joined with Joe

Byrne in his traditional "U-N-D," the cheer with which he always saw the team away after an Army game, I first heard about the Gipp speech. I wrote it for the *News*, but was annoyed to see the headline the next morning: GIPP'S GHOST BEATS ARMY.

The next time I saw him, Rock said to me: "Frank, that was the first time I ever knew you to violate a confidence."

I told him that, while it hadn't been given to me in confidence, I ordinarily would have considered it so; I had thought it over, believed it an honest and sincere bit of sentiment that belonged in the Notre Dame tradition. He thought it over, nodded, seemed to understand.

The incident certainly has lived in tradition, not just of Notre Dame but of all football. I've had to make similar decisions on some of the other material I've used for the first time in this book. One difficulty in being on the inside of a legend is to decide what should be revealed outside.

Games like the '28 Army-Notre Dame are played on down through the years. Army, for instance, will smile and still insist it had first down when the game ended. Rock first told me it was our ball; I checked my charts, found it to be true—we had forgotten the two five-yard penalties—and printed the correction. That argument went on for days as the officials, including Walter Eckersall, ducked the issue—but the head linesman finally said it was Notre Dame's ball.

We still have some fun about one phase of it back in the All-American Town where Niemiec, now a gray eagle and a high school coach, has mellowed with the years and is still as calm and poised as he was when he threw that pass. But he claims he's getting a bit fed up, after twenty years, with strangers telling him all about Johnny "One-Play" O'Brien. "When I ask them who threw that pass," he complains, "they say 'Who cares?' "

Four of the chief actors in that game died violent deaths. Rock in a plane; Chevigny at Iwo Jima; O'Brien in an automobile accident as he was returning from making a speech while a member of the Irish coaching staff in 1936; and Cagle, mysteriously on a subway platform.

I was very fond of Red Cagle, who never failed to show up at the Notre Dame rallies before the Army game, along with Elmer Oliphant. The game just doesn't end on the field and the series just doesn't end when the games are no longer played—not with the Irish anyhow, who like a good fight, which they always got at Army. Notre Dame even found things to like about those 59-0 and 48-0 games in '44 and '45—our boys never stopped trying, never stopped passing, never quit.

XXXVII

The 1928 upset of Army welded the first link in a chain of dramatic events that was to lengthen, with mounting sensation, to the flaming climax of Rockne's death.

The Gridiron Vulcan was back at his forge, fashioning magic armor for Notre Dame men.

But the next week he and they were dashed again when Carnegie Tech not only made good its boast of being an Irish jinx but gave Notre Dame that first defeat at home in twenty-two years.

Rockne continued to break records—of a different sort. At Los Angeles the following Saturday he failed, for the only time in his career, to bring his team back from a defeat; he lost his first game of the Southern Cal series, and to his old Iowa rival, Howard Jones.

But Rockne had been Rockne, fighting to live always, thinking only in terms of victory. He had drawn everything out of his bank to upset Army; when the other two came there was nothing left—physical, emotional or spiritual. Just a hollow squad, dead broke.

They began to say then that old Rock was over the hill, that the parade had passed him by; and when the phlebitis hit him they were sure that the '28 Army upset had been the last gasp of a great master.

For a lesser man it might have been; but Rockne was willing to risk his life to get back on top in that '29 Carnegie Tech game which must have been as sweet, and as deserving, a personal victory as any man has ever won.

And by now he had done something else. Coaching mostly by remote control, he had his system of player development back in smooth operation. He had a fine first unit with Carideo, Brill, Elder and Mullins in the backfield—Captain Law, Moynihan, Cannon, Twomey, Leahy, Colrick and Conley in the line. He had his shock troops—Schwartz, Savoldi, O'Connor, Gebert, Yarr, Kassis, Metzger, Donoghue, Culver, O'Brien and Kosky; and he was using a third string, mostly sophomore, for mopping up.

By the time Southern Cal came to Chicago he had already defeated three of the schools which had beaten him the year before; against the Trojans he again took a chance on his life to wipe that slate clean; after Elder's run against Army on that bitter cold day, he had his fourth perfect season in eleven years.

Rockne was on top again—with a national championship.

He was going to stay on top—after the most spectacular season any college team has ever gone through, one full worthy to climax the career of the master dramatist of the outdoor stage.

He now had his own theater—the long-awaited stadium, to which the storied sod of the old field had been transplanted, not merely as a sentimental Irish gesture but because it happens to be about the best turf in football. There has never been a muddy playing field at Notre Dame despite all that South Bend rain.

And Rockne was his old self again. He still wrapped his leg in a rubber bandage but he made a joke of that, called it his "spare tire." He was full of the old fight, zip and wisecracks, rarin' to get out there and crack 'em again.

Southern Methodist had the honor of playing the first game in the new stadium—and set the dramatic pace for the season by almost spoiling the party with a passing attack that had the score 14-all with four minutes to go. Then Marchy Schwartz, the Barrymore of this company, wrapped up the 20-14 victory.

Joe Savoldi had run a kickoff back 98 yards for the first Irish tally—and there was the story of one of Rockne's finest bits of individual coaching. Big Joe, crushed by failure as a sophomore, had not been of any real value until midway during his junior year—and then only after Rock had done a job of ego-salvaging which any psychiatrist would have applauded.

Joe still had things to learn about pass defense and blocking when, because of an injury to Larry Mullins, he started at full-back against Navy in the formal dedication of the stadium. But he could sure go to Touchdown Town, rambled for three in the 26-2 triumph.

Carnegie was coming—tougher than ever. This one was for blood. The Tartans were primed to reassert dominance. Notre Dame had another blot to erase from the '28 season—that home defeat, and none too gentle either, against a worn-out team. These regulars had been sophomores and remembered well the day.

There was also an individual joust involved. Every team has its strong man—Tech had Johnny Karcis, "the human cement barrel"; Notre Dame had Marty Brill. They had met head-on the year before and Brill had bounced back a little. In the early stages of this 1930 game, almost as if it had been arranged, the line opened and Karcis came bowling through. Brill came from his right halfback spot, they met—and this time Karcis bounced back.

To my mind that was the key play of the game and the season for both teams. Neither Karcis nor Carnegie were impressive thereafter—but Notre Dame, with a new confidence, went on not only to its greatest season but to what I believe was the finest execution of football plays ever seen on the college gridiron.

After such an emotional battle as against Tech, there was

always the danger of a letdown—and all that was coming up the next week was a Sutherland Pitt squad which had also been undefeated the year before and had gone to the Rose Bowl where it had lost to Southern Cal. This was to be the "national championship" battle of 1930, since the Trojans had already been defeated in an early game.

Notre Dame, with Schwartz leading the way, scored 35 points in the first half—and later Sutherland said, "Rockne could have made it 100."

Indiana was taken in hand 27-0.

Next was Penn, the Ivy League—and another human interest story. Brill had been at Penn as a freshman, had left embittered and come to Notre Dame to play for the best. Now he was going back to Penn and his personal vendetta was stressed in the press.

Brill was supposed to be just a blocker—but he broke the Penn game wide open with a 65-yard gallop Grantland Rice called "the finest run a football field has ever seen and it shattered the Red and Blue—a first class team." Rice continued: "Notre Dame's first team actually beat Penn 43-0 in less than 30 minutes of play. Rockne and Notre Dame passed on far beyond the Four Horsemen. With Carideo, Brill, Savoldi and Schwartz they put on a combination of four antelopes, four charging buffaloes, four dig-digs and four eels."

That was, I believe, the top day of all time for any college football team. They were so good that I asked Rock what was happening. He shrugged and said: "They're just taking the stuff, doing things right." He also said he hadn't had much to do with what had gone on that day—that the boys had taken charge, said it was Marty's day. Brill had made two other touchdowns and out of this game came a report, still printed now and then, that his father had promised and given him $1,000 for each touchdown against Penn. Both have assured me there was nothing to that. Marty is a great guy, one of Notre Dame's most beloved Protestants.

Penn was Joe Savoldi's last game. He had made two bad mistakes for a Notre Dame football player: *1. Marriage. 2. Divorce.*

He should have been the modern Jim Thorpe and might have been if he had played three full seasons, for he was just beginning to learn the game when he finished. One thing is dead certain— he was the best darned second-stringer you will ever see; and not bad with the Cloak-and-Dagger squad in Italy during the war— where his football and wrestling reputation had preceded him.

His departure left quite a gap. Mullins came back but his leg was not quite ready and, against Drake the next week, Dan Hanley, a sophomore, played quite a bit of the ball game.

The three big ones were now coming up—ever one a thriller, each with that special dramatic situation almost every Notre Dame game had had for two full seasons. Would you believe, for instance, that this super-team, after it had won eighteen straight against the best, would go into its final battle against a *beaten* Trojan team—as a 10-6 underdog?

XXXVIII

Northwestern *vs.* Notre Dame. The Big Ten champ *vs.* the National champ.

The Irish started as they had been going all season, running wild in the first period; but they couldn't get across.

In the second period the Wildcats twice penetrated the Irish five-yard line, but twice were stopped by two great Carideo kicks and a fighting defense, the strong man of which was Little Dynamite, 154-pound Bert Metzger, to whom Rock hadn't even wanted to give a uniform.

Without Big Joe to round out their running attack, the Irish took to the air, regained command—and with five minutes of the fourth period gone were on the enemy eighteen-yard line.

The perfect play! Schwartz did what he had done on the opening scrimmage against Pitt—bounced through behind blocks by Captain Conley, Metzger, Brill and Carideo, headed for the sideline. Only the safety man was between him and the goal—and then he was no longer there—obliterated by a flashy open-field block by Johnny O'Brien, who was much more than a one-play man.

Notre Dame had rubbed the bloom off another Conference champ.

Now Army was coming—and to Soldier's Field. Chicago was

to have its only glimpse of "the national game." And Chicago went for it as New York had always gone.

Down at Notre Dame Rockne was coaching *two* teams!

Somebody had thought up a charity game at Soldier's Field for Thanksgiving morning between the "Notre Dame All Stars" and the "Northwestern All Stars"—and Rock, with that characteristic Pegler had described, had agreed to coach the Notre Dame old grid grads *the week of the Army game.*

He wasn't getting much cooperation, either. Snows covered the field and both the varsity and the All Stars had to work out on the dirt floor of the gym. The All Stars were also doing most of their conditioning in West End beer joints. I thought it necessary to cover this peculiar training; and wound up early one morning in a taxicab with Moynihan, Cannon, Spike McAdams and a snow-white turkey somebody had won in a raffle. Moynihan had an intense desire to wring the gobbler's lily-white neck, but we talked him into a sporting competition. The Oliver lobby was deserted except for the scrubwomen. So we turned the turkey loose and let them scramble for it. Some fun—and some family had a good turkey dinner.

It was two above zero in Chicago on Thanksgiving morning. The charity game was played in the snow—before 2,000 crazy people. I didn't go, don't remember who won; but Rex Enright got a broken rib and Rock got clipped for $3,000 somewhere in the deal.

The night before the Army game the Chicago alumni had a big dinner with coaches of all the defeated teams on the Irish schedule as guests. I was asked for a few remarks—and complained that Notre Dame alumni were cheated of one of the great pleasures of other alumni because we never got a chance to fire our coach. Everybody thought it funny but Rockne who glared as he hadn't done since the days of the Sheik contest. I didn't think it was so funny, either, a few months later, after we had got rid of our coach.

The next day it rained, thundered and lightninged. The crowd went out anyhow, to see undefeated Notre Dame play once-tied Army. The rain became half sleet, the field was a slithering mess. Here was the day for the upset.

Larry Mullins was the best mudder, kept the Irish on the attack; but the Army line was strong enough, with the help of General Mud. It looked like a scoreless tie and that would have been the upset.

But from nowhere and without warning, just before the end, Schwartz and the perfect play again—this time for 54 yards through the duck soup. Carideo kicked the point in the mud—which nobody thought important. But it was.

In a half minute Army had its touchdown when Dick King blocked Carideo's punt and followed the bobbing ball across the goal line. The shivering crowd waited as Broshus, the place-kicking specialist came out with dry uniform, dry shoes; but the Irish line swarmed through and Broshus never had a chance to get the ball off the ground.

There was left only Southern Cal at Los Angeles. After their early surprise defeat, the Trojans had made their best record of all time, beaten California 74-0 and Stanford 41-12. The "Wonder Team," as the coast scribes called it with characteristic modesty, was getting better all the time. Notre Dame was obviously tailing off, Savoldi was missed, the eighteen-game victory streak was getting heavy—hence the 10-6 odds.

We were to leave Chicago at one on Sunday afternoon. At noon I caught up with Rock in his suite, as he was dictating last-minute notes to his secretary. One of the things he told her was to wire the Mayor's Committee in New York that "the game with the Giants was off."

Things were tough in the Big Town that year and Mayor Walker had organized a committee of sports writers to raise a relief fund. Their prize project was Notre Dame ex-stars *vs.* the New York Giants of the National League. Rock had agreed, as

260

usual, to do a favor for his friend Jimmy Walker, his friends the writers and his friends the needy of New York.

The argument about whether the pros or college teams were better had been whipping up. Rock was staking his own prestige, and Notre Dame's, with a collection of men like the Four Horsemen, who hadn't had a uniform on for six years, against a coordinated and conditioned professional team.

It was a bad match for Notre Dame and for college football—but most of all, for Rockne, who was rapidly going downhill again, obviously approaching another nervous collapse. None of his friends had wanted him to go through with this game. Perhaps they had convinced him; or perhaps he had had enough of sweet charity after that $3,000 clip and the close call against Army. So he had called it off. This was big news for my paper. He said I could use it and I got on the train in the spot every reporter dreams about, with a big "beat" all sewed up.

The next afternoon the telegrams caught up with Rockne at a town called Pratt, Nebraska. It seems, or so the story came from New York, that his secretary had failed to send the canceling message. All they knew about it was my story in the *News*.

Rock made it definite. For by now he had other troubles. Larry Mullins had come out of the Army game with his knee in such bad shape that he definitely could not play against the Trojans. The only fullback left was Hanley, the promising but inexperienced sophomore. Rock had faced such a situation two years before against Georgia Tech, with sad results.

He called Warren Brown and myself—the only two reporters with the team—into his drawing room. "These people out here always expect me to pull a rabbit out of the hat," he smiled, "so I'm going to try to give them one. I'm switching O'Connor to fullback—but keep that under *your* hats."

We stopped at Tucson Thursday to practice at the University of Arizona stadium. Five thousand people, including some Los Angeles sports writers, watched. The big news was the injury to Mullins; the big figure was the sophomore, Dan Hanley; the big question was: Could he come through against the mighty Trojans?

Nobody in that crowd knew that the fellow wearing the jersey with Hanley's number was Bucky O'Connor; or that the fellow wearing O'Connor's number was Hanley; that Rock was now trying to make a fullback out of a substitute halfback in *two days*.

Bill Henry, the present Washington correspondent and radio commentator, was then sports editor of the Los Angeles *Times*. Being a good newspaperman he wanted to talk to Dan Hanley, the key-man. He had looked a bit closer than the rest that afternoon, for in the hotel lobby that evening he said: "Introduce me to Hanley, will you?" And he pointed to *Bucky O'Connor*.

I was a newspaperman, and Bill was a friend. But I was a Notre Dame man—and anyhow, I had the secret in confidence, didn't I? Bill was already walking toward O'Connor; there was no way out—unless Bucky was sharp.

"*Hanley*," I said to Bucky, "this is *Bill Henry* of the Los Angeles *Times*. He wants to ask you how it feels for an unknown *sophomore* to start in the big game."

"Okay," Bucky grinned. "Let's go some place and sit down, away from this crowd."

I had other duties that night. People were calling Rock from Los Angeles about tickets. A civic club wanted him to talk to a meeting in the hotel. Calls were still coming from New York about the Giant game. Mrs. Rockne wanted Rock to get away from all this and to rest.

We talked him out of the speech. I answered the phone calls and made a lot of people mad from coast to coast. A little later I went down to the lobby to see how Bucky had made out with Bill Henry. I heard a familiar voice, looked in a room off the lobby —Rock was talking to the civic club!

Friday morning service was very slow in the private dining

262

room where the squad ate. Rock went to the regular dining room. An hour later I was in front of the hotel waiting for a cab. One pulled up and Rock got out, ready to explode.

"Aren't you going to practice?" I asked.

"Practice!" He snorted. "Nobody around this club is interested in practice. If they're not, why should I be? I'm going back to South Bend."

I had arranged for Jack Murphy, a movie man and an Irish fan, to make the trip from Chicago with the squad. He was aghast. All those people going crazy in Los Angeles about this game—and the Notre Dame coach was going back home!

I told Jack to take it easy, that I had seen this one before— back in 1923 when, the Wednesday before the Army game, the Master had walked off the practice field because he said nobody was interested in beating Army.

So we went to the field where, this day, secret practice was being held. Hunk had the first team and Chevigny the second. They were going through their drills—with one eye on the gate.

Finally Rock came in; walked slowly down the sideline, past the first team, never even glanced at them, stopped by the reserves, looked them over for a while, as if he were thinking: "If I do stay for the game, this will be my team."

Then: "Everybody up."

They came running from all directions as if pulled by a giant vacuum cleaner. He talked to them very quietly. I had an idea what it would be—and that's what it was. He was giving them the talk of the abused but magnanimous parent, which ended with the question: Were they really interested in the Southern Cal game? If they were and *wanted* him to stay—

The giant roar! Then, as if nothing whatever had happened, the wheels began to whir. It was a spirited practice, the boys worked up a good sweat—and in the showers after the workout, for the first time I heard a Notre Dame squad singing the "Victory March"—and really pouring it out.

Corn? Working on the emotions of boys? Sure.

But it won the game.

Every team has its "down" day when it is below par in performance, ready to be beaten or "upset." Rock suffered fewer such upsets because, more than any other coach I've known or heard of, he could smell that down day coming and do something about it in advance. Leahy is good at that, too, but he couldn't stop what happened in the last Southern Cal game.

The '48 Notre Dame squad was in almost the same psychological spot the '30 squad was. Long winning streak, flattery, autographs all the way out to the Coast, complacency. Rockne did have the advantage of being the underdog—if an artificial one—whereas Leahy's team was expected to win as it pleased. Leahy's squad didn't get its jolt until the last period, fumbled around most of the afternoon, never got hot until the last two minutes.

Rock's squad had gotten its jolt at Tucson, was hot all afternoon against the Trojans. The tip-off came when O'Connor, still supposed to be Hanley, moved flawlessly for 12 yards on his first call. I knew then that it was in. The Trojans had been expecting the big, slow sophomore—but they got the fast, smooth senior who had been running for plenty all season.

O'Connor scored the second touchdown with an 80-yard run which none who saw will ever forget—another perfect play from the blocking angle but climaxed by a change of pace on the sidelines which foxed the safety man. Bucky, now Doctor O'Connor, had perfected that stunt against Pitt and Penn—and he sure got ample revenge for the big eye and the embarrassment these same Trojans had given him the year before.

The Wonder Team was beaten 27-0, with third-string sophomore Nick Lukats scoring the final touchdown. The second national championship was won and the '29-'30 squad, after cementing their place in history and painting a sunburst around the end of Rockne's last game, went home very happy.

Of course nobody knew that was Rock's last game.

As a matter of fact, it wasn't. He did not go back on the train with the boys.

He flew back to coach the Four Horsemen against the New York Giants!

I doubt how much enthusiasm the old boys had about getting back into togs again, with their little fat bellies, to be bounced around by the pros. But when Rock called they all came to the post. The call had contained a query about what kind of shape they were in. Crowley's answer:

NEVER MIND ABOUT ME STOP GET THOSE LINEMEN IN SHAPE STOP

They lost, of course, for it was a bad match. But it was exactly that sort of thing that made Rockne—and made people like him.

He did another nice thing that year. Frank Leahy, regular tackle in '29, was the pathetic figure on the '30 squad, a silent fellow who walked around on a gimpy leg which had been hurt in a pre-season scrimmage. Here was another spot where a lesser man would have quit and cried; but Leahy wanted to be a coach, so he went out to do what he could and learn what he could.

Rock liked his spirit, took him on the Trojan trip as a reward. Out there, on the kitchen floor at Larry Mullins' house, Leahy further injured his leg playing, of all things, *tiddlywinks*.

Rock went to the Mayo Clinic after the Giant game for treatment. He took Leahy along, to have his leg looked after—also to have somebody to talk football with—and could he have picked a better man? They roomed together and one day Frank said his great ambition had been to be a coach but now he supposed everybody had forgotten him.

Rock reached for his morning mail, tossed the envelopes across to the other bed, said: "There are six jobs—take your pick."

Notre Dame was getting one of its men ready. Not quite a Rockne as a coach—just the next best. Not too successful as athletic director—perhaps because he had to talk people into trying to beat a guy named Leahy, which is not a popular pastime among coaches.

They've turned most of that job over to Moose Krause, who can talk as smoothly and eat as heartily as any all-American football and basketball player you ever saw. Together, Frank and Moose will try to make like Rockne; together, they'll do quite well, as they have always done together; and from the looks of their first efforts they might even make that football follow Notre Dame again, fashion a new orbit and a new schedule, not quite so social, perhaps, but sporting.

And behind the gridiron curtain, the academic engineers, the educational factory, the religious factory, the democratic factory—

Think-work-fight-pray-laugh—*win*!

Notre Dame.

XXXIX

by United Press

BAZAAR, Kansas, March 31—Knute Rockne, noted Notre
Dame football coach and eight other men were killed in
an airplane crash near here today.

Edward Baker, a farmer, was feeding stock on the
Stewart Baker farm, and was watching the plane when it
flew over.

Suddenly, he said, there was an explosion and the
ship fell to earth.

The plane was flying at low altitude because of the
cloudy weather.

Members of the Baker household heard the explosion and rushed to the scene, half a mile away.

The first flash to Emporia that Rockne was among
the dead shocked the entire world and business and industry halted while all sources of communication were
placed into service to determine the truth of the report.

(Houston, Texas, *Post-Dispatch*)

A copy desk man emerged from the Associated Press
printer room with a long string of copy.

He spread his paper before him on the desk, quickly

scanning the dispatches from Paris, New York, Washington, Detroit, Kansas City.

A few brief paragraphs told of an earthquake in Managua, Nicaragua. He paused for a moment, visualizing a streamer headline.

His eye ran down the string of copy—stock market, murder, romance, divorce. His expression was unchanged.

Suddenly the copyreader jumped from his chair. His face was white, his mouth open. In a moment he shouted:

"My God, Rockne's dead."

Like a flash the cry "Rockne's dead" reverberated through the *Post-Dispatch* plant.

It echoed through the editorial offices, ran down the stairs to the business office. Reporters, printers and executives stared speechlessly at the bit of paper upon which a mechanical telegraph instrument had impressed the words, "Rockne's dead."

It was a big story, the biggest of the year, someone suggested. But it was not of the story those newspapermen were thinking. Hard-boiled newspapermen! There were moist eyes in the group around the copy desk.

Not much like the movie version of a big story breaking in a newspaper office. But a true picture.

(Cleveland *Press*)

In the past generation it was Buffalo Bill.

For this generation it was Knute Rockne.

The boy had a profound respect for Knute Rockne. Knute Rockne had a profound respect for the boy.

By some sort of process each read the other's mind and heart. They were heroes to each other.

Millions of boys and men and girls and women bow in grief at the news that Knute Rockne is dead.

For millions he was greater than the president of the United States.

(New York *Times*)

Millions of citizens who knew nothing about Knute Rockne the man, regard his death, in President Hoover's words, as "a national loss." Outside the college world a profound sensation of regret was manifest. . . . His death in the crashed plane in Kansas, at the height of his career as a coach, produced a sensation in this country which reveals college football as a national institution.

(Youngstown *Vindicator*)

Anyone who can fire the manhood of others as he did is in every way admirable. . . . We all have latent powers that need to be stirred and awakened; Rockne did this, not merely for the men of the Notre Dame squad but for all the healthy young men of the country. Just as we learn history best through the biographies of great men, so in the chronicle of our own time, the life of Knute Rockne, exerting an extraordinary influence for good, will be remembered long after the Nicaraguan earthquake is forgotten.

(William Allen White)

We see nothing wrong in the President's expressing grief over the loss of a beloved football coach . . . but from a diplomatic angle it seems to leave out certain other deceased members of college faculties who worked with undergraduates in groups other than groups of eleven. . . . We are sorry we don't know their names.

(North Carolina *Advocate*, a Methodist publication)

He was king among men. We have not at any time met a man with greater personal magnetism—not even William Jennings Bryan.

(Bellaire, Ohio, *Leader*)

"The Soul of Knute Rockne" will be the subject of the sermon at the Sons of Israel Temple Friday evening. The sermon was delivered previously at Columbus by Rabbi Jacob Tarish, one of the outstanding rabbis of the country, and was broadcast.

The above are excerpts from the editorial content at the time. They were accompanied by news stories of the death—of the crowds that lined railroad routes as the body was returned, including 10,000 at Chicago; of the pouring into South Bend of messages from all over the world; and of thousands who were coming into the city but not, this time, for a football game; of the guard of honor established at the funeral parlor and later at the home on Good Friday; of the state funeral at Sacred Heart Church on the campus and the nationwide CBS broadcast of the services on Holy Saturday afternoon; of the stoppage of business in South Bend as six of the boys Rockne had carried to fame on the football field the preceding year—Tom Conley, Tom Yarr, Frank Carideo, Marchy Schwartz, Larry Mullins and Marty Brill —carried him to his grave at Highland Cemetery.

In his sermon Father Charles O'Donnell, President of the University, said, in part: "In this holy week of Christ's passion and death there has occurred a tragic event which accounts for our presence here today. Knute Rockne is dead. And who was he? Ask the President of the United States, who dispatched a personal message of tribute to his memory and comfort to his bereaved family. Ask the King of Norway, who sends a special delegation as his personal representatives to this solemn service. Ask the several state legislatures, now sitting, that have passed resolutions of sympathy and condolence. Ask the university senates, the civic bodies and societies without number; ask the bishops, the clergy, the religious orders, that have sent assurances of sympathy and prayers; ask the thousands of newspapermen, whose labor of love in his memory has stirred a reading public of 125,000,000 Americans; ask men and women from every walk of life; ask the children, the boys of America, ask any and all of these, who was this man whose death has struck the nation with dismay and has everywhere bowed heads in grief.

"What was the secret of his irresistible appeal to all sorts and conditions of men? Who shall pluck out the heart of his mystery and lay bare the inner source of the power he had?

"I do not know the answer. I would not dare the irreverence of guessing. But I find myself in this hour of piteous loss and pained bewilderment recalling the words of Christ: 'Thou shalt love the Lord thy God with thy whole heart. This is the first and greatest commandment. And the second is like unto this: thou shalt love thy neighbor as thyself.' I think, supremely, he loved his neighbor, his fellowman, with genuine, deep love. In an age that has stamped itself as the era of the 'go-getter'—a horrible word for what is all too often a ruthless thing—he was a 'go-giver'— a not much better word, but it means a divine thing. He made use of all the proper machinery and the legitimate methods of modern activity to be essentially not modern at all: to be quite elementarily human and Christian, giving himself, spending himself like water, not for himself, but for others. And once again, in his case, most illustriously is verified the Christian paradox—he has cast away to keep, he has lost his life to find it. This is not death but immortality."

Other sermons were preached over Rockne, like this one received by Father O'Donnell in a letter:

"Dear Father: I feel that I must express the sympathy and the heart feelings of myself and my family on the terrible loss suffered by the University of Notre Dame and the entire world in the death of Knute Rockne.

"I am the father of a crippled boy, twelve years of age. He

271

cannot leave the house, and lives on the radio. He is a great boy for baseball and football, and Knute heard of him last November at the time he was most hard pressed. He wrote Eddie a letter and sent him an autographed picture of himself.

"Father, when at noon Tuesday he heard the announcement over WTAM, Cleveland, that Knute Rockne was killed, he simply shut off the radio and cried; and when I came home that night he said: 'Dad, the best man in the world was killed, and I can't help him.' Well, Eddie and I knelt down and said the rosary for Knute, and I know he heard the little crippled boy pray for him, and I know he appreciated it.

"We sat and heard your wonderful sermon today at the funeral, and I am forty-six years old and am not ashamed to say I cried, for the whole world lost a friend when we lost Knute Rockne. And a man who would write to a crippled boy and try to make his life happier under the conditions Knute was fighting under last fall, is a MAN.

"Knute's picture is draped in black in my home tonight, and the kiddies all knelt before it and said the rosary for Knute Rockne. But little Dick, six years old, said: 'Dad, will there be a Notre Dame next year?' I said, 'Yes, son, next year and every year. Notre Dame will be there fighting with the Rockne spirit.'

"So, Father, when this is all over, if you see Mrs. Rockne, please tell her of Knute sending his picture to little Eddie Carty, a crippled kid out in Ohio, and that Eddie is going to pray every night for the one he calls his old friend Knute."

XL

Notre Dame *has* carried on with the Rockne spirit and—for they are the same—in the Sorin tradition.

Sorin arrived in 1842 with a capital of $400, seven teaching-working Brothers and title to a wilderness. One hundred and seven years later the valuation of the 1,700-acre campus was around $16,000,000, and the faculty numbered 433.

Most of this fabulous gain came from the flesh-and-blood endowment of men of faith, courage and good works. Football profits, averaging $200,000 a year for the last quarter century, helped mightily during the physical expansion which also saw the student body grow from 900 in 1919 to 4,500 in 1948.

There was no real financial endowment until 1921 and the figure in 1949 was only about $4,000,000. But there were hopes for a steady increase from the efforts of the Notre Dame Foundation, an alumni fund-raising group organized by Harry Hogan in 1947.

Football money has become progressively less important as the University has enlarged, and now just about cancels the annual amount allotted to student help. And Notre Dame is no longer unduly sensitive about the simple business fact that its advertising department—football—had run so far ahead of its product—education—in the public mind. It is now aggressively pointing out that its gridiron product is a fair representation of what it also turns out in education and citizenship. It invites inspection of *all* its factories, is confident that honest appraisal will declare it a national asset of intangible value.

What price, for instance, would you put on the discovery at Notre Dame of the basic formulae used to develop synthetic rubber? On the experiments in the '80's of Prof. Albert Zahm which helped lay the foundation for the work of the Wright brothers? On the achievement of Jerome Green, an Ohio State man who, while teaching at Notre Dame in 1889, sent the first successful wireless message in this country? On wartime and post-war research in chemistry and physics, in germ-free life, the atom smasher, the automatic counter of bacteria, experiments with cosmic rays and television—and the intensive wartime Naval V-7 program which commissioned 12,000 ensigns?

What value, in the current world-wide struggle against forces which deny God, and hence the dignity and integrity of the human personality, on a university which has for more than a century been a bulwark of the principles upon which the theory and practice of American government are based?

And just how would you go about beginning to reckon the good influence of Knute Rockne, George Gipp, Frank Leahy, the Four Horsemen, Johnny Lujack and all the other almost mythical heroes of the Notre Dame athletic tradition upon the impressionable minds of American youth?

There *is* a university there, much more of a university, in the physical sense, than the one Bill McGheehan discovered on his expedition from New York in 1928. And there should be twice the present facilities when the $20,000,000 expansion program of John J. Cavanaugh, the current president, is completed.

Most of this money will be spent for the research and graduate school achievements which give a university its greatest prestige. Only three residence halls are included in the estimates

274

because the intention is to limit the enrollment to the 5,000 most qualified students—who will be trained "to meet the national and international need for that moral leadership which flowers best in institutions that integrate religion and education in its highest forms."

From everywhere these days come earnest voices crying for that moral leadership. Some have even called Notre Dame by name to begin exercising the same influence in public affairs it has exercised in sports. This it has actually been doing, of course, in a substantial manner, through its more influential alumni; and its annual Laetare Medal (given in 1948 to Irene Dunne, the motion picture actress) is an award to Catholic lay leaders. Notre Dame people have begun, humbly, to believe that their school, providentially or not, may really have such a mission—to, by and for America and Americans, particularly to such areas as show signs of being too tired to fight for traditional liberty against the advocates of a human-herding master state.

Notre Dame, certainly and definitely, is not too tired. Three fourths of its 15,000 alumni have been graduated since Rockne's death in 1931; the classes are getting bigger right along; and all these are but officers in that amazing army of associate alumni who have voluntarily brought themselves within the school's orbit.

Notre Dame believes that it thinks straight and hits hard; that while it accepts the new things which are also good, its teachings are based upon the fundamentals of the good, the beautiful and the true; that it has the qualifications of the winning team—physical vitality, mental hunger, emotional dynamics and spiritual inspiration; that it is still on the march, on the *attack,* on the *offense,* not in there to die gamely but fighting to live and to win for the things in which it believes.

Notre Dame stands, in its second century and to its own people, as a Midwest fort and cathedral, dedicated and devoted to God and the melting pot, to country and individual rights.